BONDS OF ORGANIZATION

An Appraisal
of Corporate Human Relations

BONDS OF
ORGANIZATION

An Appraisal
of Corporate Human Relations

BY

E. WIGHT BAKKE

Sterling Professor of Economics
Yale University

SECOND EDITION

ARCHON BOOKS
HAMDEN, CONNECTICUT
1966

Library of Congress Catalog Card Number: 66-14603
Printed in the United States of America

To

The Staff of the
Yale Labor and Management Center
Who Are in Reality
Joint Authors of This Book

CONTENTS

PREFACE

Everyone on the staff of the Center has contributed greatly to this book. The contributions of those specifically involved in interviewing, in observing the life and work of participants in this company and union, in the laborious task of recording and analyzing the data, in the production of first reports from which this summary was made, in the clerical tasks of copying, duplicating, and checking the original material and the successive drafts through which the manuscript has gone, are obvious. They are partners in an enterprise, each of whose product is an essential and valuable part of the whole. Moreover, at all stages of the project, we have had the stimulating counsel and criticism of the senior members of the staff who were directing their own projects.

Our efforts would have yielded few results, however, without the extraordinary co-operation of the people of the Southern New England Telephone Company and the Connecticut Union of Telephone Workers. Fifteen hundred of them gave from three to eight hours each in responding to the interviewers' questions. Not only did they respond readily (only one refused to be interviewed) and fully to our questions, but they caught so thoroughly the methodological importance of keeping the questions to themselves after being interviewed that the last of the 1500 came to the questions with the same possibility of spontaneous responses as the first. The general officers of the company and the executive board of the union not only spent considerable time before the field work began in familiarizing themselves with the theoretical framework of the study, but they constituted themselves into advisory committees to which we reported at intervals so that we might profit by their counsel and criticism. They placed the physical and organizational facilities of the company and union at our disposal and have withheld no information or records we considered essential. Officials of both organizations have been free with their time in helping us to clear up details of their operations whenever we faced that need. Officials of the A.T.&T. have encouraged us by their genuine expressions of interest in the significance of the study, though current information on the content of our findings was not made available to them since, by agreement with the S.N.E.T. and the C.U.T.W., no results were to be released until cleared by both groups. Incidentally we should report that not a single change in our manuscript was made or even suggested by the readers of either group. It stands as it was written.

Although we are under heavy obligation to every individual referred to above, we are impelled to give a special vote of thanks to Clarence Bennett, the president of the union, and to Ellis Maxcy, assistant vice-president of the company, whose guidance and sponsorship have been indispensable at every stage of the project, and to Roland Calkins, who was our liaison man arranging facilities and interview schedules, obtaining records and seniority lists from which we drew our sample, and in general keeping the wheels of operations well oiled.

Since it was understood that the results of the study of both organizations were to be made available to the other as well as to the general public, the leaders of both groups assumed considerable risk in opening up their organizations to careful and comprehensive study. In doing so they demonstrated a type of "risk taking" in the public interest and a courage and faith which are worthy of high commendation. Needless to say, the staff of the Center shares in this commendation and is committed to the presentation of results in a manner which, while accurate and truthful, will reward and not punish men for the confidence they have placed in the value of the Center's scientific efforts.

At this point we cannot but call attention to the character given to this study by the fact that both the management and the union are co-operating and that both have consented to be simultaneous objects of investigation. Here is labor-management co-operation of a high order, a collaboration in ascertaining the facts of human relations upon which must be based an intelligent approach to improving them, a collaboration with a research organization in building a science of utility to a multitude beyond their own organizations.

Although our major objective, as indicated in the last chapter, and explained to all involved at the beginning, was the advancement of science, we hope that, both in the specific and in the more general findings, the people of the Southern New England Telephone Company and the Connecticut Union of Telephone Workers will find real help in carrying on their tasks. We trust they will realize that there is not only no conflict between scientific results and practical wisdom but a very real consistency between the two. If they do, we shall feel our heavy debt to them is partially discharged.

E. WIGHT BAKKE

New Haven, Connecticut
March 1, 1950

BONDS OF ORGANIZATION

Development of a Concept of
an Organization

INTRODUCTION

DEVELOPMENT OF A CONCEPT OF AN ORGANIZATION

BONDS OF ORGANIZATION, first published in 1950, was the seventh in a series of studies of going organizations in which I had been involved. The organizations studied included an English employment exchange (1931), several self-help cooperatives of the unemployed, the assembly department of a hardware plant, a business machines plant, a steel rolling mill, and a local trade union. Each study was concerned with a number of problems in human relations peculiar to the particular situation. But in each case a major objective was to gather data useful for the development of a model or concept of the structure of organizations, a concept which would provide a framework of "parts" and their relation to each other and to the whole, a framework which would be universally applicable to the study of behavior related to any kind of specific purpose social organization.

Many of us who were engaged in research on activities and relationships within and between organizations sensed the need for what might be called an "anatomy" of organizations which would provide a framework within which the problems of organizational "physiology" could be studied. There were available, in the early 1930's, models or concepts of organizational structure useful in the study of problems of particular kinds of organizations: the navy, the army, the church, the business firm, the political party, the government bureau, the trade union, municipal, state, and national governments, etc. But few social scientists had given their attention to a model or concept which would be equally useful in the study of all of them on a comparative basis. This lack became particularly obvious when the object of study was a problem in the relationship of two or more organizations to each other, for example, of a company to a union or to a government bureau.[1]

Since the publication of *Bonds of Organization,* my empirical study

---

[1] An extended discussion of the need for and uses of such a model in the study of the behavior within and between organizations will be found in the Chapter (2) which I contributed to *Modern Organization Theory,* Mason Haire, (ed.), Wiley, 1959.

of going organizations has continued, and always with a major objective of refining and redefining that model or concept of the structure of a social organization. The types of organization in the study of which I have participated since that date have been a local union, a commercial bank, a research organization, a hospital, and an educational institution. In addition, as a consultant, I was concerned with structural and operational problems of organization in two foreign productivity centers, several university research institutes, three management training institutes, a government department, a number of companies including a machine tool plant, and a small but geographically dispersed, diversified product, multiplant corporation. Since in each case I utilized the model of organization as developed to date as a framework for investigation, its utility and applicability to a going organization was constantly being tested—and corrected.

From the point of view, then, of the search for empirical data useful for the construction of a universally applicable model or concept of a special purpose social organization, this book, involving the study of a telephone company and the union of its employees, stands midway in the process. The model of organizational "parts" used in that study was that which had been formulated to that point, and specific attention was directed to the degree of participant satisfaction with certain characteristics and features of five of those parts. The parts focused on were defined as (a) the Organizational Charter, (b) the Functional Specifications, (c) the Status System, (d) the System of Rewards and Penalties, and (e) the Communication System.

The findings of the study were, quite understandably, presented within the framework of the categories utilized in gathering the data. But among the questions asked of the 1500 employees and officers of the company and union with respect to several "bonds of organization" (including four others in addition to the five the satisfaction with which is reported in this book) was one which stimulated them simply to describe what sort of activities related to each of these bonds they participated in, with the use of what resources, in relationship to whom, and with what personal and organizational objectives in mind.

The data, provided by answers to this question, were gathered with the specific intention of correcting, modifying, and elaborating the model of a social organization which had structured the research at the telephone company and union. Analysis of the data produced, as is to be expected when data are examined in the hope that they will extend rather than confirm one's existing knowledge, evidences a number of weaknesses and inadequacies in the model used. This evidence, together with that gathered from its use in the additional research and consultant projects named above, led to a continuous modification of the categories of "parts" and the systemization of their relation to each other and to the whole so that they might approximate ever more closely to, and picture more accurately, the reality of the structure and dynamics of operating organizations.

Very little modification has resulted, however, with respect to the nature of the five bonds of organization described in this book. They have stood the test of successive application in the projects named.

It was felt desirable, however, in reissuing this book after 15 years, to set forth briefly the most recent version of the model of a social organization to the elaboration and systemization of which the data gathered in connection with this study and the others mentioned have contributed. It will then be possible for the reader to see how the five parts herein discussed are related to the total pattern of parts and their relationship as defined in 1966.[2]

THE CONCEPT OF ORGANIZATION—1966 VERSION

It will be helpful to start with an overall definition which can then be amplified and made operational by more specific definition of the parts implied. A social organization is a continuing unique system of differentiated and coordinated human activities utilizing, transforming, and welding together a specific set of resources (people, materials, money, ideas, operational field, allies, time, and nature) into a unique problem-solving whole engaged in satisfying particular human needs in interaction with other systems of human activities, resources, and constraints in its environment.

2 The most recent published version of the Concept of a Social Organization here summarized is in *Modern Organization Theory*, Mason Haire, ed., Wiley, 1959, Chapter 2. That version stands unchanged with the exception of the addition of "Operational field," "Allies," and "Time," to the basic resources, and of the processes "Cultivation," "Association," and "Scheduling" related respectively to their perpetuation quantitatively and qualitatively. Also to the Homeostatic processes has been added one named "Legitimization."

The major features essential to a more specific definition of a particular social organization would therefore be:

1. *The Organizational Charter* or the image and "character" of the organization's unique wholeness.
2. *The Basic Resources,* people, materials, money, ideas, operational field, allies, time, and nature, utilized in organizational activities.
3. *The Essential Activity Processes* essential to the acquisition, maintenance, utilization of these basic resources in the performance of the organization's function, and for the maintenance of the stability and viability of the organization.

The Organizational Charter

In many relationships of participants and outsiders to a social organization, it is essential that those involved have an adequate image of the uniqueness and wholeness of the organization. It is essential that the organization as a whole mean something definite, that the name of the organization shall call to mind unique identifying features. This image and its content we label *The Organizational Charter.* The Organizational Charter facilitates the relation of people and other organizations to a specific organization in the same way that the concept of "personality" or "character" facilitates the relation of individual people to each other.

It is the conception held by participants in the organization of what the name of the organization stands for, its purpose and major policies, together with the basic organization oriented values shared by these participants. Efforts to maintain the integrity of the organization will be governed by what is necessary to actualize and perpetuate this image of unique wholeness.

The Basic Resources

The basic resources essential to the operation of an organization are the People, Materials, Money, Ideas, Operational Field, Allies, Time, and Nature which are employed by the agents of the organization in their activities on behalf of the organization. The nature of these resources, their quality, their quantity, and their specific attributes are of a high level of importance in determining the structure of the organization, for they necessarily dictate the kinds of activities which are appropriate to their acquisition, maintenance, transformation, and utilization, and they determine the scope within which the Organizational Charter can be actualized and limits on that actualization. One of the most important factors leading to the "steady state" of organizational activities will be the degree of persistency of the quantity and quality of the resources employed, and therefore the need for the adaptation of actions to these continuing attributes.

The nature of these resources is almost self-evident. A brief comment, however, with respect to Ideas may be necessary. The ideational resources are the Ideas used, or available for use, by agents or members of the organization, and by those outside the organization whose behavior affects the operations of the organization, and the Language in which these are expressed and communicated. Particularly important are the major premises which serve as foundations for the thinking the actors do about their relationships and activity. Significant elements of such ideational resources are the operational targets, plans, the set of codes or the "web of rule" which govern the activities of the participants.

In sum, the resource Ideas comprehend the whole of the mental constructs (and the Language used for their expression) which reflect the perceptions and interpretations people have of themselves, of others, of the aspects of their world which affect them, the appropriate and actual activity relationships among all these, and the principles, targets, plans, codes, and rules which govern these relationships.

Essential Activity Processes

The concept of the social organization serves to reflect realistically the dynamic character of going organizations only if that concept portrays the pattern of activities through which the resources available are acquired, maintained, transformed, and utilized.

Before outlining these Processes, it is desirable to indicate that their dynamic content is *all* of the actual behavior of participants in the organization which persists in response to the recurrent situations calling for activity. The behavior which is the substance of the organization will therefore include that which actually takes place:

1. Whatever the source of the expectancies to which it is a response (e.g., the expectancies of the organization through its responsible managers or leaders, expectancies of the functional and common interest groups with which the individual is associated, and expectancies that the individual has for himself);
2. Whether the activity is one of initiation or response;
3. Whether or not it is normal or deviant with respect to certain norms existing among those concerned;
4. Whether it is directed inwardly or outwardly, that is, toward participants in the organization or toward outsiders, whether it brings the actor as an agent of the organization into contact with people and other resources internal to the organization or with those in the external environment.

The concept of organizational *structure* is, therefore, not a static one. In reality, that structure is a system of dynamic activities in their continuing and normally steady state.

Classification of Essential Processes

The following classes of activities would appear to be necessarily required in order to attain the objectives of any organization, in the sense that the attainment is critically imperiled if such activities are performed ineffectively and is impossible if they are not performed at all.

1. Activities to define, make clear and symbolize the image or character of the unique wholeness of the organization, including the main features which group it with and distinguish it from other organizations. We shall call these *Identification Activities.*

   If effectively carried out, the result is the development of a commonly understood and accepted Organizational Charter, and its symbolic representation.
2. Activities to acquire, maintain, develop, and renew the basic resources utilized by agents of the organization in the performance of their work within and for the organization. We shall call these the *Perpetuation Activities.*

   If effectively carried out, the result is the availability of all basic resources adequate in quantity and quality for organizational operations.

Subclasses of activities of this sort are defined by reference to the basic resources utilized and which it is the specific function of the subclass of activities to perpetuate.

a. *Personnel* activities perpetuate People and their qualities.

b. *Service* activities perpetuate Materials, Equipment, and Plant.

c. *Finance* activities perpetuate Money and Credit.

d. *Thoughtways* activities perpetuate Ideas such as alternative targets, strategies, premises, decisions, plans, organized bodies of data and knowledge, rules and codes, and concepts of values.

e. *Conservation* activities perpetuate Natural Resources and access to them.

f. *Cultivation* activities perpetuate conditions in the Operational Field (e.g. the market for products or services) favorable to successful performance of the organization.

g. *Scheduling* activities perpetuate the resource of Time.

h. *Association* activities establish and perpetuate supporting relationships with the resource Allies.

3. Activities to create or produce an output, i.e., the product or service satisfying the human need which it is the organization's function to supply, and to distribute the output advantageously to the continued operation of the organization. We shall call these the *Workflow Activities*. These are the central activities of every organization. All other activities are justified, and their effectiveness measured, by the degree of their contribution to the output of the "Workflow," that is the product or service the organization is set up to produce.

If effectively carried out, these activities result in Work and an Output of a quantity and quality adequate to sustain the continued contributions to and support for organizational operations by participants and "outside" recipients of the output.

Subclasses of activities of this sort are defined by reference to the stages in the workflow which they occupy. The major subclasses are:

a. *Production* activities which create or make the output, i.e., the service or product.

b. *Distribution* activities which distribute the product or service to its consumers or clients often in exchange for that which the organization can employ as an input.

4. Activities that assure and control the performance, coordination, and the focusing on organizational and participant objectives of all activities carried out by agents and facilities of the organization. We shall call these the *Control Activities.*

If effectively carried out, these activities result in an Administration unifying and coordinating all differentiated activities with a minimum of leakages, i.e., irrelevant or negative activity.

Subclasses of activities of this sort perform the following functions:

a. *Directive activities* are those which initiate action and the type and direction of action for people and machines. The most important are those which (1) determine the target for performance, (2) make known to those from whom performance is desired the details of that target, the performance, and the results expected, (3) assign, order (or request), and sanction the performance, (4) obtain acceptance for, or compliance with the order or request, (5) oversee performance, (6) adapt type and direction of action in accordance with guidance from feedback information. Directive activities are normally considered to be initiated by those in the managerial hierarchy at a stage above the actor expected to carry out the directed activity. This is, of course, an important species of directive activity; but we consider as directive activities all those that proceed upward in the hierarchy of participants, laterally among participants at any level, diagonally among participants at any levels, as well as those which proceed downward.

b. *Motivation activities* reward and penalize, or promise rewards or penalties, for behavior in the interest of making it conform to the type desired by the person or persons administering the rewards and penalties.

c. *Evaluation activities* review, appraise, and rate performance, performers, and results according to standards established; assign people (as well as other resources) to positions on scales pertaining to a number of dimensions (such as prestige, importance, power, ability, acceptability, etc.); compare the relative advantages and costs of alternative courses of action; predict probable consequences of alternative courses of action; assess the impact of changes in one part of the organization on other parts and the whole; assess periodically the state of the whole organization internally and in relation to its environment.

d. *Communication activities* are those which *supply* participants with the premises and data (including feedback data) which they need in order to perform other activities.

5. Activities which serve to stabilize and vitalize the organization as a whole in an evolving state of dynamic equilibrium. These activities we shall call the *Homeostatic Activities.*

They differ from the Perpetuation, Workflow, and Control activities discussed above both in purpose and in character. Perpetuation, Workflow, and Control Activities are intended to achieve *effective and efficient operation* of the organization in its effort to fulfill the purpose for which it is established. The Homeostatic activities together with the Identification activities provide for the *maintenance and survival of the organization as an evolving, active, unified, integrated, and unique whole.*

They differ also from the specific purpose operational activities (Perpetuation, Workflow, Control) in that they are *combinations* of the other activities. They are *synergic* in character. They therefore add no new *elementary* activities to the concept.

One could call them simply "synergic" activities and thus avoid the impression of definition by analogy created by the use of the word "homeostatic." The use of this latter word is, however, intended to indicate a very real function necessitated by a continual problem every organization faces. That problem is the maintaining, with respect to the organization as a whole, an evolving state of dynamic equilibrium consistent with its Organizational Charter in the face of internal and external conditions and changes in those conditions. These conditions and changes cause strains and stresses within and pressures from without which, if unattended to, can threaten the stability, the integrity, and the viability of the organization. They pose this problem whether they are negative dangers or positive opportunities.

The Homeostatic activities we now are considering are those which marshal and bring into action the other activities in a concerted adaptive effort to maintain the continuing integrity of the organization, integrity with respect to the relationship of its "parts," and integrity with respect to its relations with the external environment.

There are at least four synergic processes which can be observed to function in a social organization to fulfill this need: the Fusion process, the Problem-solving process, the Leadership process, and the Legitimization process. Disintegration of an organization can result from a failure of any one of these processes.

Fusion Process. The function of the Fusion Process is to maintain the integrity of the organization in the face of centrifugal forces including the divergent interests of individuals, of groups, of particular departments or divisions, of other organizations, and of the organization itself, which each hopes to realize through its contact with the other. Its aim is to establish and maintain for the organization an internal and external integration which will at least leave its capacity to perform its function unimpaired, and at best will improve that capacity.[3]

The Problem-solving Process. The need for the Problem-solving Process is so obvious as to need little elaboration. The problems here referred to are non-routine in character for which there has been developed no adequate customary routine for solution. Many such "routines" of course are the results of the previous operation of the Problem-Solving Process here under discussion, at the time when the problem to which the routine is directed first arose. Indeed it might be said that the "routines" assume as given the results of the steps in the Problem-Solving Process between the first step, i.e. *awareness of stimulus* and the step *action.* Whether the problem is in the form of a disturbance to, or difficulty in, operations and achievement of results, or in the form of an opportunity for activity which, if adequately exploited, promises advantageous and desirable results, it calls for the marshaling of the organization's resources and activities and their co-ordinated combination in a more or less systematic problem-solving process.

[3] See Bakke, E. Wight, *The Fusion Process,* Yale Labor and Management Center, New Haven, Connecticut. 1953.

It involves, in addition to steps frequently referred to in analyses of "the decision-making process" (i.e. setting and clarification of objective, search for alternatives, appraisal of alternatives, choice or decision) those steps which both proceed and follow these tasks of "deciding." Those steps preceding the ones named above are: (a) Awareness of stimulus, (b) Exploration of nature and implications of the problem, (c) Structuring of results of exploration, (d) Simplification of the problem sufficient to make action feasible. Those steps following the task of "deciding" are: (a) Mobilization, (b) Action, (c) Appraisal or Judgment of results, (d) Closure or Renewal. They provide for a carry through of the choice of alternatives or decision and for a judgment and evaluation as to the results of that carry through. In a very real sense the *organizational decision* has not been made until the carry through in action is finished.[4]

Leadership Process. In defining homeostasis we used the phrase "an evolving state of dynamic equilibrium." Such a concept of the organization's steady state is not the product of a value judgment that an organization *should* grow or evolve as a dynamic whole, but the product of the observation that it *does* grow or evolve because:

1. It operates in a dynamic environment which is constantly making changes necessary in the parts of the organization.

2. Such changes in parts impose the necessity for adaptive changes in other parts.

3. Such adaptive changes inevitably modify the requirements for cooperative unity and therefore the character of that cooperative unity.

4. The result, unless the organization disintegrates, is that it *does* grow or evolve into a new state of dynamic equilibrium, a new form of the whole.

It is this set of circumstances which creates the need in the case of a social organization for some synergic process that provides:

1. The anticipation, vision, or imagination as to developments in the

4 See Bakke, E. Wight, "Concept of the Social Organization" in Haire, Mason (ed.), *Modern Organization Theory*, 1959, pp. 61 ff. for a more extended discussion of this process.

environment and within the organization itself, and as to their significance for parts of the organization, and the organization as a whole.

2. The vision or conception of what this implies as to modifications in the characteristics of an evolving whole organization if it is to maintain its integrity and functional effectiveness, to grow, and to survive.

3. The initiative for launching activity which is concerned with adaptation of the organization while maintaining its integrity.

4. A spur and guidance to cooperation of participants in this development.

It will be observed that this process incorporates a number of classes of activities we have already discussed, and focuses them on achieving a homeostasis in the face of the opportunity and necessity for *adaptation, development, and growth.*

The Legitimization Process. The need for a Legitimization Process arises from the fact that the stability, viability, and growth of the organization is vitally affected by the acceptance by persons and other organizations of its right to exist, to possess or have access to the resources it requires, to pursue the ends for which it is established, to maintain the structure of relationships it has built, to engage in the kinds of activities characterizing its work, and to have the effects on itself and the environment which flow from these activities.

The right to exist, and the other rights named, are just as strong as the reciprocal duties voluntarily fulfilled or legally or extralegally imposed on others not to interfere with or prevent that existence and the activities essential to it. The obtaining of charters, articles of incorporation, franchises, and the building of many types of protective armament are ways of insuring against such interference which could weaken or destroy those rights. And such attempts are significant examples of the Legitimization Process.

We have now come the full circle in classifying the activities essential for an organization's survival and its capacity for performance of its function:

1. From the Identification Activities which develop, and symbolize the image of the organization, that is its Organizational Charter;

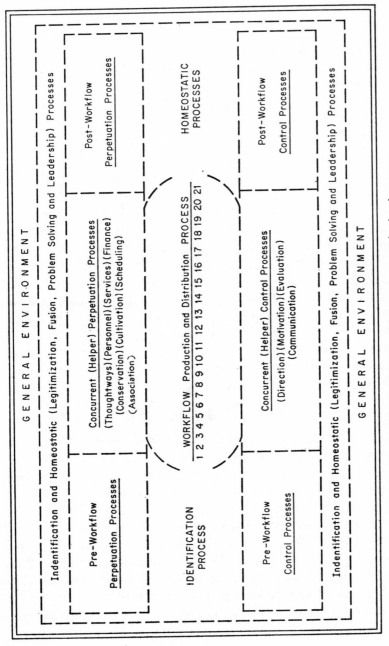

CHART A. Model of relationships among organizational processes.

2. Through the Perpetuation, Workflow, and Control Activities which, so to say, bring that image to life in operations;

3. To those Homeostatic Activities which preserve the integrity of the operating organization (i.e., which actualize that image) in the face of changes required of the whole by changes introduced into the parts as adaptations to internal or external stimuli, and which envision, initiate, and guide its evolving steady state of dynamic equilibrium.

These processes are interdependent in the sense that each requires some degree of help and support from all the others. Actually, therefore, if we are concerned with a problem arising in the operation of any one of them, we would eventually find such operations being affected by the character and quality of operations associated with all the others. This relationship of interdependence is pictured on the preceeding Chart A. The broken lines indicating a uniqueness of the types of processes also indicate their openness to impact from the other types of processes. Centrally important for every organization are its Workflow processes. These are immediately supported (effectively or ineffectively) by the Perpetuation and Control processes. And the whole is integrated and supported by the Identification and Homeostatic Processes. Through the operation of these processes the organization as a whole affects and is affected by the external Environment.

BONDS OF ORGANIZATION

In the foregoing discussion of the model or concept of an organization I have not referred to the concept "Bonds of Organization." The constituent elements, however, have all been presented, the Organizational Charter, the Basic resources, the Essential Activity Processes. The concept, *Bonds of Organization,* arises from the need to represent the way in which these elements are related to each other in a state of functional interdependence. To each Essential Process corresponds a Bond of Organization. The heart of that Bond (say the Communication Bond) is the Essential Process (the Communication Process). But the welding together task of Communication is accomplished not alone by communicating *activity* but by all elements in the organization which support that type of activity. To be more specific, the Communication Bond (as well as all Bonds):

1. Has an *objective* indicating the contributory relationship of this process to the function of the organization as defined ultimately in its Organizational Charter,
2. Utilizes *instruments* which are specific items of the Basic Resources need for that kind of activity
   a. People
   b. Ideas (including premises, specifications, plans, criteria, bodies of data or knowledge)
   c. Materials and Equipment
   d. Funds
   e. The organization's Operational Field (e.g., its Market)
   f. Nature
   g. Time
   h. Allies
3. Receives aid and reinforcement from the other essential activity processes considered as *helper processes* (e.g., from Direction, Evaluation, Motivation, Thoughtways, Personnel, etc.).

A description of each Bond of Organization would therefore be organized around the description of its:

1. Objective
2. The Essential Activity Process predominantly involved
3. The Instruments (specific resources) utilized
4. The aid and reinforcement from other (helper) Essential Processes

It may be helpful to summarize the model or concept of a social organization in a chart. (See Chart B.)

This concept of social organization has proved to be applicable to the description of the several types of specific purpose organizations in the study of which I have been involved (See page xiii f.). It has been particularly useful in understanding some of the problems in the active bargaining, conflict, and supporting relationships between two

Chart B. THE BONDS OF ORGANIZATION

IDENTIFICATION BOND
Developing, symbolizing, and making acceptable
The Organizational Charter

PERPETUATION BONDS
Acquiring, maintaining, and developing
Basic Resources

Thoughtways (Ideas)	*Personnel* (People)	*Services* (Materials)	*Finance* (Money)	*Conservation* (Nature)	*Cultivation* (Operational Field)	*Scheduling* (Time)	*Association* (Allies)

WORKFLOW BONDS
Producing and Distributing
the Output

Production　　　　*Distribution*

CONTROL BONDS
Directing, coordinating, stimulating, regulating, appraising
All Operations *i.e. Administration*

Direction　　*Motivation*　　*Evaluation*　　*Communication*

HOMEOSTATIC BONDS
Preserving *integrity of the organization* in an
evolving state of dynamic equilibrium

Fusion　　*Leadership*　　*Legitimization*　　*Problem Solving*

or more organizations (e.g., between company and union, local union and national union, national union and federation). It has also been useful in the study of a company and its divisions or departments (Research and development, manufacturing, personnel, marketing, etc.) since the dynamic structure and activity of the latter can be described within the same framework, that is they can be considered as organizations in their own right.

RELATION OF THE 1950 TO THE 1966 CONCEPTS

In this book five Bonds of Organization are described and subjected to a degree-of-satisfaction-level evaluation. The Status system herein described corresponds to the Direction Bond in the revised concept. The Reward and Penalty system corresponds to the Motivation Bond. The Communication system corresponds to the Communication Bond. The Organizational Charter described in this book is a *product* of the Identification Bond. The emphasis in this book is on the product rather than the process, but the nature of the process is clearly suggested by its results.

The System of Functional Specifications is closely related to the Workflow Bond in the revised concept. In the 1966 model, however, the Workflow Bond appears at first reading to be much more specifically and narrowly defined; the central activity core of the Workflow Bond is the process providing the output the organization is established to produce. As used in this book, "Functional Specifications" is less a description, for the company as a whole, of a specific process (like Workflow, Direction, Motivation, Production, Communication, Evaluation, Services, etc.) than a concept of how tasks related to these several specific processes were sequentially linked together in the accomplishment of the Workflow function of specific task teams, each of which can, in fact, be defined as an organization. Each of these teams is of course also a suborganization within the overall company or enterprise organization. The tasks, which constitute the Workflow (i.e., an output-producing and distributing process) of each of these teams as an organization, are performing for the company organization helper activities to the company's Workflow, which is "Completing Customer Calls."

For example, the two charts indicating the flow of work involved for the "station trouble correction team" (Chart A)[5] and for the "installation of residence equipment team" (Chart B)[6] would, in accordance with the 1966 revised model, and from the point of view of the overall company, depict the performance of two aspects of the "Services" bond. That is, the teams are concerned with the dominant function of supply and maintenance (perpetuation) of equipment. The example of the flow of work involved for the union's "preparations for negotiation team" (Chart C[7] would be classified, in accordance with the revised model, and from the point of view of the Union as an organization, as predominantly related to "Thoughtways" since the activity of that team is concerned with the decision making involved in the preparation of plans and a case (Ideas) for use in collective bargaining by the Union. The example of the flow of work carried on by both company and union personnel in the "settlement of grievances team" (Chart D)[8] would be classified now, from the point of view of the comprehensive organization, as depicting an aspect of the "Fusion" bond, since the activity is concerned with maintaining or restoring an integration of the interests of the company and its employees, the lack of which can threaten the stability and operation of both the company and union organizations, and the organized enterprise which comprehends them both.

In other words the dominant objectives of the flow of work presented graphically in Charts A & B are those appropriate to "Service" activities; the dominant objective of the flow of work indicated in Chart C is that appropriate to "Thoughtways" activities; the dominant objective of the flow of work indicated in Chart D is that appropriate to "Fusion" activities.

Looked at from the point of view of the total organization then the flow of tasks represented in those charts are appropriately designated as "Service," "Thoughtways," and "Fusion" activities, respectively—the function which they perform within the total organization. When, however, attention is focused on the team carrying out these functions, as in itself an "organization," these tasks are appropriately called *their* workflow for they are activities producing *their* output.

[5] p. 25.
[6] Opposite p. 26.
[7] p. 27.
[8] p. 29.

The concept of the Homeostatic Bonds, which occupies so prominent and important a place in the 1966 model of the social organization, became an obvious necessity when we studied further the data from interviews with those in the Executive Department, including of course the top management and those who carried on tasks in such areas as public relations, personnel, and legal matters. It became clear that their tasks were largely concerned with the maintenance of the organization as a whole, in the face of difficulties or opportunities, with its integrity and internal harmony, with its acceptability and legitimacy in the eyes of its own employees, and before the public and public agencies, with its analysis of, its response to and solution of, non-recurring problems, and with its continuous adaptation and development in the light of anticipated changes in the environment. Once such institution maintaining functions as Fusion, Legitimization, Unusual Problem Solving, and Leadership became as obvious as the all but dominant concern of the people performing roles in the Executive Department for the company as a whole, it became evident that these functions were also performed on behalf of each subdivision, (or suborganization) of the company, whether a Department or a specific task team.

We turn then to the discussion of five of the Bonds of Organization which are of major importance in the functioning of these two organizations, the Southern New England Telephone Company and the union of its employees, The Connecticut Union of Telephone Workers. We shall also explore the degree to which each of these Bonds (or systems of activity) is experienced as satisfactory by management and employees in each of three operating departments (Traffic, Commercial, Plant) in the company organization, and by officers and members in the union organization.

The five Bonds are:

1. *Identification* (Herein discussed in terms of its "product," the Organizational Charter)
2. *Workflow* (Herein referred to as Functional Specifications, and illustrated by reference to the flow of work in specific task teams (organizations) providing a particular "product" supporting the overall company's Workflow, namely, the completion of customers calls)

3. Three Control Bonds providing the company with its Administration, namely,

   a. *Direction* (Herein referred to as the Status System);

   b. *Motivation* (Herein referred to as the Reward and Penalty System);

   c. *Communication.*

BONDS OF ORGANIZATION

An Appraisal
of Corporate Human Relations

I

A RESEARCH PARTNERSHIP

H UMAN relations in industry is our big unfinished job." Again and again in recent years leaders of management and labor have made such a declaration. The problem has been frequently discussed in management and labor publications and conferences. That is an encouraging and important development. Articles and speeches provide many descriptions of particular devices and techniques for improving human relations. Occasionally an author or a speaker suggests that the recorded experience points to certain general rules of human organization and principles of human relations. The need to understand the forces and factors that contribute to good teamwork within management, employee, and union leadership groups, and between these groups, is widely recognized. There are many who sense that the success not only of single companies and unions but of the American way of private enterprise and democracy depends on the adequacy of that understanding and the effectiveness of those procedures.

One thing obviously required to meet this practical need of managers and labor leaders is better *methods* of dealing with people: training programs for union and company officials, communication techniques that really get across, manuals for persons in authority in both groups, grievance procedures that really settle grievances, and other techniques. Able people in both organizations are working hard on those techniques. They have made real progress.

Particularly important is the training of those responsible for policy and administration in the leadership of organizations. Many outlines of training courses, classes, and conferences have come to our attention which indicate systematic thinking and action on this matter.

When one talks to managers and union leaders who are engaged in or interested in this sort of training, however, they all eventually come back to the same question: "What are the principles of human relations which we ought to get hold of?" Intuitively they know that there must be some fundamental principles about how human beings act and why they act that way. There must be some cause-and-effect laws in the way human beings behave, just as there are cause-and-effect laws in the way steel or wood or oil or rubber behaves. Any engineer knows that when he devises methods or tools for dealing with these materials, the success or failure of his efforts is determined by whether or not he takes these principles of physical science into account. The "human relations" engineers sense the same things. As one of them said, "We are just playing around with one method after another until we have a fundamental grasp of what makes human beings tick and why." So the most thoughtful of them are looking for a set of principles on that matter which will make their job something more than trying out one technique after another until they find one that works.

Where can they look for those principles? One could suggest several sources, none of them completely satisfactory. We might call in the psychologist, the anthropologist, the economist, the political scientist, or professional men like doctors and ministers and say: "What can you tell us?" As a colleague of these people one can say that there would be value in that method. They have done a lot of work on the determinants of human behavior that is potentially of real service. Why are the results of their effort not used more frequently? First, because practical men don't understand their jargon; second, because their conclusions and generalizations didn't grow out of the analysis of the kind of human relations with which leaders of management and unions are familiar. It's too big a jump, for instance, from findings having to do with the rat cage or the Hottentot society or the "free competitive market" to the factories and union halls or the picket line.

Let us, then, turn to people who do speak the right language, who do base their conclusions on experience with the kind of facts with which the leaders of management and labor have to live, that is, to successful leaders themselves. Do their comments add up to a set of principles of human relations? Here and there one strikes pay dirt; but on the whole their suggestions do not add up. Why? Either these men do not state their principles at all, or for the most part their statements are so general and so unrelated to the facts that they record that one cannot apply them to any specific set of facts.

What is the trouble here? It is not that these generalizations from either source are unplausible or the product of dreamers. The basic difficulty with them, so far as furnishing practical men with guideposts to action, is this: they do not state in precise terms the causal relations between things over which they have some control and the reaction of human beings to those things. They do not attempt an explanation, supported by systematic analyses of observed facts, of why men behave as they do.

So, in the search for usable principles of human relations, leaders of organizations are disappointed both by the offerings of the academic and professional fraternity and by those of the practical men. What then are we to do?

If we cannot find our principles ready made, the action suggested is that we proceed by careful observation and analysis, experimentation and study, to supply what we lack. It seems unlikely, however, that such effort can be fruitful if carried on independently by either practical or academic men. The former are normally too close to details of daily operations to generalize effectively from their experience. The latter are normally too far away from the details of daily operations to make their generalizations realistic. The former frequently have too many fires to put out. The latter are frequently not concerned with fighting fires at all. If the so-called academic man and the so-called practical man could start analyzing these problems of human relations basically in the same way, using the same framework for classifying and describing their experience, every man's observations could be added to those of every other man. Then when we came together to discuss what our observations meant, we would be talking the same language. Our discussion might have a chance of "adding up."

It goes without saying that both practical and academic men engaged in such a partnership have their own specific objectives, which are of importance to each of them. The academic man is interested particularly in the development of a systematic science of human relations. The practical man is interested in the application of that science to his immediate and long-range problems of operation. In the carrying on of such a partnership each must respect and understand the objectives of the other, and recognize that, in the long run, the objectives are not only not in conflict but are actually two ways of phrasing an identical goal.

Early in 1947, the Yale Labor and Management Center in collaboration with the Southern New England Telephone Company and the Connecticut Union of Telephone Workers entered such a partnership. Together they undertook the ambitious project of describing, analyzing, and evaluating the structure and dynamics of human relations in the latter two organizations. Both organizations anticipated that information of practical value to them would result from this project. Since the basic evidence was to come from comprehensive and intensive interviews with participants, management and employees, union officers and members, several practical results were probable. Those responsible for the operation of the organizations would get a clearer picture of the organizational structure *as experienced* by all participants; and, since the primary basis for evaluating the efficiency of the structure was to be the degree of satisfaction experienced by the participants who carried on their work within it, management and union leaders might be furnished with suggestions as to the aspects of the structure most in need of attention to improve the quality of teamwork in their respective organizations and in the relations between them.

These anticipations were also shared by the staff of the Labor and Management Center, and constituted one legitimate and worthy reason, from our point of view, for undertaking the study. The staff of the Center had another objective, however, which was of a long-range character, an objective both practical and scientific. This objective is set forth and defended in several publications of the Center[1] and need not be here defined in detail. Briefly, it was the development of principles of human relations, answers to the question, "Why do people behave as they do?" answers which could contribute to a sound and usable science of human relations. It was the testing of certain hypotheses which had already been developed concerning these matters at the Center. It was the correction, amplification, and filling with realistic content the terms, cause-and-effect relations, and the systematic framework in which these hypotheses were expressed and organized. It was the sharpening of research methods essential for a continued testing and correction of the seeds of a theory of adaptive human behavior already formulated in preliminary fashion. These objectives are described more specifically in the final chapter.

In other words, to the staff of the Center, the willingness of the two organizations to collaborate furnished a laboratory, the only kind of a laboratory available for the carrying on of many types of social-science research.

This objective was fully explained to the officers of both organizations

---

[1] *Plans and Progress; From Tactics to Strategy in Industrial Relations; Frontiers of Industrial Relations Research.* These may be obtained from The Yale Labor and Management Center, New Haven, Connecticut.

before the project was undertaken, and was communicated to the participants in both groups by their officers and, to all who were interviewed, by the interviewers. It is a matter of great satisfaction to the staff of the Center that this objective was accepted and understood by all concerned, and that the furtherance of this objective has from the beginning been considered of importance equal to the acquisition of practical and immediately useful information. Indeed it is clear that the participants in these organizations have accepted the time-consuming and time-costing procedures involved as much in the interest of producing findings useful to industry, unions, and the community in general as in the hope of improving teamwork within their own organizations.

In all, 1500 participants in the two organizations were interviewed. This report records, in the text, primarily the responses of those who were attached to the three operating departments at headquarters and in the fifteen local exchanges chosen for investigation. The responses from other departments are set forth in tabular form in the appendixes.

The number and distribution of respondents attached to local exchanges in the three operating departments is set forth in Table I.

TABLE I

TOTAL NUMBER OF INTERVIEWS WITH LOCAL EXCHANGE PERSONNEL*
BY DEPARTMENT AND CLASSIFICATION

| Department | Management | Classification | | Union Officer |
		Employee I†	Employee II†	
Traffic	53	273	71	38
Plant	76	143	181	43
Commercial	46	74		24

* Totals include only those individuals attached to a local exchange; i.e., for management and employees they do not include those employed at the district, divisional, or headquarters level. Union officers include local and general representatives and local officers.

† In the Plant Department, Group I is inside; Group II is outside. In the Traffic Department, Group I is operators and clerks; Group II is supervisors (an employee classification).

NATURE OF THE PRESENT REPORT

Since this study is the first of a series to be made in a number of organizations, a series which will extend over many years, a major objective was to clarify, by reference to actual observations of the company and union "society" in action, the terms and categories to be used throughout the series. Of special importance is the concept of the organization as a

small society, that is, a group of individuals welded together into a functioning team by certain devices, or *bonds of organization*. This concept is basic
to our whole approach to the study of human relations. The several bonds
must therefore be clearly understood. The first objective of this report,
then, was to build up a realistic definition of these bonds of organization
as they were revealed in the experience of participants.

The first half of each chapter is such a definition in general terms,
applicable to any organization, of the bond under discussion, illustrated
where necessary by examples from this company and union. This part of
the chapter will be of interest alike to the general reader and participants
in the company and union—indeed to anyone who is searching for a pattern of observation and analysis by which systematic sense can be made
out of organizational life and activity. This clarification and definition of
terms, not by analogy, but by generalization from observed facts will, we
hope, appeal to practical and academic minds alike as an essential, though
small, step in laying the foundations for a science of human relations.

The second part of each chapter is a preliminary demonstration of the
possibility of developing tests of efficiency for these bonds by formulating
questions suggested by asking how the bond might affect participants' desires for certain goal experiences and how the answers to these questions
may be summarized to get a first approximation to the degree of efficiency
with which the bond is functioning for several groups within the organization. All questions were formulated with this demonstration in mind.
Many of them were "open-ended" questions, the answers to which are
difficult to. treat statistically.

Some of the questions asked in the course of our interviews, however,
could be answered in *yes* or *no* terms initially. The *yes* or *no* could be in-
terpreted as indicating satisfaction or dissatisfaction with some experienced
result of the functioning of the organizational bond under consideration.
In the case of other questions, a direct inference could be drawn from
the answers as to whether the bond was of such a character that a particular goal was or was not being realized. In a sense these questions and
answers could be considered to form a basis for a survey in which participants in the organization indicated their satisfaction or dissatisfaction with some particular feature of their environment. We have decided
to present an analysis of these questions relative to five of the organiza-

tional bonds in this preliminary report, leaving the analysis of answers to the open-ended questions to a later report.

The specific findings in the second part of each chapter will be of interest, of course, primarily to the participants in these two organizations. To the general reader that part will prove interesting, however, as an illustration of how a similar plan of analysis might be applied to other organizations, and to suggest a pattern for thinking about and studying the effect of organizational experience upon the satisfaction of participants. Moreover some of the implications suggested by these findings may stimulate an answer to human-relations questions raised by the reader's experience.

OBJECTIVES RESTATED

There is no short cut to a sound understanding of the essentials of effective teamwork in companies and unions or between them. The traditional rules of effective co-operation between two individuals, rules which embody the wisdom of experience, are helpful and indispensable. But standing alone, they do not suggest all the principles of effective co-operation among individuals who are related to each other as *members of groups*.

The problems of relationship in a company and union are of this nature. They arise not merely because individuals have differing personalities, but because these individuals have several positions within these "societies" and their subdivisions, positions which carry functions, responsibilities, rights, and privileges which pertain to *any* individual occupying them regardless of his individual characteristics.

Even to understand and deal with individuals, therefore, it is essential to know the compulsions placed upon him and his behavior by the social system of the society of which he is a part. Though it may be true that "A man's a man for a' that," the content of the concept "man" includes elements he has taken unto himself by virtue of his necessity to *be* "a man occupying a position related to that of other men in a particular society and defined, as to appropriate behavior, by the social system of that society."

Although much attention has been given, particularly by anthropologists, sociologists, and historians, to clarifying these terms for tribes, communities, and even nations, their meaning with respect to smaller societies such as companies and unions has been developed largely by analogy and not by reference to empirical evidence resulting from on-the-spot observations of such smaller groups in action. Those meanings have, therefore, had for the practical man a hazy outline and content, and their relevance to his pressing and very real problems of management and leadership did not have a sharp focus. If, however, we want something more than analogies with which to understand the nature of our practical problems, we must be prepared to await with patience the careful fact-gathering and analysis in the area of human relations which presents us with those day-to-day problems.

Our conception of a company and union as a small society of individuals bound together by a social system is therefore central to our whole approach both to the development and to the application of science, both to the suggestion of techniques and to the formulation of principles which in the end will test the validity and practicability of those techniques. That conception imposes upon us the task of describing and evaluating the particular social system within which the individuals we are studying live.

In this report we are dealing with only five elements of that social system—the five *bonds of organization*—each of which is the subject of one chapter. They are important elements, however, for they weld men together as partners in production (Functional Specifications); as directors and directed, representatives and represented (Status system); as givers and receivers of information (Communication system); as agents of reward and penalty (Reward and Penalty system); and as sharers of a conception of the organization as a whole (Organizational Charter).[2]

In each case we have described what we mean by the bond and have indicated what aspects of it were essential as categories for reporting how it actually appeared in the experience of members of these organizations. We have then in the second part of each chapter attempted a preliminary evaluation of the bond in terms of its contribution to the goal realization of these individuals.[3]

Though this investigation is, in a sense, a "case study," we hope that those who are in positions of responsibility in any organization will sense that the approach used and the findings recorded suggest a useful way of

[2] Other bonds not discussed in this report are Technology, Services, Thoughtways, and the Educational System. See Appendixes, Framework of Analysis.

[3] See Appendixes, Framework of Analysis for list of these goals.

trying to understand the human-relations problems in their own organizations and clues to an explanation of why some of their efforts in eliciting satisfactory teamwork from their many partners in the organization are successful and others unsuccessful. And we trust that all who are concerned that group life in America shall be so organized and arranged that individuals may develop and maintain to the maximum their individual potentialities and dignity will find here useful suggestions for their thought and effort in relation to this most important and worthy concern.

II

FUNCTIONAL SPECIFICATIONS

EVERY member of an organization has a particular set of functions he is expected or required to perform as an individual. These may be detailed and may differ from those of another individual whose craft label is the same as his. If any individual is asked what his job is, he will probably answer with the name of his craft; and then, if he feels talkative, he will explain the nature of his activities and responsibilities: he will explain what he does, how he does it, where and when he does it, what is expected of him in effort and results. In other words *his* function can be described in terms of work process, method, place, time, energy, and product requirements. These are the terms in which *job descriptions* are normally written.

Such individual job descriptions are essential elements in the system of Functional Specifications. But a collection of such job descriptions does not constitute the *system* of Functional Specifications in an organization. For any individual, his own framework of activity, so described, is the most intimately and vividly experienced part of that *system*. But participants, in describing their jobs, frequently spoke of relations they had with others in performing their individual tasks. Particularly in discussing whether the job was satisfactory or not, their comments turned to the influence of the activities and attitudes of other people with whom they were associated in the performance of their tasks. Their testimony of experience was that their job was defined not only in terms of individual tasks but in terms of doing these in association with others. As we observed the actual activities of the many people in the organization and listened to their comments, what had been a formal concept of the system of Functional Specifications was filled with realistic content.

The clue to the relation of the individual's job description to the rest of the system of Functional Specifications was the fact that individuals performing their individual functions are grouped into several types of teams. Each of these teams also had a defined function. These teams in turn were grouped into more comprehensive teams, each with its more comprehensive function to perform, until the most comprehensive team of all, the company or the union itself, was formed. Its function is identical with the purpose and function of the organization as defined in the Organizational Charter. We came to define the system of Functional Specifications as including the functions of the organization as a whole, those of individual participants, and those of the several groupings of individuals which brought the first two together.

These groupings of teams appear to be of four sorts. Only the first two concern us in describing the nature of the organizational bond, Functional Specifications. They are stated and identified here merely for purposes of orientation. They may be labeled briefly as (a) work-flow, (b) staff-line, (c) supervisory, and (d) clique groupings.

The purpose of the *work-flow* and *staff-line* teams is to carry forward the service or finish the product which the organization is set up to furnish. We shall describe them in more detail in a moment.

The purpose of the *supervisory* teams is to provide for stimulus, control, co-ordination, and uniformity of direction of the efforts of a number of individuals or groups of individuals. This type of team relationship (say between repairmen and foremen of repairmen, or between operators and chief operators, or between the union's general representative and local representative) we describe as a part of the Status system. So far as the system of Functional Specifications is concerned, our definition of function is in terms of performance of or staff assistance to a step in the flow of work toward a completed service or product as a contribution to the building up of that service or product. From this point of view the foreman of repairmen and the repairmen are performing the same function, though one has the status of "boss" and the other that of "the bossed" in the performance.[1] Likewise in processing a grievance the general representative and local representative are both performing the same work-flow function, though one "ranks" the other.

The purpose of the fourth type of grouping, or team, the *clique*, is to supply the individual with the support of a group in the satisfaction of

[1] We believe this distinction between the status and functional relationship to be a useful one, as we shall hope to demonstrate. We are aware that certain of our colleagues lump the supervisory and work-flow relations under the label Status system. Although work-flow and supervisory activities are intimately related, the analysis of the structure and dynamics of human relations loses sharpness and preciseness if their differences in character are not understood.

any personal needs or ambitions the members may have in common. That need may be as simple and elementary as the desire for friendship or as complicated as an ambition "to run the business or the union from behind the scenes." Clique groups are to be distinguished from the others on the basis of their incidence. Cliques arise in response to personal needs of the members; the other three from the needs of the organization. Actually a functional work-flow group or even a supervisory unit *could be* identical in membership with a clique. It is conceivable but hardly probable. For analytical purposes, however, the several concepts should be kept clear. Identical people in their clique relationship may, in the satisfaction of their personal needs or ambitions, either further and re-enforce or retard and undermine the functional purpose of the organization as a whole.

We may now return to the description of the work-flow and staff-line groupings of functions and of the people who perform them, recalling that our purpose is to indicate how the functions performed by such teams help to define and elaborate the system of Functional Specifications. We observe two major kinds of such work-flow and staff-line groups. The first may be labeled an *activity area* and the second a *specific task* group.

ACTIVITY AREA TEAMS

Consider first the *activity area* team. In considering how this concept applies to the company organization, let us ignore for the moment any division of function smaller than the craft. Our first example comes from the Plant Department. Let us say that John Jennings is a testman. How do his Functional Specifications get defined? Being a testman involves a daily routine, the performance within specific requirements of a set of functions that distinguish him from, let us say, a PBX repairman. But, as indicated above, we do not comprehend the *system* of Functional Specifications if we simply collect job descriptions of all crafts utilized in the operations of a company. To comprehend the system of Functional Specifications we must see how an individual craftsman is grouped with a team and how the teams, each with a particular function, are grouped and built up in the ever more comprehensive teams. Here is the picture which results, starting with a testman as the base:

1. *Testman Team*
   Individuals A, B, C, and D are grouped in the Testman Team. They work in close proximity to each other on the testboard.

2. *Repair Service Team*
Testmen are grouped with repairmen and PBX repairmen to form the Repair Service Team.

3. *Equipment Team*
Repair servicemen are grouped with Central Office wiremen and installers to form the Equipment Team.

4. *Field Plant Team*
The Equipment Team is grouped with the Construction Team and the Clerks Team to form the Field Plant Team.

5. *Plant Department Team*
The Field Plant teams are grouped with Plant Engineer, Plant Personnel, Methods, Buildings, Supplies, and Motor Equipment teams to form the Plant Department Team. At this point we have both work-flow and staff-line teams, although the latter may be associated in specific contacts with the preceding work-flow teams also.

6. *Operations and Engineering Team*
The Plant Department Team is grouped with the Commercial Department, Traffic Department, and Engineering teams to form the Operations and Engineering Team.

7. *Management Team*
The Operations and Engineering Team is grouped with the Accounting, Public Relations, Secretary-Treasurer, Personnel, and Legal teams, and the President, to form the Management Team.

8. *Organized Enterprise Team*
The Management Team is grouped with the Union and Stockholders teams to form the Organized Enterprise Team. The union, of course, through its own organization makes contact with the members of subordinate teams all up the line.

From the point of view of the object of our study we may stop at this point. It is tempting to suggest one further degree of comprehension, however, namely that the Organized Enterprise Team is grouped with the Customers and the Government teams to form what might be called the Public Service Team.

In one sense the job description of testmen is incomplete unless it includes the succession of statements: These functions are to be performed in collaboration with the members of Team 2 and are an integral part of that team's functions; the functions of Team 2 are to be performed in collaboration with the groups in Team 3; and so on. One can start with every function performed in Plant operations and follow through to the most comprehensive activity area grouping of functions as we have done in the case of testmen. This is one way in which the system of Functional Specifications in an organization is built up.

Let us take another example of how Functional Specifications are elaborated by activity area groupings, this time from the Commercial Department. Let us follow through the groupings of functions and those who perform them, starting with one craft, service order clerks, in the Commercial operations:

1. *Service Order Team*

   This is a group of service order clerks who work together performing several functions, but chiefly taking orders for new or changed service and typing up orders which are distributed to the several departments for their attention.

2. *Business Office Team*

   The Service Order Team is grouped with the Service Representative, Commercial Representative, and Teller teams to form the Business Office Team.

3. *Field Commercial Team*

   The Business Office Team is grouped with the Customers Service, Coin Telephone (now part of Customers Service), Coach, and Directory Sales and Service teams to form the Field Commercial Team. At this point a staff-line team enters the picture.

4. *The Commercial Department Team*

   The Field Commercial teams are grouped with the Directory, Commercial Engineering, Methods, Results, and Training, Special Business Units, and Commercial Personnel teams to form the Commercial Department Team.

5. *The Operations and Engineering Team*

   The Commercial Department Team is grouped with the Traffic Department, Plant Department, and Engineering teams to form the Operations and Engineering Team.

From here on the development of the grouping is identical with that described in the example from Plant operations. The above picture would seem to indicate that a *group* of people actually performed a team function in the activity area smaller than the Field Commercial Team. This is true in the larger exchanges. In a smaller exchange one person may perform the functions of one or more crafts or even teams. This in no way destroys the point we are making that the functions of an individual are defined as related to, a part of, and contributory to the functions of the series of more comprehensive teams of which he is a part. Indeed, in the smaller exchanges the relationship is established within a single person rather than among several persons. We consider a team as a grouping of definable functions as well as of the individuals (or individual) who perform them.

Now let us follow through the grouping of functions and those who perform them starting with one craft in the Traffic Department:[2]

1. *Toll Switchboard Team*
   Inward, outward, delay, through, and assistance operators and their supervisors[3] are grouped to form the Toll Switchboard Team.

2. *Local Operating Team*
   The Toll Switchboard Team is grouped with information, intercepting, mobile service, teletypewriter, route and rate, and company PBX operators to form the Local Operating Team.

3. *Field Traffic Team*
   The Local Operating Team is grouped with the Clerical and the Training and Development teams to form the Field Traffic Team. At this point a staff-line grouping enters the picture.

4. *The Traffic Department Team*
   The Field Traffic teams are grouped with the Methods, Reports, Force, and Observation, the Traffic Engineering, and the Traffic Personnel teams to make the Traffic Department Team.

5. *The Operations and Engineering Team*
   The Traffic Department Team is grouped with the Commercial Department, Plant Department, and Engineering teams to form the Operations and Engineering Team.

From here on the development of the grouping is identical with that decribed in the example from Plant operations.

When we turn to the definition of Functional Specifications within the union organization, we are faced with two difficulties. First of all the job description for being a union member is indefinite and hazy in the minds of union members. This statement involves no criticism of this union or of any union. It simply reflects the fact that, in a political organization (union), the rank and file are less concerned with *their own* functions than with the functions of those whom they have elected to perform a

[2] Assuming a dial exchange at the local level.
[3] In the Traffic Department, "supervisor" is an employee classification.

service for them. In a business organization, on the other hand, they have agreed to perform particular functions in return for compensation from the company, and their own functions are therefore more clearly defined in their minds.

What we have to say about the typical rank-and-file member of a union applies equally to the typical nonofficial citizen of a community. The fact is that the *job* of being a union member is so indefinite, the *member* responsibilities, processes, methods, and the time, place, and performance requirements are so infrequently clearly realized among the rank and file, that this organizational bond is significantly meaningful as one which holds the organization together only when we reach the local officers. The definition of responsibilities and expected activity *as a part of the union* begins to take form when one becomes a local officer. Up to that time, the only universally accepted function of members are (a) to attend meetings if they feel like it, (b) to ask or demand services of elected officers, (c) to give attention to information passed on by officers, (d) to accept occasional requests from officers to undertake specific services, and (e) to pay dues. Such an understanding by the rank and file of a political organization is much more hazy and indefinite than the understanding of employees of a business organization of their individual functions as employees.

It will be noted that the function of voting has not been included. This is a part of the operation of the Status system. We include in the Functional Specifications system only those items that have to do with the performance of the work of the organization, not those having to do with the source of authority for doing that work.

The second difficulty is that when we study the job descriptions of union officers, they are general in character. There is much less of a division of labor from the point of view of the kinds of work to be performed. There is not, for instance, a "grievance settling," a "social affairs," a "fund solicitation," a "legal," a "collective bargaining," or an "educational" craft. By and large, for different departments, areas, and level of operations, *all* union officers perform *all* union duties in this union.

The elaboration of the Functional Specifications system through a succession of activity area teams therefore takes its definition much more by reference to departmental and geographical areas than from activity areas. As such it is much more closely related to the supervisory groupings than to the work-flow or staff-line groupings. Nevertheless, the officers in defining their jobs are aware of "teamwork *in performing functions* with other individuals and teams" as well as "teamwork with superior and subordinate union officers." Indeed, in the explanation of the duties of union officers put out by the union, the concept of "boss" and "bossed" is warned against and the functioning relationship heavily stressed.

Tentatively, however, the following picture results from indicating how successive team groupings of this activity area sort, connect and integrate the functions of local union officers with those of the organization as a whole. We shall start with a local representative in a Plant local:

1. *Local Representative Team*
   In a large local there may be several local representatives representing several craft divisions, or combinations of these, who comprise a Local Representative Team.
2. *Local Plant Team*
   Local representatives are grouped with other union officers and especially the Plant general representative to form the Local Plant Team. (In this team the staff-line type of team enters the picture, although the general representative, who performs certain advisory "staff" functions, is also an integral part of the work-flow group.)
3. *All-Union Plant Team*
   The Local Plant teams are grouped with other Local Plant teams to form the All-Union Plant Team. This is done through the instrumentality of the Central Committee, which includes the general representatives and the Plant Executive Board member. Another instrumentality is the Central Board.
4. *Union Team*
   The All-Union Plant Team is grouped with the All-Union teams from Commercial, Traffic, and Headquarters on the Union Team. The visible instrument of this team is the Executive Board, its officers and committees. The Executive Board, in addition to members of the several departmental groups, includes four members at large and the general officers of the union.
5. *The Organized Enterprise Team*
   The Union Team is grouped with the Management and Stockholders teams to form the Organized Enterprise Team.

We are again tempted to suggest the further degree of comprehension, namely that the Organized Enterprise Team is grouped with the Customers and Government teams to form what might be called the Public Service Team.

The job description of the Plant local representative is incomplete unless it includes the succession of statements: These functions are to be performed in collaboration with the members of Team 2 and are an integral part of that team's functions; the functions of Team 2 are to be performed in collaboration with those of the groups in Team 3; and so on. One could start with the local representative of any other department (including Headquarters) and follow through to the most comprehensive activity area team in the same way. This is one way in which the system of Functional Specifications in the union is built up.

We have now elaborated our concept of the bond of organization called Functional Specifications by tracing the grouping or teaming up of functions and the people who perform them into ever more comprehensive activity area teams, each with its own defined function. Such an elaboration could be developed from a detailed organizational chart of the company or union, at least through the description of the Management Team and the Union Team. It is a conception with which all management people above first-line supervisors and union officers, particularly general officers, are familiar. It is the definition of Functional Specifications to which the definitions of status positions are most closely related. It is basically the military concept of organization. I suspect that if most management personnel or union officers were suddenly called upon to explain "how our company or union is organized," it is this concept of the elaboration of Functional Specifications which they would develop.

Because this concept of Functional Specifications is visualized by charts, because to some extent the Status, Reward, and Communication systems are geared to it, and because this is the picture of operations which is clearest in the minds of management or union leaders, it is important for any student of the structure and dynamics of human relations to have it clearly in mind. It is real, but it has at least three shortcomings: one from the point of view of the realization of the purpose and function of the organization as a whole; the second from the point of view of defining the system of Functional Specifications as actually experienced and understood by the participants *at all levels* of the organization; the third from the point of view of the student of human relations.

The first shortcoming is evidenced when a need arises for co-ordination of the activities of several activity area teams on a specific problem or project. The activity area concept develops inevitably into the concept of a number of department teams. Each department is concerned with its own defined functions; it has built up an *esprit de corps* based in part on pride in accomplishment of those departmental functions. Status for individuals within the department is dependent on success or failure in attempts at such achievement. Rewards and penalties are linked with success or failure as reported by departmental superiors. Communications are ordered in part with the objective of making departmental success more probable.

Now occurs a problem which is defined, not in departmental, but in management or union terms, or in *organized enterprise* terms. We have already suggested that the activity area concept is essentially a military one. Analogies from military history are not, therefore, irrelevant. The record of military operations in World War II is not lacking in illustrations of this problem. The project is, say, a landing on a particular island which involves collaboration of Army, Navy, and Air Force departments. Those ultimately responsible for the success of that project will testify that a major difficulty is the acceptance of "operations" functions and their implementation by commanders of the several departmental services who by tradition and training have conceived of their Functional Specifications in departmental terms.

The memoirs of almost any president of a major corporation will include a description of experiences in getting the sales, production, and comptroller's departments together in the solution of a particular company problem. One of our unit studies of the operations of this particular company, our study of the transfer problem, illustrates the difficulties involved in co-ordinating the activities of executives whose functioning has been shaped in terms of departmental problems and goals. The union faces a comparable problem in the co-ordination of the efforts of the several departmental teams on an all-union problem. The problem may arise at any level of the organization at which collaboration with individuals on the same level across departmental lines is called for.

The second difficulty arises from the attempt to put reality into the team-work concepts and activities of individuals at all levels of the organization. Actually only a small part of this system of functions defined in activity area terms is experienced in the daily routine activities of any particular person. This is particularly true of those at the employee, foreman, or local officer level, but it is also true of those in intermediate management and union positions as well. Beyond their own associations at work, the system of activity area teams is a concept, not an experience. Moreover, the responses of our informants to our questions about teamwork focus as heavily on a discussion of their relations with their co-ordinates in other departments as upon their collaboration with other crafts or team groups within their own departments. Perhaps the Telephone Company and Telephone Workers Union operations involve an unusually large number of such horizontal cross-department relations. But to the extent that they exist, the system of Functional Specifications must include the elaboration of individual functions through the functions of such cross-departmental groupings. The activity area method of elaboration is not inaccurate; it is merely incomplete.

This fact raises the problem for the student of the structure and dynamics of human relations. In order to interpret human behavior in an organization as a response to the structure of living of those participating in the organization, he must comprehend the nature of the bonds of organization, including Functional Specifications, as actually experienced by the participants.

SPECIFIC-TASK TEAMS

All of this is said, not to minimize the importance of or to criticize the implementation of Functional Specifications defined in activity area terms, but to highlight the importance of another type of grouping of functions which stands out from answers to our questions put to employees and management of this company, and to members and officers of this union. We have labeled this type of grouping *specific-task* teams.

We have said that the system of Functional Specifications includes the job descriptions of individuals, of the organization as a whole, and of the teams which join the one to the other. Obviously, the scope of functions performed by these teams, and the number of individual tasks which are co-ordinated within that function, vary. A team of two individuals may have a specific task which involves the joining of activities which are only a small part of their total job. That they do work together on this specific task may or may not be known and recognized by management or union leaders. This informal specific-task type of team is a characteristic feature of organization both in the company and the union, and especially in the former. Other teams may perform major tasks contributing to the function of the organization, and involve practically the whole time of many individuals having positions in most departments of the organization.

In illustrating the character of these teams and their functions, we shall refer only to these major specific-task groupings.

Company Teams

In the study by F. L. W. Richardson, Jr., of the work-flow within the company, eight specific tasks were identified which have to do with the major function of the company, supplying customers with telephone service:[4]

End Services	1. Completing Customers' Calls
Direct Subsidiary Services	2. Installing and Removing Telephones
	3. Providing Directories
	4. Providing Call Information and Assistance
	5. Clearing Reported Trouble
	6. Monthly Billing
Indirect Subsidiary Services	7. Rerouting Flow of Calls
	8. Expanding Telephone Network
	a. Local Office Expansion
	b. Cable Expansion
	c. Authorization and Cost Estimates

How are the functions of individuals woven together to provide for a flow of work which accomplishes these team functions? Ideally, if each participant in the organization is to understand not only the job description governing his individual activities but his job description as a member of the team, he should be able to see his individual task as an integral part of the team task. We have tried to provide the basis for this understanding by describing the steps in the team task in tabular and in chart form. We may illustrate this process in the company by reference to two of the major team tasks (5 and 2) listed above.

Both table and chart are given for the specific task team responsible for Station[5] Trouble Correction. The same type of table is involved in preparing the other charts, but, to conserve space in the text, the relevant tables have been placed in the Appendixes.

---

[4] This study will be published in the autumn, 1950.

[5] Station is the word used to designate a single instrument.

STATION TROUBLE CORRECTION TEAM

Step	Person	Status	Others	Function	Papers	Inflow	Outflow
1			Customer	Experiences trouble, e.g., buzzing noise or no dial tone, etc. Dials 114 according to instructions in telephone directory or dials "O" to reach operator or calls Commercial Office.			
2				Direct connection with repair service clerk (Step 3).			
2a	Operator (Tr.)	VII	Customer	Receives call from customer who has dialed "O." During business hours connect customer with repair service clerk (Pl.), advising customer that in case of future trouble he should dial 114, rather than "O." Prepares Form E-696 trouble ticket. During night hours operator receives call and records complaint on Form E-696, which is forwarded to repair service clerk following morning. (Where there is no repair service clerk, the operator connects customer with testman or forwards information to testman.)	Form E-696	From Customer	To Plant
2b	Service Rep. (Comm.)	VII	Customer	Receives call from customer who has called Business Office. Takes report and gets information on trouble. Records name, address, date, and information on trouble on Form 1532. Relays information to repair service clerk (or testman where there is no repair service clerk) and closes out Form 1532.	Form 1532	From Customer	To Plant
3	Repair Service Clerk (Pl.)	VII	Customer	Receives call from customer who has dialed 114, or from Traffic (2a) or Commercial (2b). Records complaint on Daily Log (Form E-694). Pulls Line Card, verifies name, address, enters date, time, and detail of trouble on Line Card, and gives it to testman. (Where there is no repair service clerk, the testman does this work.)	Form E-694, Line Card	From Customer	

4	Testman (Pl.)	VII	Customer	Receives *Line Card*. May confer further with customer. Tests circuit to determine location and source of trouble, which may be in the Central Office equipment, the outside cable plant, or in the plant beyond the cable terminal. The procedure for clearing the trouble depends on the determination of the location in one of these types of plant. Testman will call a Central Office repairman, cable repairman, or station repairman as the case demands.	Line Card
5	Station Repairman (Pl.)	VII	Customer	Receives *notification* of trouble from testman. Locates trouble under direction of testman. Corrects trouble and reports clearance and cause of trouble to testman. May also advise customer trouble has been cleared. Makes up *Form 343* trouble ticket which is filed locally and may be of assistance in clearing trouble on the same line at a future date.	Form 343
5a	C.O. Repairman (Pl.)	VII		Receives *notification* of trouble from testman. Locates and corrects trouble and reports clearance and cause to testman. Prepares a trouble ticket, *Form 748*, which is used to compile a record of trouble in C.O. equipment.	Form 748
5b	Cable Repairman (Pl.)	VII		Receives *notification* of trouble from testman. (Under normal conditions a cable repairman would not be called for a one-pair cable failure; the customer's circuit would be shifted to another good pair.) The cable repairman locates, corrects, and reports clearance and cause of trouble to testman. He also makes up *Form 500*, giving data on location and cause of trouble. This form is used to compile history of the cable and as a notification to the Plant engineers in certain cases where further work may be required at the location of the trouble.	Form 500

Step	Person	Status	Others	Function	Papers	Inflow	Outflow
6	Testman (Pl.)	VII	Customer	Receives *Report*. Ascertains that trouble has been cleared. Makes entry in code on *Line Card* indicating cause of trouble and corrective measures taken, date and time of completion of trouble clearance. When necessary, advises customer trouble has been cleared. Puts *Line Card* in return till for repair service clerk.	Line Card		
7	Repair Service Clerk (Pl.)	VII		Picks up *Line Card* from till and enters trouble record on *Daily Log (Form E-694)*, using code. Prepares a daily sheet, *Form E-2703*, recording a summary of number of complaints and trouble by code. At the end of the month these forms are forwarded to Headquarters where they are analyzed to determine if corrective action is required.	Line Card, Form E-694, Form E-2703		

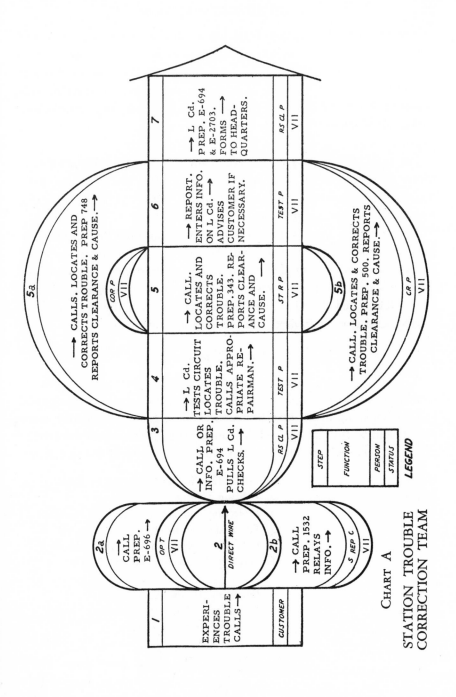

CHART A

STATION TROUBLE
CORRECTION TEAM

The Residence Installation Team has a function more complicated and involving more people in every operating department of the company, as well as in Accounting. The task of this team must be completed before the company is ready to provide telephone service and to carry on subsequent relations subsidiary to that service such as correcting trouble, providing information, furnishing directories, receiving and accounting for payments, etc.

The basic paper forms which accompany this flow of work are the six copies of the Service Order, Form 250, and, after the telephone is installed, the six copies of the Completion List, Form 251. But many other forms and records are involved.

The successive steps in the work-flow from the time the customer requests telephone service to the time he pays $3.50 for this complicated series of activities is indicated on the following chart. The relationship of the members of the team is revealed by their positions along the flow of work. The dotted lines indicate the holding of a form by the person indicated until it is again used in a subsequent activity.

Union Teams

Within the union, as in the company, specific-task teams may be informal, small, and scarcely recognized or they may perform recognized tasks contributing to the main function of the organization, involve many people, and be fully recognized. The major specific-task teams involved in providing services to members in this union we have identified as follows:

Direct Services	1. Preparation for and Conduct of Negotiations
	2. Policing Contract
	3 Protection and Advancement of Members
	4. Education and Informing of Members
	5. Enlarging Social Activities for Members
	6. Participation in Community Affairs
Supporting Services	7. Financing Union Activities
	8. Maintaining Internal Discipline
	9. Building Group Solidarity
	10. Recruitment
	11. Keeping Records

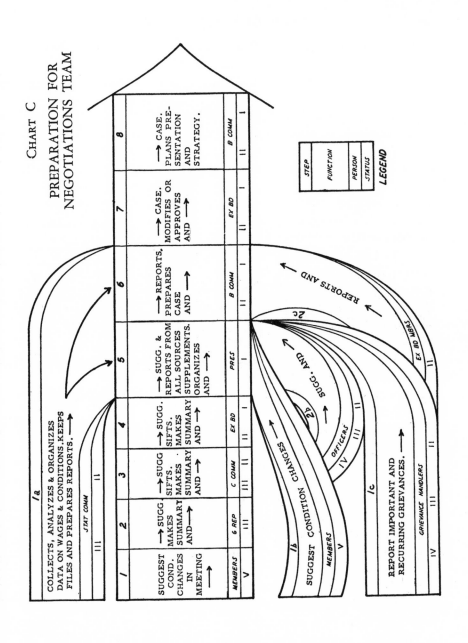

CHART C

PREPARATION FOR
NEGOTIATIONS TEAM

| STEP |
| FUNCTION |
| PERSON |
| STATUS |

LEGEND

As an example of the work-flow by which the functions of individuals in the union are caught up in the functions of a specific-task team, consider the following chart describing the Preparation for Negotiations Team.

Organized Enterprise Teams

To this point we have considered specific-task teams organized within the framework of either the company or the union as such. It will be re-called that in discussing the successive stages of generalizations of the activity area teams we ended with one which included *both* the union and the company, which we labeled the *organized enterprise*. One of the functions of that team we might specify as the maintenance of fair and satisfying relations between the employees and management of the com-pany. In this report we have not developed this concept of a unified society. This we shall do with respect to all bonds of organization in a later report. But as an illustration that such a concept is real, and that it has its own bonds of organization, it may prove interesting to indicate how individual tasks are caught up in that function of a specific-task team—the Grievance Team—which has its own personnel, process, and its own function contributing to a function of the organized enterprise. It will occur to some that several other functions such as negotiating, writing, and administering the contract are also specific-task teams within this uni-fied society.

In considering the steps outlined in the accompanying chart, it should be kept in mind that there may be hour-to-hour personal difficulties which are cleared up between the employee and his supervisor without reference to the grievance procedure, and therefore would not be a problem for this Grievance Team at all. Only if these were unsatisfactorily dealt with in the face-to-face meeting would the employee experience a grievance, as indicated in Step 1. Also it should be noted that although the employee may approach management without the aid of a union official (though the latter must be in on any adjustment), it is always possible that he may break off in his direct dealings and decide to proceed via the regular alternative grievance procedure. This fact is indicated by means of the dotted line from Step 2a to Step 2.

This chart represents the Grievance Team work-flow as formally de-fined. We find that it is possible to skip one or more steps in this process if, by mutual consent of union officers and management, the grievance is

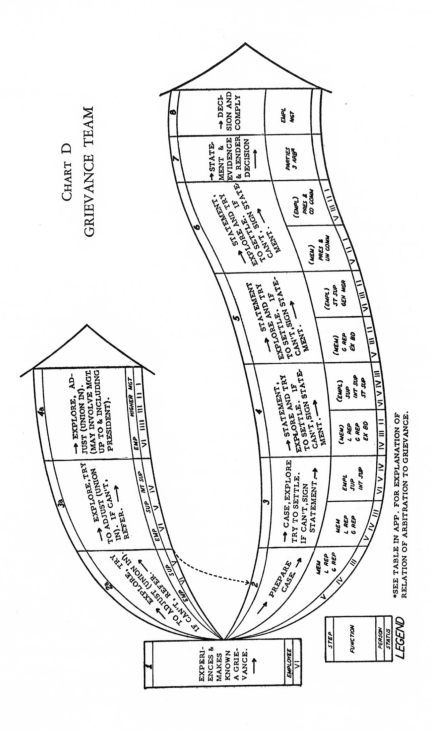

CHART D

GRIEVANCE TEAM

*SEE TABLE IN APP. FOR EXPLANATION OF
RELATION OF ARBITRATION TO GRIEVANCE.

LEGEND

| STEP |
| FUNCTION |
| PERSON |
| STATUS |

of sufficient importance to warrant such action; that the person on the in-
take of the report from the employee may be not only the general or local
representative but an executive board member or the president himself (in which case it is normally referred back to Step 2 on the chart);
and that the employee who takes up a grievance directly with management
occasionally skips one or more managerial levels in doing so (in which
case it is normally referred back to Step 2*a* on the chart).

The contribution to the system of Functional Specifications made by
the specific-task team functions, examples of which are given above,
is harder to discern than the individual job descriptions or the activity area
team functions. The reason is that so many of them have arisen informally.
Those illustrated above, of course, are planned and stabilized. In many
cases, however, the relationships are the inventions of practical men with
jobs to do and an eye for the shortest path to its completion. In some
cases higher management or union leaders are not aware of them. Even if
they are, their definition is not so clear-cut and their description as precisely recorded as are the activity area functions.

SUMMARY

We may now summarize briefly our concept of the organizational bond
labeled Functional Specifications. It may be defined as the system of job
descriptions and of arrangements for association in work-flow operations
which ties the function of the organization as a whole to the functions
of individual participants in the organization through the functions of
teams. It is most clearly seen as having the numerous individual job
descriptions at its base. These are in terms of the individual's responsibilities for personal performance in the creation of the product or service which
comes out at the end of the work-flow. Each one includes what he does,
how, when, and where he does it, and the requirements in terms of
energy expenditure and product demanded or expected of him.

The individual's functions are elaborated and woven together with
those of other individuals by their groupings into teams of ever more
comprehensive and general character in the functions assigned to them
in the work-flow, until at last the largest team, the organized enterprise,
is formed to perform its over-all purpose and function.

We have seen that many of these teams and their functions are formally
defined and recognized. That is true also of the occupational positions and

functions of individuals and the organization as a whole. Such definition and recognition help to visualize the "formal" system of Functional Specifications. In the course of operations, however, men redefine, by their actual thought and behavior, each of these. How men define their jobs and what they actually do may, and, as we have seen, frequently does, depart from their formal job specifications. So it is in the case both of activity-area and specific-task teams. Indeed there were many specific-task teams the functions or even the existence of which were not fully known to higher management. The concept of the organization as a whole and its function varied as between groups of participants, as we shall see in the chapter on the Organizational Charter.

It is our impression that this "informal" system of Functional Specifications is the one which actually operates as a bond welding the participants of these organizations together, since it is the one which describes the pattern of their actual thought and behavior. This is what they were reacting to when giving the responses reported below.

This is the first and, in some respects, the most important of the bonds of organization which weld individuals in an organization together in a team. It is the first feature of an organization which provides a framework for experience of participants, and, therefore, furnishes a category for the description of the organization and an element whose efficiency and effectiveness can be the object of appraisal.

Degree of Satisfaction with Functional Specifications

We may now turn to the analysis of the responses of the several groups of participants in the organization and to an appraisal of the degree of satisfaction they indicate with the system of Functional Specifications as experienced.

The eight questions asked of respondents relevant to the degree of satisfaction with certain aspects or results (hereinafter referred to as results) of Functional Specifications[6] are as follows. The headings are the shorthand descriptions used to identify the questions in the tables and discussion. The heading includes in parenthesis the goal to which the question is relevant.

---

[6] It should be noted that management and employee questions refer to the company organization while union officer questions refer to the union organization.

Job Instructions (Understanding)

Is the arrangement for getting to you instructions on what to do and how to do it satisfactory? If not, what is wrong?

Use of Abilities (Capacity Performance)

Are you dissatisfied on the score that some of your abilities or capacities aren't being used on your job? If so, could your job be changed to use them?

Scope of Freedom (Control)

Do you have enough freedom to do your job your own way to satisfy you? If not, what changes would you like to make?

Teamwork (Integration)

Your job obviously requires considerable teamwork, that is, working together with other people. Illustrate. Are you satisfied with the teamwork? If not, could you suggest improvements?

Respect for Job (Respect)

Within the company do you feel you get the respect which you think your job deserves? That's true of people above you, on the same level, those you supervise, union officers, management?

Fatigue (Creature Comforts)

Does your job normally make you excessively tired at the end of the day? What is responsible?

Steadiness (Security)

When your duties are changed do you have ample warning and preparation?

Fairness (Justice)

Is there anything about what you have to do or how you do it which you consider unfair to you? If yes, what about the job produced this reaction?

Perhaps the best way to get an over-all picture of the degree to which company Functional Specifications are contributing to the goal realization of management and employees, and union Functional Specifications are contributing to the goal realization of union officers,[7] is to consider Table II.

---

[7] The question naturally occurs to the reader: Why are not union members included in the group whose responses help to evaluate the adequacy of Functional Specifications in the union, just as responses of employees are used to evaluate the adequacy of Functional Specifications in the company? The answer to that question should be clear from the discussion of the work-flow organization of the union above. For all practical purposes the definition of work to be performed within the union starts with the job descriptions of local officers. This does not mean that members do not have tasks to do or responsibilities as members. But the definition of these tasks and responsibilities is sufficiently indefinite so that member responses on adequacy of Functional Specifications would not have a positive and clear-cut referent.

This table records (in tenths) the proportion of individuals in the groups indicated who said that Functional Specifications were adequate with respect to the specific results of that bond about which they were questioned. Thus, with respect to Job Instructions, .8 of the Traffic Management indicated that the bond was adequate.

TABLE II

PROPORTIONS SATISFIED WITH CERTAIN RESULTS OF FUNCTIONAL SPECIFICATIONS
(In tenths)

Question and goal	Department	Management	Employee I	Employee II	Union
Job Instructions	Traffic	8	7	8	6
(Understanding)	Plant	8	6	7	8
	Commercial	8	8		7
Use of Abilities	Traffic	9	7	7	8
(Capacity Per-	Plant	9	6	7	9
formance)	Commercial	8	7		10
Scope of Freedom	Traffic	7	7	7	8
(Control)	Plant	9	8	8	10
	Commercial	7	8		8
Teamwork	Traffic	5	6	5	6
(Integration)	Plant	9	8	8	8
	Commercial	7	7		6
Respect for Job	Traffic	8	7	7	7
(Respect)	Plant	9	6	8	7
	Commercial	7	8		5
Fatigue	Traffic	2	8	8	8
(Creature	Plant	6	8	9	9
Comforts)	Commercial	7	9		9
Steadiness	Traffic	8	7	7	8
(Security)	Plant	8	8	9	9
	Commercial	7	8		9
Fairness	Traffic	7	6	7	9
(Justice)	Plant	8	7	7	7
	Commercial	9	7		9

This table records the responses of all groups at the local-exchange level; that is, it does not include management at the district level and above, nor the union officers of the executive board. Later tables make reference to higher management and union officers.

These questions for which the proportions of satisfied responses are recorded do not refer to the total organizational environment, but primarily to that part of it labeled Functional Specifications. Thus the question on Steadiness (Security) does not refer to the steadiness of work in terms of tenure, but to the dependability of job specifications and adequacy of preparation for any change in them. Nevertheless in the case of Scope of Freedom, Teamwork, and Fatigue the response may be stimulated by a situation in connection with some bond or bonds in addition to Functional Specifications. Only through a more thorough analysis of the comments accompanying the direct answers could the factors responsible for the response be separated.

One other comment is necessary before proceeding to a discussion of this table. It will be noticed that in the case of the Traffic and Plant departments two groups of employees are indicated. In the case of Plant, Group I is inside Plant; Group II is outside Plant. In the case of Traffic, Group I is operators and clerks; Group II is supervisors.[8]

Danger Spots

Several conclusions are suggested by a study of Table II. First of all, so far as the proportions of satisfaction with Functional Specifications are concerned, where are the danger spots? At the moment we have no way of knowing what proportions of satisfied individuals in a group are equated with different degrees of *danger* to productive, effective, and efficient teamwork. Arbitrarily, however, we might suggest that normally any group in which .8 or more were predominantly satisfied had little to worry about so far as employee morale is concerned, that any group in which only .5 to .8 were predominantly satisfied should arouse definite concern, and that any in which less than half were satisfied presented a real problem. Call these three groups Satisfactory, Questionable, and Unsatisfactory.[9] A summary of this analysis is represented on Chart E.

Consider the management responses in the light of this arbitrary basis for judgment. We have three departments responding to eight questions, making a total of 24 responses. Of this number 14, or more than one half, fall in the Satisfactory group, 9 in the Questionable group, and only

[8] The reader is reminded that, in Traffic, supervisors are considered employees.

[9] These terms, it will be noted, refer to a classification of participant reactions. They therefore may be considered to throw light on the degree of "efficiency" as we have used that term. The relationship of "efficiency" to "effectiveness" we have not explored in this report. That must await further analysis.

QUESTION AND GOAL	DEPARTMENT	Company			Union
		Mgt	E I	E II	Off.
Job Instructions (Understanding)	Traffic				
	Plant				
	Commercial				
Use of Abilities (Capacity Performance)	Traffic				
	Plant				
	Commercial				
Scope of Freedom (Control)	Traffic				
	Plant				
	Commercial				
Teamwork (Integration)	Traffic				
	Plant				
	Commercial				
Respect for Job (Respect)	Traffic				
	Plant				
	Commercial				
Fatigue (Creature Comforts)	Traffic				
	Plant				
	Commercial				
Steadiness (Security)	Traffic				
	Plant				
	Commercial				
Fairness (Justice)	Traffic				
	Plant				
	Commercial				

LEGEND

Satisfactory

Questionable

Unsatisfactory

Irrelevant to this group

CHART E

Proportions Satisfied with Certain Results of Functional
Specifications

1 in the Unsatisfactory group. The latter involves Traffic Management's appraisal of the degree of fatigue produced by their jobs.

Plant management appears to be the most nearly satisfied with its Functional Specifications. Of the 10 responses falling in the Questionable and Unsatisfactory groups only 1 is attributable to Plant Management, while 4 are attributable to Traffic Management, and 5 to Commercial Management. Both Traffic and Commercial are less than Satisfactory with respect to Scope of Freedom permitted by the jobs, the adequacy of Teamwork, and amount of Fatigue. Commercial adds to this list of Questionable results Respect for Job and Steadiness of job specifications, and Traffic adds Fairness. The responses of Plant Management are classified in the Questionable group only in the matter of Fatigue, a situation characteristic of the responses of both the other departments.

If we turn now to the employee group we find a slightly smaller portion of responses falling in the Satisfactory group. Since there are two groups of employees in Traffic and Plant, we have a total of 40 responses in all departments to consider. Seventeen of these, or considerably less than one half, fall in the Satisfactory group, the rest in the Questionable group. None fall in the Unsatisfactory group. Of the 23 responses in the Questionable group, 7 are attributable to traffic operators and 6 to traffic supervisors.[10] In other words over half (13 out of 23) of the Unsatisfactory responses are attributable to the Traffic Department. Indeed, only the response relative to degree of Fatigue is in the Satisfactory group for traffic operators, and that response and the one relative to Job Instructions fall in the Satisfactory group as far as traffic supervisors are concerned. In the case of both inside and outside Plant the responses with respect to Job Instructions, Use of Abilities, and Fairness fall in the Questionable category, and inside Plant is also less than Satisfactory relative to Respect for Job. The responses of Commercial employees must be classified in the Questionable group in relation to Fairness, Use of Abilities (a situation characterizing all employee groups), and Teamwork.

The questions put to union officers had to do with their appraisal of Functional Specifications of their own organization. Sixteen of the 24 responses, or two thirds, fall in the Satisfactory category. It will be noted that, as far as Functional Specifications are concerned, union officers indicate a higher degree of satisfaction with this bond in their organization than do

[10] Supervisor is an employee classification in Traffic.

either management or employees with the bond in the company organization. Certain factors may be responsible for this. Only the union officers and management responses are directly comparable, since we have indicated that the concept of Functional Specifications for union members is so indefinite and hazy that it is relatively insignificant in their appraisal of the contribution of the union to their goal realization. But when company management and union leadership are compared, it is found that union leaders express with regard to their organization greater satisfaction with those results of Functional Specifications that have to do with realizing their goals of Capacity Performance, Control of their own affairs, Creature Comforts, Security, and Justice; and less satisfaction than management with those results which have to do with Understanding (Job Instructions), Respect, and Integration (Teamwork).

The 8 responses of union officers falling in the Questionable group are fairly well distributed by departments, Plant having 2, and Commercial and Traffic having 3 each. All are less than satisfied with the degree of Respect accorded them as union officers. Less than four fifths of Commercial and Traffic union officers find Job Instructions adequate and are satisfied with respect to Teamwork. Less than four fifths of Plant union officers are satisfied that all elements of their jobs as union officers are fair to them.

Variations Among Departmental Groups

The findings as developed to this point have suggested certain variations as between departments in the proportions expressing satisfaction with certain results of Functional Specifications. Those variations may be brought to a focus by considering the ranking of the departments.

Turn first to management. We may eliminate Job Instructions as revealing insignificant variations among the management of the three departments. Plant Management indicates the highest proportions among the three departments satisfied in the case of three of the remaining seven results of the bond being considered (Scope of Freedom, Teamwork, Respect for Job), and is tied for first, or the second highest, with respect to the other four (Use of Abilities, Fatigue, Steadiness, Fairness). Commercial shows the highest proportions satisfied relative to two results (Fatigue and Fairness), and the second highest with respect to one other. Traffic reveals the highest proportions satisfied relative only to Steadiness, is tied with Plant in the case of Use of Abilities, and is second highest with respect to only one other.

If the departmental standings are rated by adding the number satisfied with respect to the eight items and dividing by eight times the total number, we get the following relative ranking of proportions (in tenths):

Plant	.8
Commercial	.7
Traffic	.6

When the employee groups are considered, and rankings are computed in the same way, it is found that the differences are not great. The averages are as follows:

Outside Plant	.7
Inside Plant	.7
Commercial	.7
Supervisors	.7
Operators	.6

The same method of ranking the satisfaction of union officers in the several departments with the several results of Functional Specifications in the union produces the following results:

Plant	.8
Commercial	.7
Traffic	.7

VARIATIONS AMONG EMPLOYEES, MANAGEMENT, AND UNION OFFICERS

Another point of interest in these findings is the variations to be observed among management, employees, and union officers in the proportions of these groups satisfied with the several results of Functional Specifications in their own organizations. If a reference is made to the averages just discussed, it will be seen that only in the case of the Plant Department is the management average substantially better than that of the employees and approximately the same as that of the union officers. This fact is revealed in Table III.

Actually the average for Traffic management is slightly lower than that for the employees in this department. It is also lower than the average for the union officers.

In other words it is the high degree of satisfaction of Plant Management with its Functional Specifications which made it possible to indicate that in general the management of the company demonstrates a greater degree of satisfaction with this bond than do the employees of the company. In one department, the problem of producing increased satisfaction with Functional Specifications is actually greater in the management group than it is in the employee group.

TABLE III

AVERAGE PROPORTIONS SATISFIED FOR EIGHT RESPONSES WITH RESPECT TO FUNCTIONAL SPECIFICATIONS

(In tenths)

Department	Management	Employee I	Employee II	Union
Traffic	6	6	7	7
Plant	8	7	7	8
Commercial	7	7		7

The problem of teamwork in industry is customarily discussed in terms of getting greater *employee* co-operation. This is a shallow concept for many reasons. One reason is revealed here. Teamwork involves the co-ordination of functions of *all* participants in the organization. The study of employee reactions indicates only a part of the problem. Our survey would seem to suggest that, with limited resources for improving satisfaction with Functional Specifications, this company would be well advised to give some attention to increasing the satisfaction of local *management* in Traffic and Commercial.

FOCI OF SATISFACTION FOR MANAGEMENT, EMPLOYEES, AND UNION

The foregoing types of averages, however, do not reveal another interesting comparison, that is, what results of the bond under consideration give greatest, and what ones least, satisfaction. A rough approximation to the order of satisfaction with the several results as indicated by the proportions expressing satisfaction can be seen by a glance at Table IV.[11]

[11] This order was derived by the simple and rough method of adding together the number of satisfied individuals in all three departments with respect to each result and arranging the results in the order resulting from these totals.

Several interesting suggestions arise from a consideration of this table. The first is that, in all three classifications, management, employees, and union officers, satisfaction with Teamwork is in next to the last position. We have already indicated that the question asked with respect to Teamwork did not produce answers which enable us to say that the lack of clear-cut definition of teamwork requirements in Functional Specifications relationships is alone responsible for this result. But the lowly Satisfactory position of Teamwork should cause those responsible for job specifications to question whether they have sufficiently stressed the nature of and responsibility for relation with other people and groups as a part of the job specifications for participants in the organization.

TABLE IV

RESULTS OF FUNCTIONAL SPECIFICATIONS IN ORDER OF NUMBERS
EXPRESSING SATISFACTION

Order	All Management	All Employees	All Union Officers
1	Use of Abilities	Fatigue	Use of Abilities
2	Respect for Job	Steadiness	Steadiness
3	Job Instructions	Scope of Freedom	Scope of Freedom
4	Fairness	Job Instructions	Fatigue
5	Steadiness	Respect for Job	Fairness
6	Scope of Freedom	Fairness	Job Instructions
7	Teamwork	Teamwork	Teamwork
8	Fatigue	Use of Abilities	Respect for Job

Another conclusion which is immediately suggested is that whereas, in the management group, full Use of Abilities by job requirements is rated as satisfactory *more* frequently than is any other result of Functional Specifications, in the employee group it is rated as satisfactory least frequently. Union officers, however, find their Functional Specifications as union officers as satisfactory as management on this score.

We have here an interesting suggestion for further exploration. Why this result? Does the high ranking of satisfaction with Use of Abilities in both management and union leader groups indicate that executive and leadership tasks appeal to men as those having broader scope, and that equivalence of capacity to the task is harder to achieve? The remark of one high management official to this question, "Man, I'm fresh out of capacities," and the response of an executive board member of the union,

"Brother, this job is so big I'll never catch up with it," might indicate such an explanation.

Another interesting preliminary observation from one of the analysts, that the dissatisfied responses from employees seemed to come from the most highly skilled men with longest service, furnishes the basis for a generalization which will be further expounded and tested in a later report.

If the ratings are divided into those in an upper and those in a lower half according to their standing, the following comparison results: as between management and employees, Teamwork is in the lower half and Job Instructions in the upper half of the several results as indicated by both groups in the company. Aside from these two results, however, the positions of the satisfaction ratings of the other results are exactly opposite. Use of Abilities, Respect for Job, and Fairness are rated as satisfactory *most* frequently among management and *least* frequently among employees. On the other hand, Fatigue, Steadiness, and Scope of Freedom are rated as satisfactory *most* frequently by employees and *least* frequently by management.

These results run counter to popular conceptions of the results to be expected from the experience of management and employees at several points. Dissatisfaction with the amount of Fatigue involved in the performance of management tasks is greater than that involved in the performance of employee tasks. Indeed, it is the greatest cause for dissatisfaction among management and least among employees.

We may anticipate the results of our more thorough analysis at this point. Reports of interviewers indicate that the sense of fatigue is increased to the extent that Functional Specifications involve dealings with other human beings. Those whose primary responsibilities involve the manipulation of human beings report greater fatigue than those whose primary responsibilities involve manipulation of materials. The nature and character of human beings is less well understood, less predictable than that of materials. Adaptive behavior for the organizer or leader is, therefore, less clearly indicated. The uncertainty, the possibility of mistakes, the range of alternative actions in dealing with human beings, present problems which are productive of the experience of fatigue more frequently than are those problems connected with the manipulation of materials. Since the job specifications of management involve a considerable amount of responsibility for human relationships, the result is not unexpected.

One cannot refrain from indicating, however, that the problem of fatigue in industrial life is normally discussed in physical terms, a result of concentration on the circumstances of *employees* who manipulate materials. The organization includes management as well as employees. The fatigue of the former is produced by frustration in attempts to manage human materials. At least this is an important factor.

The other unexpected result is not so marked, yet it is clear. Employee groups rate Scope of Freedom as third from the top in their rating of results of Functional Specifications, whereas management groups rate this result as third from the bottom. This is a finding which we shall wish to explore in some detail in the analysis-in-depth report to come later. It is at variance with customary conceptions of the characteristic features of capitalistic enterprise. The popular conception is that it is management which experiences freedom of activity, employees who experience a regimentation and restriction of personal activity. On the basis of the present study, we are inclined merely to report the finding that management and employees in this company do not respond in a way consistent with this popular conception, and to suggest no generalization applicable to industry in general.

Even at this point in our study, however, we are able to point out several characteristics of the organizational life of people involved in the telephone business which may help to explain this contra-expectancy result. Management in this company is aware of two limitations on individual freedom which are of considerable importance. In the first place they work for a public utility. Restrictions unknown to more competitive enterprise are experienced by those who manage such an enterprise. In the second place, although the Southern New England Telephone Company is relatively independent of the Bell Telephone System, every manager is aware of the influence of the American Telephone and Telegraph Company upon his specific activities. Time after time management expressed to our interviewers the awareness of a certain restriction on their local freedom and inventiveness arising from suggestions and standards that stemmed from the research activities of the A.T. & T. Fully aware of their freedom to challenge such suggestions and standards, and thoroughly appreciative of their value, they nevertheless sensed a compulsion to follow indicated patterns.

Another feature of the experience of employees in this company helps to explain the relatively high rating accorded to Scope of Freedom permitted to employees. To be sure, the descriptions of what one has to do and how he is to do it on the job are unusually detailed. These details of the job descriptions for those assigned to specific tasks are clearly and definitely presented in the various training programs and by elaborate written specifications. Such a program might be assumed to be excessively restrictive on the activities of individual employees. But two unexpected (to us) consequences of this clear-cut job description are observed. Because job descriptions are so precise and so thoroughly explained in job-training programs, an individual is fairly clear in his mind as to how he should proceed to do his job. To the extent that he is aware, in detail, of how to proceed, he is first of all less subject to guidance and correction by his immediate superiors. He is therefore less subjected to the experience of interference in his activities by other people, his immediate supervisors. Moreover, understanding his own operations well, he can be left freer to follow or invent those informal specific-task arrangements which are so important a part of the system of Functional Specifications.

In this situation we become aware of the fallacy in judging job satisfaction in terms of parts of particular bonds of organization without reference to the whole. In terms of the job-description element in Functional Specifications, the employees of the Southern New England Telephone Company are restricted to some extent. Yet restriction in this aspect of the bond makes possible greater freedom in establishing and carrying out informal functional relationships which are also aspects of the bond. Moreover it helps to reduce limitations on personal actions which stem from the Status system. Because these requirements are driven home with clarity and precision, individuals are relatively free from the personal direction and criticism of superiors. Restricted by job descriptions, they are relatively free from regimentation by individuals occupying a position superior to theirs in the Status system. Restriction of freedom in one aspect of Functional Specifications is the prerequisite for a large degree of freedom in another aspect and for less rigid restriction of freedom through the Status system.

The generalization suggested by this train of thought is that the goal of Control of one's own affairs may be realized in terms of the possibility of establishing working relations to get the job done and in the degree of freedom from control by supervisors, in spite of a relatively small degree of freedom permitted by the job descriptions as such.

It has already been noted that union officers share with management and employees a relatively low satisfaction with Teamwork, and that they agree with management in expressing a larger amount of satisfaction with the opportunity given by their jobs for utilizing all their capacities than with any other result of Functional Specifications. Two other comparisons between the union leaders and management stand out. Respect for their job is satisfactory to a proportion of management, second only to Use of Abilities. But Respect for Job is the least satisfactory result of union officers' Functional Specifications. Although the fact is not recorded in any of the tables here presented, it is worthy of note that dissatisfaction with the degree of respect accorded to their (the officers') job by union members occurs more frequently than dissatisfaction with that accorded by other union officers or by management.

Also, Job Instructions for union officers are less clear and adequate than they are for management. When this fact is added to the observation that Job Instructions in the case of union *members* are indefinite and hazy, this aspect of the devices of organization would appear to call for serious attention from the union. The director of this study has ample evidence, not only from the responses to questions in the formal survey, but from informal contacts with members of the Executive Board that they are aware of this problem. The written job descriptions are clear and in simple and direct language. The area of improvement would seem to lie in training.

VARIATIONS IN SATISFACTION BY SIZE-OF-EXCHANGE GROUPS

It will be recalled that the exchanges to be studied were selected to represent all sizes of exchange. The average numbers employed by the exchanges studied in each group were as follows: Group I (2), 1250; Group II (3), 385; Group III (3), 211; and Group IV (7), 66.

The question now arises as to whether any significant variations can be observed in the degree of satisfaction expressed by company and union personnel among those working in different-size exchanges. Did size of exchange influence the results in any way?

The basic data for conclusions on this point are contained in Table V below. This table presents the average proportions (in tenths) satisfied with respect to all Functional Specifications aspects for each of the groups indicated.

TABLE V

AVERAGE PROPORTIONS SATISFIED WITH ALL RESULTS OF FUNCTIONAL SPECIFICATIONS
(In tenths)

Department	Status	Size of Exchange Group				Hdq.	Div.	Dist.
		I	II	III	IV			
Traffic	Mgt.	6	7	7	6	7	8	7
	E.I	7	6	7	7	7		
	E.II	6	7	8	7			
	Off.	6	6	7	8	8		
Plant	Mgt.	8	8	8	.8	9	9	7
	E.I	7	7	7	7	7		
	E.II	7	8	7	8			
	Off.	9	7	8	9	8		
Commercial	Mgt.	7	8	7	6	7	9	8
	Emp.	7	7	7	7	8		
	Off.	8	8	7	8	8		

Variations Among Employees and Management

Certain variations departmentwise are indicated. If we consider the individual groups of employees we get the following results:

Employee Groups	Proportions Satisfied	
	Highest in Groups	Lowest in Groups
Traffic Operators	I, III, IV	II
Traffic Supervisors	III	I
Inside Plant	All the same	All the same
Outside Plant	II, IV	I, III
Commercial	All the same	All the same

If we consider the individual departmental groups of management we get the following results:

Management Groups	Proportions Satisfied	
	Highest in Groups	Lowest in Groups
Traffic	II, III	I, IV
Plant	All the same	All the same
Commercial	II	IV

An added point of interest is that only Commercial headquarters has a proportion of employees satisfied with Functional Specifications greater than any local exchange groups. For management this is true only in Plant. Also division (but not district) management has a considerably higher proportion than the highest groups of local management.

Union Officers

The proportion of local union officers in the several size-of-exchange groups satisfied with the Functional Specifications within their own organization indicates that except in Commercial, officers in the smaller exchanges on the whole exhibit greater satisfaction than do those in the larger exchanges. Headquarters officers, except in Plant, indicate a proportion satisfied equal to that of the highest-ranking local group. All local and headquarters officers, except in Traffic (in Groups I & II), show a higher proportion satisfied than, or one equal to, executive board members.[12]

If we consider the individual departmental groups of union officers we get the following results:

	Proportions Satisfied	
Union Officer Group	Highest in Groups	Lowest in Groups
Traffic	IV	I, II
Plant	I, IV	II
Commercial	I, II, IV	III

SUMMARY

For the general reader the first part of this chapter will have the greatest interest. It is an attempt to define in meaningful terms the nature of this organizational device or bond, Functional Specifications, by which a group of individuals is welded into a team. Its essential contribution is to indicate that the system of Functional Specifications must be described by reference to three of its aspects: the job description or functions of individuals, the job description or function of the organization as a whole, and the job description of those activity-area and specific-task teams by which the first are amplified and organized so that the second may be achieved.

The most obvious type of such work-flow and staff-line teams in the

---

[12] Not in table. 7/10 satisfied.

case of the company is that which groups individuals performing certain functions into crafts, crafts into sections, sections into subdepartment teams, subdepartment teams into departments, departments into the management team, and the management team together with the union and stockholders into the organized-enterprise team. Because of this type of elaboration called activity-area elaboration, the individual's job description includes: You shall make your functional contribution to the function of your craft, your craft will make its functional contribution to the function of the section, and so on until the last and next most comprehensive team makes its functional contribution to the function of the organized enterprise.

In the case of the union the most obvious type of work-flow and staff-line teams are those which group the local officers together on a departmental basis first locally, then systemwide, then these systemwide groupings into an all-union group, then the union together with management and stockholders in the organized enterprise. The implication for the most junior union officer is an elaboration of his job description to include collaboration with and contribution to the functions of the several more comprehensive teams.

The other type of work-flow and staff-line teams is that which groups individuals together, frequently across departmental lines, in the performance of specific tasks. Because of this type of elaboration, giving rise to specific-task teams, the individual's job description includes: You shall, in the carrying out of this particular task, work in the following way with this person or these persons. You will perform your function in collaboration with his performance regardless of your departmental affiliation.

The individual's functions, as elaborated and woven together with those of other individuals through these two types of work-flow and staff-line groupings and their defined team functions, plus the job description of the organization as a whole, are what we mean, therefore, when we refer to the organizational bond labeled the system of Functional Specifications.

The second point of interest to the general reader is the idea that the efficiency of this bond of organization can be tested by ascertaining the proportions of participants who find that the bond as experienced provides a framework for activity within which they can realize their goals, their standards of successful living.

To the members of this particular company and union the specific findings in the second part of the chapter should be helpful in ascertaining at what points and to what degree the Functional Specifications are succeeding in accomplishing this objective and at what points and to what degree they are not. To the general reader, however, who is not responsible for affairs in this company and union, this part merely serves as a demonstration of how this pattern of analysis might be used to disclose the strengths and the weaknesses of any organization, although certain implications pointed out may suggest clues to the understanding of human-relations problems which he may have faced.

Both should be cautioned that we have been considering not the efficiency of the organization as a whole, but of only one aspect of that organization. At this point one would be ill advised to hazard any general judgment as to the relative efficiency with which the organization is serving particular groups of its participants. We must first consider the efficiency of other devices or bonds of organization. This we shall do in succeeding chapters.

III

STATUS SYSTEM

IT IS obvious in every group that a division of labor and the resulting system of Functional Specifications is an essential device or bond of organization. Teamwork among members of the group is a meaningless term without both. Considerable debate has taken place in the course of human history, however, about the necessity for a Status system, that is, an arrangement whereby some exercise power to direct and represent others, which results in a system of status positions in the group and the behavior which supports this system.[1] Even the most casual observation of group activity, however, suggests that any group of people organized to accomplish a common purpose will tend to develop a Status system as one of its important bonds of organization. This is particularly true of a group organized to provide a product or service for economic consumers or for political constituents.

The needs of the group which lead to this consequence are basically two: the organization's need for direction of many people functioning as a team toward the accomplishment of a team goal, and the participants' need for representation in the determination of matters affecting their welfare and satisfaction. The first results in a downward-looking *delegation* of directive authority and function; the second results in an upward-looking *designation* of representative authority and function. The behavior devised and relationships established to satisfy both needs help to define these first two aspects of the Status system.

DIRECTIVE STATUS

We turn first to the more particular needs which result in the establishment of what we shall call the *directive* aspect of the Status system, as we have seen them revealed in discussions with participants in these organizations. In a group organized to provide a product or a service, many specific tasks must be performed before the product or service is delivered. Objec-

---

[1] It will be noted that we are here using Status in a more restricted sense than is customary among anthropologists and sociologists in their discussion of "status" and "role."

tives must be determined and stated. The demands of consumers and the compulsions, opportunities, and limitations stemming from contacts with other societal institutions must be analyzed and adjustment made to them. Decisions must be made as to *what* is to be done. Administrative methods designed to determine *how* tasks are to be done must be devised. Appropriate directives must be issued. Execution of the methods determined upon must be undertaken.

It is improbable that all participants in the organization will understand equally the facts relevant to these tasks or will have equal abilities to carry them out. A division of labor is called for. This division of labor alone might lead merely to a horizontal or work-flow functional arrangement were it not for certain other circumstances involved.

In the first place, suppose we have all of these tasks stretched out on a work-flow line; permission must be granted or directives given to act and the permission or directive must specify the area of discretion permitted to the actor in terms of the fulfillment of the directive received from those involved in the preceding step. This is true even if the "permission" is merely in terms of an announcement that a necessary preceding step in the work-flow process has been completed and of a statement of what the decisions made in the preceding step imply for activity along the line.

In the second place, as the work process of the organization proceeds from setting of objectives, through the analysis of controlling factors, through issuing of directives, through administration, to execution and particular performance, *compliance* must be obtained at each and every step if the process is not to bog down. Unwilling participants must be persuaded or compelled to act, and even the most willing must be advised, persuaded, requested, or ordered to act in ways consistent with the most effective total performance of the group and with the action necessitated by previous decisions. Reports must be received and modified performance suggested after analysis of and conclusions from these reports.

In all of these circumstances the person responsible for granting permission to act, giving directions for action, and obtaining compliance finds that the occupation of a "higher" status than those with whom such functional relationships are established is helpful. The possession of directive authority facilitates the process. This is the case not merely because of the occasional need for compulsion on recalcitrants but because of the need to heighten the effectiveness of persuasion and advice and to provide those directed with an assurance that the direction is authentic and may be acted upon with security. Moreover, as we shall see in discussing the next aspect of the Status system, if, from those directed, any reaction, critical or otherwise, is to be expressed, or any modification suggested in the performance required, those making the expression or suggestion appreciate the value of doing so to someone "in authority."

The carrying on of the processes indicated above need not involve an elaborate hierarchy of authority. Indeed in some cases it could involve only two levels. Several additional factors, however, lead almost inevitably to the elaboration of such a hierarchy in any large group and usually to a degree in proportion to its size. The first is the fact of *numbers* of participants. The number of persons who can be directed by any one person is limited. The possible number decreases as a supervisor, in addition to his function as a transmitter of directives, is responsible for a wider range of decision-making and the study of factors required for such decisions.

Because the number who can be personally directed and upon whose compliance one can personally check is limited, it becomes necessary in large organizations to limit supervisory duties by defining their scope and the numbers supervised. That definition attempts to provide each supervisor with the responsibility for obtaining that amount and type of performance from a group of subordinates which he can plan for, explain to them personally, and upon which he can check. The decisions from which this responsibility stems are left to "higher-ups."

This leads to the next factor which produces a hierarchy of authority, the varying degree of general applicability of directives. With the transmission of every directive from a higher-up, that directive becomes more particularized. Reversing the process and looking up the line, it is more generalized. A corollary of this fact is that the influence of the decision at each higher point is felt more broadly throughout the organization. The decision by the general officers to institute a particular transfer practice has a more generalized effect upon the whole organization than the decision of a particular junior officer to agree to the transfer of a particular employee from one job to another within the Plant Department.

The next fact which leads to the elaboration of a hierarchy of authority grows out of those just mentioned. Performance of the function of supervision at each higher stage of generalization requires a higher level of capacity and of willingness to shoulder a heavier load of responsibility for the *organization as a whole.* Parenthetically we wish to underscore the fact that we are not referring here to capacity in general but to a particular kind, *supervisory capacity.* Experience apparently suggests that the incentive to develop these supervisory capacities and to assume these responsibilities is increased by the arrangement that those who do so shall be awarded a higher status position in the organization than those who do not, and shall be accorded a degree of authority and recognition commensurate with their responsibilities. That some are able and willing to assume such responsibility and are not selected for a status position matched with their ability and willingness does not destroy this necessity.

It is not simply that a hierarchy provides the possibility of reward and functional security for the more capable and willing (in a supervisory sense), however, which makes it a legitimate device of organization from the point of view of promoting good teamwork. The progressively particularized definitions of function as one descends the status ladder provide supervisory functions potentially coincident with decreasing amount of supervisory abilities of men whose supervisory capacities and willingness ripen at lower levels of competence. There is no reason to suppose that the curve of the number of participants in an organization possessing supervisory capacity and desire for responsibility of varying degrees coincides with the curve of the number of supervisory positions calling for such degrees of capacity and desire. Indeed if the former curve were a normal one, that result would not be expected. But the fact remains that the efficient organization must provide positions that do not extend individuals beyond their capacities as well as those which offer full opportunity for maximum use of their capacities.

The first or downward-looking or *directive* aspect of the Status system may be defined then as the hierarchy of positions in the organization endowing the holder with authority to direct and supervise the functions of a certain group of people, and the behavior and relationships which characterize these positions. The positions move from "low" to "high" as the decisions made and actions taken become more generalized in nature and involve responsibilities for an increasing area of organizational activity, and as they affect an expanding number of participants in the organization. The simplest means of identifying these positions is to ascertain who "reports to" whom and who "directs" whom, or to peruse an organizational chart.

The basic status functions of each position in the minds of those who occupy them in this company and union are (a) to accept the directive from the next higher level of authority and to take terminal action in accordance with it if no action by subordinates is necessary; (b) to transmit directives from the next higher level of authority and to interpret the directive and the objectives set by those at that level and above; (c) to particularize directives from the next higher center of authority so that they point to actions which are within the competence of those from whom performance is expected; (d) to stimulate and supervise performance and compliance of the individuals subordinate to the person in that position in line with these particularized directives; (e) to resolve conflicts arising among these individuals or the subgroups in the organization whose performance these individuals supervise; and finally (f) to report to the next higher level.

REPRESENTATIVE STATUS

If we were to stop at this point we would have a definition of the Status system which is frequently assumed to be adequate. It is a definition which fits the conception of organized activity as a series of operations delegated *down the line* by persons with authority to do so. Any realistic observation of the activities of men in status positions will, however, disclose behavior that does not fall within this framework. Our observation in this company and union disclosed an abundance of such behavior. Every supervisor is aware that he not only "acts for" higher management or leadership in relation to his subordinates but also "represents" his people to higher management and leadership. The representation may be infrequent, but it is a part of his so-called supervisory function.

A function which stands midway between the "carrying out of directives from higher executives" and "representing subordinates to higher executives" is the appraisal of the performance of subordinates. Supervisors, in every section of the organization perform this function. Another commonly performed function is the presentation of grievances or dissatisfactions to higher executives, the settlement of which requires an exercise of authority beyond that permitted at the level involved. Less frequently the supervisor passes on suggestions for improvement in operations or conditions of work presented to him by his subordinates.

We may note parenthetically that in cases where the conception of status did not stress the representative function, a tendency arose for supervisors at a particular level to "stretch" the definition of discretion permitted to them to include discretion to institute practices necessary to solve the problem brought to their attention by subordinates. Or a tendency developed to devise alternative methods of representation.

The second or upward-looking or *representative* aspect of the Status system may therefore be defined as the hierarchy of positions in the organization endowing the holder with authority to represent the needs, wants, and suggestions of a certain group of people. The positions move from low to high as the consideration and decision and action with respect to these problems involve effects on an increasing number of persons and areas of organizational activity and hence involve increasing degrees of responsibility for generalized effects. The simplest means of identifying these positions is to ascertain "who brings his problems to whom" when the solution of problems involves action the initiator is not authorized to take.

The resulting picture was not always identical with the organizational chart. One reason is that it frequently involved "level-skipping." Another reason is that the representative function was sometimes shared with a person in another organization, say a union or company officer.

The basic status functions of each position in this upward-looking or representative aspect were summarized as follows: (a) to accept the representation and take terminal action on it if no action by superiors is necessary; (b) to transmit representation from one's own or lower levels of authority to the next higher level (as a report either of a solved or unsolved problem) and to interpret the needs or objectives stimulating those initiating the communication; (c) to generalize the problem presented so that it is stated in terms consistent with the discretionary *area* of decision of the position or the person to whom it is transmitted; (d) to stimulate and ascertain performance by those at the level to which the problem is submitted; (e) to assist those at this level in resolving the problem; (f) to report to the initiators the outcome of the action taken and to explain their reasons; and finally (g) to "live with" the decision made.

The need for a hierarchy in this representative aspect arises from precisely the same factors which lead to the development of a hierarchy in the directive aspect: the limitation on numbers who can be directly represented; the increasing generalization of the representations and effects of decisions relevant to them; the increased representative capacities and desire for responsibility needed at each higher level of generalization; and the utilization, as a reward, of higher representative authority both in obtaining qualified personnel and in making their actions effective.

This representative function is frequently excluded from the definition of the Status system because authority is defined in "from top to bottom" terms. But when, as we have found, a function is actually performed by an individual because of his status position, that function cannot be ignored in defining the character of the Status system.

The importance of this representative function in defining the Status system will become more apparent when we discuss the third aspect of the Status system, the *source of authority*.

SOURCE OF AUTHORITY

It was clear that the authority for the performance of both of these sets of functions, i.e., direction and representation, accompanying each position in the Status system was derived from sources both higher and lower in the hierarchy of status. That from above in the case of the directive function originates in the authority granted the officers of the organization as a whole by the group whose interests the organization is designed to serve. In the case of the company this is the community (acting through government and a charter grant) and the stockholders. In the case of the union this is the membership (acting through a convention or assembly).[2] The delegated authority from above includes that to receive and transmit directives and representations, although it must be observed that the authority to transmit representations is frequently less explicitly set forth and clearly defined than the authority to transmit directives in the case of the company. The situation is frequently but not always reversed in the case of the union.

Authority from below, in the case of the downward-looking or directive-status function, originates in the acceptance of the directives on the part of those receiving them and in their willingness to act accordingly. That

[2] The fact that the union may be organized under charter from a larger unit simply elaborates the hierarchy but does not destroy the logic of authority delegation.

both sources of authority are important in defining the actual status of an individual or of his position in the directive aspect can be seen by assuming a consistent and continued refusal on the part of subordinates to accept and act upon directives received. No amount of modification in the kind and degree of authority "delegated" to that position from above would furnish a bond of organization for a functioning organization until it was coextensive with the kind and type of authority "granted" to that position from below through acceptance and action.

In the case of the representative functions, the authority from below comes from designation of a position or the person occupying it as the *representative* of those from whom the communication comes. Those represented are the source of authority. The authority from above is constituted by the acceptance by superiors of that representative, and of his case as an appropriate and persuasive or compelling basis for their action. As we have seen, this acceptance is determined not merely by personal inclination but by authority delegated from above to accept.

Whether we are considering a position in the Status system in its directive or in its representative aspects, therefore, that position and its occupant receive authority from two directions in each case. A lack of authority from either direction makes the occupant's position insecure and his performance ineffective. If he is functioning in his directive capacity, his security and effectiveness can be disturbed both by an inadequacy in authority delegated to direct and by an inadequacy in the acceptance of that authority to direct. If he is functioning in his representative capacity, his security and effectiveness may be disturbed both by the failure of those whom he represents realistically to designate him as one with authority to represent them and by the failure of those to whom the representation is made to accept him and his authority to represent. In either a directive or representative capacity, the actuality of his status depends on the sources of his authority from both directions furnishing an amount and degree of authority that keeps his position in equilibrium. This is the vertical axis on which the equilibrating forces act.

They might also be considered to act on a horizontal axis to determine not only his effectiveness and security in the Status system but that of the Status system as a whole. That is, in an organization in our culture it is probable that a balance must be maintained between the directive and the representative aspects of the Status system, as on the whole it appeared to be in the organizations we studied.

This is not to say that each of these pairs of types of authority nicely cancels out, or that they balance each other. But a hypothesis suggested by our preliminary explorations which we shall want to examine carefully is that, when that balance of types of authority is not present, equilibrium must be obtained by compensating means in some other aspect of the Status system or in the Reward and Penalty system which sanctions it. Neglect of the representative arrangements in either company or union, for instance, might require either extensive rewards to persuade men to take orders or extensive discipline to compel them to do so when directed. A failure of direction to be balanced by acceptance in the directive aspect might be compensated for in the same manner (i.e., by extensive reward and penalty) or by enlarging the operations of the upward-moving, representative functions in the Status system itself. That is to say a disequilibrium between direction and acceptance might be corrected either by penalties or rewards which caused men to put up with such an unbalanced situation or by enlarging their representative functions so that they had an increased opportunity to change it. But in one way or the other the disequilibrium must be corrected if the organization is to function effectively to achieve its organizational objectives and efficiently to satisfy the goals of its participants.

This concept of the Status system, in so far as the source of authority is concerned, might be represented by the following diagram:

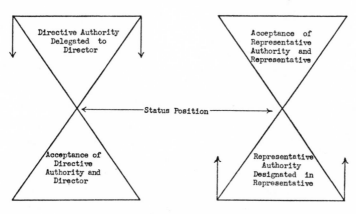

CHART F

Directive and Representative Aspects of the Status System

At this point one warning should be given. It is clear that both company and union, considered as independent organizations, have Status systems characterized by both a downward-looking or *directive* aspect and an upward-looking or *representative* aspect. Union officers no less than company officers are responsible not only for representing their men but for directing them. The failure, in the case of a union, of directive authority to balance representative authority is as fatal to effective teamwork as is the failure, in the case of a company, of representative authority to balance directive authority. The label given the first situation is anarchy; the label given the second situation is dictatorship. Neither, within our culture at least, describes an effective Status system conducive to effective teamwork within the organizations and to effective teamwork between them.

It should also be clear, even when we describe the organized enterprise which encompasses both management and the union (which we are *not* doing in this report), that it is a fallacy to equate the union with the representative aspect and the management with the directive aspect of the Status system in *that* social system. Both perform *both* types of functions in the combined organization, though the Organizational Charter of each may imply a heavier emphasis on one function than on the other.

SCOPE OF AUTHORITY

In describing the realities of the Status system as experienced by participants, we found need for additional categories of features. Important among these is the *scope of authority* which defines the content and boundaries of responsibilities expected of any person in a status position. From some *source* it is indicated that a position carries authority and responsibilities for a specific area of directive and representative functions, and this is usually accompanied by explicit and implicit indications of the limits of such authority. Specifically stated instructions on this point are usually so general and minimal that the actual content is built up in particular situations by an accumulation of interpersonal expectancies which vary with the people involved. The power of these expectancies to stimulate, and to make one secure in, appropriate behavior rests, in some cases, on the same basis as that of written definitions, namely that the person expressing them is in a recognized *line* of delegated or designated authority. But informally this is not always the case, and when the source of authority we have labeled acceptance is considered, it will be seen that there are many chances for informal modification of the scope of authority by virtue of the degree of informal acceptance of authority on the part of those directed or those to whom representations are made.

We also became aware of another important factor which determines the scope of authority which is not attributable to the behavior of specific individuals as such. It might be called the group expectancies embedded in the customs or norms of the organization. The best illustration of this is found in the complaints of certain staff people that they did not have sufficient authority to "control" the activities of line executives in areas related to their staff functions. To be sure we were unable to find specifically spelled-out formal statements of such authority. But in interviews with other staff and line management it became clear that, in this company, there was a recognized pattern of relations between staff and line people which adequately defined the scope of authority in the exercise of such control, a pattern of possible relations involving not only permissive functions but expected responsibilities of staff people in such relations. Such a pattern had become so customary, and was so widely understood and accepted, that it was a stronger factor in defining the scope of staff authority than any written or verbal pronouncement on the matter.

Methods of Administration

Another feature of the Status system revealed in its description by respondents was the *methods of administration* by which delegated or designated authority was implemented in action. This feature is sufficiently self-explanatory, and need not be amplified here.

Techniques

The final aspect of the Status system which constitutes its substance is the set of techniques by which the system of positions and their accompanying definitions of authority are established, by which authorization to occupy them and function accordingly is given or withheld, and by which occupants maintain themselves in these positions.

Needless to say, the Status system is frequently visualized by means of charts, charters, and other written documents, but these simply mirror the system and are not necessarily of its substance.

The substance of any of these aspects of the Status system is the *actual* behavior and relationships among the people involved. This may or may not correspond with the charts, bylaws, manuals, etc., which picture the Status system *as it is supposed to be*. The difference between the first, or informal, and the second, or formal, Status system has been pointed out by a number of observers. Too great a divergence between the two may result in conflicts and confusion destructive of the effectiveness of the organization and its efficiency in satisfying its participants.

In this description and definition we have not mentioned the means by which this Status system and the relationships and behavior it involves are *sanctioned*. Nor have we mentioned the symbols, traditions, slogans, philosophies, etc., by which it is re-enforced. This is not an oversight. The sanctions for the Status system are included as parts of the bonds labeled Organizational Charter and Reward and Penalty system.[3] The symbols traditions, slogans, philosophies, etc., are elements in the Re-enforcements[3] which support the "structure of living" and the behavior which takes place within it.

Nor to this point have we used another word frequently associated with the Status system, the word *power*. This omission has been deliberate to this point, for we are now in a better position to comprehend its content. Power is the resultant of behavior and relationships carried on within the framework not only of the Status system but of the other organizational bonds as well. But even if the opportunities for and limitations on behavior provided by the Status system only are considered, such behavior results in power which has many aspects. It is expressed, not only as "power of superiors over subordinates" by means of delegated directive authority and the granting or withholding of acceptance of representations, but as "power of subordinates over superiors" by means of representative authority and the granting or withholding of acceptance of directives. It is implemented not only by delegation of directive functions to directors but by the designation of representative functions in representatives. It serves both to further the objectives of the organization and to realize the will of the participants. It is revealed not only in conflict but in co-operation. It is sanctioned not only by penalties but by rewards. It can and does operate both to restrict and to expand both personal and organizational opportunity and achievement.

The actual nature of power possessed by any person in an organization may arise from either delegation of authority for direction, or from

---

[3] See *Adapative Human Behavior*, rev. ed. (New Haven, Yale Labor and Management Center, 1949), for explanation of these terms.

acceptance, or both, or from designation of authority for representation, or from acceptance, or both. His actual degree of power is determined (so far as the Status system can determine it) by the degree to which either his directive or representative authority is accepted as well as the amount of authority delegated or designated. The security of his power is determined by the degree to which the balance between the directive and representative aspects of the Status system is such that the purposes of the organization *and* the goals of its participants are being realized.

SUMMARY

As we review the realities of experience of participants in these organizations with what we have labeled the Status system, we find that a summary description of that system would involve the discussion of the following features: (a) the *organization* of positions into a hierarchy, each carrying directive and representative responsibilities of a more generalized nature and involving direction or representation, through subordinates, of an increasing number of people as we move up the hierarchy; (b) definition of the *scope* of authority for each position; (c) definition of the *source of authority* in delegation and acceptance relative to the directive aspect, and in designation and acceptance relative to the representative aspect; (d) *methods of administration* utilized in implementing the authority to direct and represent; (e) *techniques of assignment* to status positions and *maintaining the authority of the positions and the persons occupying them*. Since status relations are always those between persons, we are inclined to add another realistic element involved in the operation of the Status system, (f) the *personal attributes* of those in status positions.

Any first-hand contact with a Status system in an organization will reveal what we have found in this company and union, that each of the first five of these features has both formal and informal aspects. Few organizations lack organizational charts, written specifications, and explanatory memoranda which outline the pattern of formally recognized status relationships and functions. But one who derived his description of the system from these sources, even utilizing the verbal explanations of top management or leadership, would scarcely capture the reality of the Status system as actually experienced and utilized by the participants.

The modification of the formal system by the inventiveness and adjustments of the very "human" people in the organization, in response to personal and social as well as to operational needs, is extensive. This is evident not only when considering the methods of administration and techniques of assignment and maintenance, where extensive informal action would be anticipated since they are obviously dynamic in character, but in the organization of positions and the scope and source of authority, which are more specifically structural in character. Since less attention has been given by executives to formalizing the representative aspects of the Status system than the directive aspects, these observations are particularly pertinent to the former, though of real significance in relation to both aspects.

In our final report, utilizing all materials gathered in our investigation, these points will receive adequate descriptive support. Such a result is already indicated by the progress of analysis to date. Here we may safely indicate that the reactions recorded below are stimulated not by the formal Status system alone but by the Status system *as experienced,* which has a large informal content.

Degree of Satisfaction with Status System

We may now turn to the analysis of the responses of the several groups and to the degree of satisfaction they indicate with the Status system as experienced in this company and union.

The ten questions relevant to the degree of satisfaction with certain aspects of the Status system follow. The headings are the shorthand descriptions used to identify the questions in the tables and the discussion. The letters in parentheses indicate those groups of whom the question was asked—i.e., Mgt. = Management, E = Employees, with respect to company Status system, O = Union Officer, M = Member, with respect to union Status system.

Directive System

General Reaction (Mgt., E, O, M)

Every company or union is organized so that certain people have authority over some individuals and, in turn, must recognize the authority of others. Is there anything about such arrangements in this organization which you don't like? What?

Position Fair (Mgt., E, O, M)

Are you satisfied that your present position in this organization is fair in comparison to that of other people?

DIRECTIVE AUTHORITY

Double Reporting (Mgt., E, O)

To whom do you report? Does there sometimes seem to be more than one?

Backing of Higher Management or Officers (Mgt., O)

Do you feel that you have the backing and support of higher management or officers?

DIRECTIVE ACCEPTANCE

Of Superiors (Mgt., E, O, M)

If you could, would you make any changes in the kind of people superior to you in the organization? What?

By Employees or Members (Mgt., O)

Do you feel you have the backing and co-operation of your employees or members?

REPRESENTATIVE SYSTEM

Grievance (Mgt., E, O, M)

Is the procedure satisfactory for expressing dissatisfaction with the way the company or union does things or has treated you?

Suggestions (Mgt., E)

Is the procedure satisfactory for making suggestions for improvements in operations?

Attention above Supervisor (Mgt., E)

Does anyone in management above you know about what you are doing and how well you are doing it beside your immediate supervisor, and is this found out through him only or also in some other way?

TECHNIQUES

Promotion Requirements and Methods (Mgt., E, O)

Would you make any changes in the requirements and methods of promotion in status positions?

These were not the only questions asked about the Status system. They are, however, key questions, the general reaction to which can give us a first approximation to an understanding of the varying proportions satisfied with this system in the several groups.

As in the case of the other bonds, our understanding of their nature and operation has increased as the reported experience of respondents has been analyzed. Were we to reformulate the questionnaire used as a basis for interviews in the light of what we have learned, the questions would be put differently in some cases and would be amplified. For instance, the representative aspect of status functions was revealed as a prominent and significant feature during the course of our interviews. It should have been more adequately and pointedly represented in our questions. The same thing can be said of acceptance of direction and representation as a factor actually defining the realistic adequacy of authority on the part of one occupying a status position.

In our later reports based on the analysis of all evidence, including that which cannot be treated statistically, due weight can be given to a consideration of such matters. Yet, even in this initial report, some indication is possible as to how much satisfaction is expressed with these aspects of the Status system as experienced in the company and union.

The first two general questions were asked toward the end of the "status" section of the interview so that the thinking of the respondent has been focused for some time on this area of experience. They represent a general reaction to the directive aspects of the Status system.

The next two questions suggest whether the source of directive authority from above is clear and whether it is reinforced by the backing of higher management or officers.

The next two questions approach the matter of acceptance of authority from two directions. First did those whose actions are directed feel satisfied with those who direct them? The way the question was asked suggested comments relative to the directive rather than to the representative aspects of the behavior of superiors. The second question asks whether those who were doing the directing felt that those whom they directed were responding with support and co-operation—that is, accepted them.

The next two questions reveal a general reaction to three types of representative functions: grievance, suggestion handling, and opportunity to have one's qualifications and performance called to the attention directly of those higher in the Status system than the immediate superior.

The last question has to do with only one technique, though an exceptionally important one, for implementing the Status system—namely, the requirements for and method of assignment to (election to, in case of union officers) status positions up the line.

While it would be unwise to generalize from the findings reported below as to the over-all efficiency of the Status system in these two organizations, we do have, nevertheless, the reaction to a number of factors vitally affecting the efficiency of that system. They are interesting both because of their independent importance to the operations of the organization and because of their relationship to the adequacy of the Status system.

Perhaps the best way to get an over-all picture of the degree to which the several aspects of the Status system in the company and union are satisfactory to the participants is to consider Charts G and H.[4]

STATUS SYSTEM		Traffic			Plant			Comm.	
		Mgt	E I	E II	Mgt	E I	E II	Mgt	E
Directive System	General Reaction								
	Position Fair								
Directive Authority	Double Reporting								
	Backing Higher Mgt.								
Directive Acceptance	Of Superiors								
	Backing of Employees								
Represen- tative System	Grievances								
	Suggestions								
	Attention above Supv.								
Techniques	Promotion Requirements								

LEGEND

Satisfactory

Questionable

Unsatisfactory

Irrelevant to this group

CHART G

Proportions Satisfied with Company Status System

The participants in the union conscious of the nature of the directive Status system are chiefly the officers. Relatively few questions were, therefore, directed to union members.

In the case of those questions in which the respondent gave no indica-

[4] The tables on which these charts are based (VI and VII) will be found in Appendix A. They record (in tenths) the proportion of individuals in the groups indicated who said that the particular feature was satisfactory. A guide to the interpretation of these tables has already been set forth in Chapter II.

tion of dissatisfaction, though no positive satisfaction was indicated, the answer was classified as Satisfactory, thus giving an upward bias in the findings to satisfaction.

DANGER SPOTS

Several conclusions are suggested by a study of Charts G and H. First of all where are the danger spots? Where is satisfaction with the Status system relatively low? We again use the following arbitrary classification: Satisfaction (.8 or more), questionable (.5 to .8), and Unsatisfactory (less than .5).

Company

Consider first the management response in the light of this arbitrary basis for judgment. We have three departments responding to 10 questions, or a total of 30 responses. Of this number 21, or over two thirds, are in the Satisfactory group; 8 are in the Questionable group; and only 1 in the Unsatisfactory group.

Plant Management has only 2 items in the Questionable column. Traffic and Commercial have 3 in that column, and Commercial has 1 in the Unsatisfactory column.

Promotion Requirements and Acceptance of Superiors are less than Satisfactory for more than one department. The General Reaction to the Status system, the Grievance Procedure, and the Promotion Requirements are Questionable for Commercial; and the low proportion in this department who desire no changes in their superiors definitely places their responses in the Unsatisfactory column. Traffic Management has a proportion less than Satisfactory with respect to Acceptance of Superiors, Attention above Immediate Supervisors, and Promotion Requirements. Plant Management records the Suggestion system as less than Satisfactory, and the .3 who desire changes in their superiors place this group in the Questionable column with respect to this item. With the exception of the situation in the Commercial Department, however, there are no serious dissatisfactions among management relative to the Status system revealed by the responses to these questions.

If we turn now to the employee group we find, on the whole, that a considerably lower proportion are satisfied with the Status system as it is experienced by them. The leading question on General Reaction warns that this may be true when it is observed that, with the exception of employees in outside Plant (in which .7 are satisfied), all other groups report either .5 or .6 satisfied with the directive Status system.

We have recorded the responses of 5 groups of employees (two each in Traffic and Plant, one in Commercial) with respect to 8 questions, or a total of 40 responses. Of this number only 10, or one fourth, fall in the Satisfactory category; 26, or over three fifths, fall in the Questionable category; and the other 4, or one tenth, fall in the Unsatisfactory category. Moreover, since the Questionable category includes all groups in which from .5 to .8 expressed satisfaction, it is worthy of note that 11 of the 26 responses, so classified, reported only .5 satisfied and an additional 5 reported only .6 satisfied. Of the 26 responses rated as Questionable, 6 are attributable to traffic supervisors and 5 each are attributable to the other four groups of employees. Of the 4 responses rated as Unsatisfactory, 2 are attributable to traffic operators and one each to inside and outside Plant.

This generally low satisfaction with aspects of the Status system among employees suggests the desirability of considering what aspects are particularly weak in their ability to produce satisfaction.

The two aspects of the Status system with which the lowest proportions are satisfied are the representative aspect in so far as it has to do with the Suggestion system, and the Promotion Requirements and Methods. Although .7 of Commercial employees are satisfied with these two aspects, the employees in the other departments reveal relatively low proportions satisfied. Representation in the making of suggestions is satisfactory to only three fifths of traffic supervisors (an employee group) and to only two fifths of traffic operators and the two Plant groups. The Promotion Requirements and Methods are satisfactory to only about half of each group of employees in Traffic and Plant.

A possible weakness in that authority of supervisors which is based on their acceptance by employees is revealed in inside Plant, traffic operators, and Commercial, where half of the employees indicated that they would like to see changes made in their superiors.

Some question about the clarity and adequacy of directive authority would appear to be indicated in Traffic in which .3 of the operators and .5 of the supervisors reported more than one person to whom they felt they were expected to be responsible. This finding will not surprise those familiar with the organization of operations of the Traffic Department in the local exchanges in which the chief operator is the formally designated first line of supervision, but in which operators feel they have supervisory relations to assigned or division supervisors, to a home supervisor (both employee classifications), and in some cases to an assistant chief operator, as well as to the chief operator. The nature of the work apparently makes necessary this division-of-supervision labor, but its effect on the clarity of lines of authority from the employees' point of view should be noted. It is possible that this situation with respect to the Status system is related to some of the low proportions of satisfaction reported by Traffic employees in connection with other bonds of organization.

Union

We now turn to the danger spots in the Status system of the union organization. Chart H presents the situation graphically.

Consider first the union officers' responses. We have three departments responding to 8 questions, or a total of 24 responses. Of this number 14, or nearly three fifths, are in the Satisfactory group, and all but one of the remainder are in the Questionable group. Officers of Plant locals show less than satisfactory proportions in the case of half the items, Traffic and Commercial in 3 items each.

All three departmental groups of local officers show proportions satisfied which can be classified in the Satisfactory group with respect to the fairness of their position in the union, and to the clarity and adequacy of their directive authority (i.e., *re* questions on Double Reporting and Backing of Higher Officers). The representative aspect of the Status system in so far as it is exemplified in the procedure for expressing Dissatisfaction with Union is satisfactory to .8 each in Traffic and Commercial and to .7 in Plant. The only pronounced danger spots are with reference to two items in Traffic and Commercial. In Traffic only half of the officers report satisfactory Backing from Members; in Commercial only two fifths and in Traffic one half are satisfied with Promotion Requirements and Methods.

In view of this generally favorable picture it is not surprising that .7 of the officers in every department report satisfaction with the union Status system in general.

Now consider the responses of members. Since there are five member groups, we have a total of 20 responses to consider. Of this number 7, or over one third, are in the Satisfactory column and the rest in the Questionable column. It is not surprising, therefore, to find that the General Reaction to the Status system in the union finds .7 or more of members satisfied in every group.

STATUS SYSTEM		Traffic			Plant			Comm.	
		O	M I	M II	O	M I	M II	O	M
Directive System	General Reaction	/////	/////	/////	/////	///	/////	/////	/////
	Position Fair	///	///	///	///	///	///	///	///
Directive Authority	Double Reporting	///			///			///	
	Backing of Officers	///			///			///	
Directive Acceptance	Of Superiors	///	/////	/////	/////	/////	/////	/////	///
	Backing of Members	///			///				
Repr. System	Dissat. w/Union	///	/////	/////	/////	/////	/////	///	///
Techniques	Promotion Requirements	///			///			■	

LEGEND

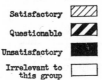

Satisfactory   ///
Questionable   //
Unsatisfactory   ■
Irrelevant to this group   ☐

CHART H

Proportions Satisfied with Union Status System

The members were asked only four questions about the Status system. Eight or nine tenths in every group were satisfied that their position in the union was fair. Only .3 in Traffic and Plant and 1 in Commercial would make changes in their officers. Indeed the only point at which they indicate marked dissatisfaction is with respect to the procedure for expressing Dissatisfaction with Union, only one half of members in Commercial and three fifths in Traffic being satisfied on that score.

VARIATIONS AMONG DEPARTMENTS

Variations among departments in proportions satisfied with respect to the several aspects of the Status system have already been referred to with respect to both the company and union organizations. The interest in these comparisons is chiefly focused on differences in proportions satisfied with respect to the several individual aspects, a matter which has already been covered. No over-all summary is therefore made.

VARIATIONS BETWEEN STATUS GROUPS

Company

Variations have also been noted between management and employees in the proportions satisfied. If the numbers satisfied with those items about which both management and employees were questioned are averaged, the following table results.

TABLE VIII

AVERAGE PROPORTIONS SATISFIED FOR ALL RESPONSES RELATIVE TO COMPANY STATUS SYSTEM (In tenths)

Department	Management	Employee I	Employee II
Traffic	8	5	6
Plant	8	6	6
Commercial	7	6	

It will be noted that management displays a higher average proportion satisfied than do employees in all departments, although the difference is not great in Commercial.

Another way of stating this fact is that management revealed higher proportions satisfied than did employees in the case of all eight of the items about which both were questioned in Plant, seven of the eight in Traffic, and only three in Commercial.

Union

Since union members were questioned with respect to only four items relevant to the Status system in the union, it is possible to make only a brief comment concerning their degree of satisfaction compared to that of union officers. The General Reaction reveals almost identical proportions

(.7) of officers and members satisfied in all departments. Union officers show a slightly, but not notably, greater proportion satisfied that their position within the union is fair. But the proportions satisfied in all groups is high. Union officers in Traffic are highly satisfied (.9) with their higher officers, whereas the members' proportion is .7. The situation is reversed in Commercial, in which department it is .9 of the members who are satisfied.

The union officers in Plant show the greatest desire of any group to make changes in their officers, and the .4 who do so is higher than the proportion (.3) of Plant members who would like to do so. The representation situation, so far as means for expressing dissatisfaction with the union is concerned, is considerably more satisfactory for officers than for members in Traffic and Commercial, but is about the same for the two groups in Plant.

Foci of Satisfaction

If the two questions the answers to which reveal a general reaction to the Status system are not considered, the remaining questions can be related to the following four aspects of the Status system: Directive Authority (two questions for management and officers, one for employees), Directive Acceptance (two questions for management and officers, one for employees), Representation (three questions for management and employees, one for officers), and Techniques of Promotion (one question for all groups). If we rank the numbers satisfied with these several aspects in management, employee, and officer groups as a whole by the rough method of averaging the numbers expressing satisfaction in answer to the questions relevant to each aspect, we get the result indicated in Table IX.

TABLE IX
STATUS SYSTEM ASPECTS IN ORDER OF NUMBERS EXPRESSING SATISFACTION

Order	Company		Union Officers†
	Management*	Employee*	
1	Directive Authority	Representation	Directive Authority
2	Representation	Directive Acceptance	Representation
3	Directive Acceptance	Directive Authority	Directive Acceptance
4	Techniques	Techniques	Techniques

* Relative to company organization.
† Relative to union organization.

Several interesting suggestions arise from a consideration of this table. The first is that within each group the aspect labeled Promotional Requirements and Methods is the least relatively adequate aspect of the Status system. The second generalization is that management and union officers rank the aspects of the system in the identical order for their own organizations. We have noted this similarity between the two groups before in the case of Functional Specifications.

The chief difference between management and employees in their response to questions on the Status system is the relatively low satisfaction expressed by the latter with the clarity and adequacy of directive authority. This aspect ranks first for management and third for employees.

RELEVANCE TO GOAL ACHIEVEMENT

The questions on the Status system used as a basis for this preliminary report are so general in character that it is not possible to infer from the response to a particular question the impact of some aspect of the system on a particular goal. Such inferences can be made more legitimately after we have analyzed in greater detail the content of the responses participants made to these questions. The discussion of this point in so far as the Status system is concerned is therefore reserved for our final report.

VARIATIONS BY SIZE OF EXCHANGE

One would anticipate that satisfaction with the Status system would vary as between large and small exchanges. The character of the variation, however, can not be predicted a priori. Indeed it is doubtful whether, on the basis of responses to the general questions considered in this report, we are justified in doing much more than indicating a general trend which will have to be explained by reference to the analysis of more detailed questions in our final report. Since we have a question which sought to elicit a reaction to the Status system in general, we shall use it as the clue to these variations by size-of-exchange groups. That question was this: "Is there anything about such arrangements (i.e., the Status system) which you don't like? What?" A summary of the proportions indicating complete satisfaction in the responses of management and employees to this question is found in Table X. It will be recalled that the size-of-exchange groups range from Group I (largest) to Group IV (smallest).

TABLE X

SATISFACTION RATING WITH RESPECT TO GENERAL REACTION
TO COMPANY STATUS SYSTEM

(In tenths)

Department	Status	Size-of-Exchange Group				Hdqt.	Div.	Dist.
		I	II	III	IV			
Traffic	Mgt.	9	7	7	8	8	10	8
	E.I	4	4	6	7	8		
	E.II	1	5	6	8			
Plant	Mgt.	8	9	7	6	8	7	6
	E.I	7	5	6	8	8		
	E.II	8	7	6	10			
Commercial	Mgt.	5	7	5	10	8	10	5
	Emp.	6	7	3	8	8		

Company

Departmentally, Commercial Management is the only group which has the greatest proportion satisfied in the smallest exchanges. The smallest exchanges rank second for Traffic Management and last for Plant Management. In these two departments, Group I shows a relatively high proportion satisfied.

If we consider the individual departmental groups of management, we get the following results:

Management Groups	Proportions Satisfied	
	Highest in Groups	Lowest in Groups
Traffic	I	II, III
Plant	II	IV
Commercial	IV	I, III

The above discussion has concerned local management. How do matters stand with those at the divisional and district level? Traffic and Commercial divisional management show higher proportions satisfied than any local size-of-exchange group. Proportions satisfied in all three departmental district managements are at the level of the lowest proportions revealed by any local size-of-exchange group. Headquarters management would rank in proportions satisfied about at the average of management in local exchanges, except in Commercial where the proportion would be greater.

The proportion of employees satisfied with the Status system in the smallest exchanges is outstanding. It is a trend characteristic of every departmental group.

If we consider the individual groups of employees, we get the following results:

Employee Group	Proportions Satisfied	
	Highest in Groups	Lowest in Groups
Traffic Operators	IV	I, II
Traffic Supervisors	IV	I
Inside Plant	IV	II
Outside Plant	IV	III
Commercial	IV	III

The Headquarters employees in all three departments reveal proportions satisfied equal to or greater than those in any local size-of-exchange group.

Union

We may next consider the variations in reactions to the Status system in the union on the part of officers and members in the several size-of-exchange groups.

We again turn, for our clue to the variations, to the responses to the question concerning their over-all appraisal of the Status system in the union. A summary of the proportions indicating complete satisfaction is found in Table XI.

TABLE XI

SATISFACTION RATING WITH RESPECT TO GENERAL REACTION TO
UNION STATUS SYSTEM
(In tenths)

Department	Status	Size-of-Exchange Group				
		I	II	III	IV	Hdqt.
Traffic	O	6	5	10	9	10
	M. I	7	7	8	7	7
	M. II	6	7	6	9	
Plant	O	8	9	5	8	10
	M. I	7	8	7	7	6
	M. II	7	7	9	7	
Commercial	O	7	3	8	10	7
	M	7	6	7	7	8

The highest and lowest ranking groups for union officers are as follows:

| Officer Groups | Proportions Satisfied | |
	Highest in Groups	Lowest in Groups
Traffic	III	II
Plant	II	III
Commercial	IV	II

Officers of headquarters locals in Traffic and Plant show complete satisfaction; those in Commercial indicate a proportion equal to the average of the exchange locals. The proportion satisfied on the executive board is .7.[5]

The variations in proportions of members satisfied with the union Status system in the several size-of-exchange groups is not significant.

The highest and lowest ranking size-of-exchange groups by member department groups is as follows:

| Member Group | Proportions Satisfied | |
	Highest in Groups	Lowest in Groups
Traffic Operators	III	I, II, IV
Traffic Supervisors	IV	I, II
Inside Plant	II	I, III, IV
Outside Plant	III	I, II, IV
Commercial	I, III, IV	II

SUMMARY

The Status system provides for the placing and action of people in a vertical hierarchy of authority and deference. It provides a system which defines who shall *direct* whom and who shall *represent* whom. The first of these aspects looks down the status hierarchy; the second looks up the hierarchy.

The *source* of authority for direction is the power delegated to the director from above and the acceptance of his direction by those subordinate to him. The source of authority for representation is the power given to him by those who designate him as their representative and the acceptance of his representations by those to whom they are made. No Status system provides security and adequate power to participants which reveals a lack of balance between the directive and the representative aspects, and between authority received and authority recognized and accepted in both aspects.

[5] Not shown in Table.

In other words, the Status system says to every member in the organization: This is your status; you are (say) a foreman. You will *direct* workers *a, b, c,* and *d,* in accordance with directions given to you by manager *X*. He has delegated certain authority to you which he, in turn, has been delegated in more general form by *Y*. That is one source of your authority. The other source is in workers *a, b, c,* and *d,* in their recognition and acceptance of your power to direct—that is, the degree to which they accept and follow your direction. You will also *represent* workers *a, b, c,* and *d* before manager *X* or those higher up the line. The source of your authority to represent is your *designation* by them to represent, and the recognition and acceptance of that authority by *X* and those above him—that is, the degree to which they accept and act on your representation.

Clearly revealed in such statements is the need for defining not only the *source* but the *scope* of authority in each case and the need for supplementing such definitions by a clarification of *administrative methods* by which the authority is implemented.

The Status system also involves the *techniques* by which persons are assigned or elected to Status positions, and the *means* by which they maintain themselves in those positions.

Closely related to the last point is another feature of the system as experienced which we have found necessary to label in order to classify descriptive comments of participants—namely, the *personal attributes* of those who occupy status positions.

The strong and weak points in the Status systems of the company and union were indicated in so far as they were revealed in the comments of our respondents. These were chiefly found among the employees (for the company organization) and were with respect to both directive and representative aspects of the Status system. Particularly noticeable was the low proportion of satisfaction with the suggestion system and the methods and standards for assignment to status positions. In the case of the union, the chief danger spot was with the representative system for expressing dissatisfaction with the union in the case of members and the methods and requirements for election to status positions in the case of officers.

A much more elaborate description and appraisal of the Status system will be made in our final report, but enough has been said to indicate its great significance for the effective or ineffective functioning of any organization.

IV

COMMUNICATION SYSTEM

THE purpose and function of any group is fulfilled through the acts of individuals working together in teams, as we have indicated in the discussion of the systems of Functional Specifications and Status. The transmission of information is essential to both individual and team functioning. We label the system by which this is accomplished the Communication system.

In our interviews with the participants in this company and union we sought information on seventeen different types of communications we considered essential to the effective and efficient operation of the organizations. From the descriptions given and the reactions expressed, we have concluded that if one were to describe the Communication system of an organization he would have to focus on a number of items. These are listed below:

1. Subjects
2. Objective
3. Route
   a Between origin and initiator
   b. Between initiator and recipient
4. Techniques
   a. Media
   b. Language and composition
   c. Manner of giving and receiving
5. Timing (including frequency and speed)
6. Authentication and control

Most of these features are self-explanatory, but a brief comment on each may make them clearer.

SUBJECTS OF COMMUNICATION

The chief subjects of communication are determined mainly by the fact that the Communication system is a *helper* to the functioning of the other systems which give patterns to the behavior of people in the organization.

Below are listed the chief subjects noted in our investigation. In the left-hand column is indicated the organizational bond to which such items of information are chiefly relevant. This notation helps to clarify the concept of the Communication system as a helper system.

Relevant to
Functional
Specifications
(also *t* and *u*)

  a. Job instructions.

  b. Specific problems of operation of associates, superiors, and subordinates in the department.

  c. Specific problems of those in other departments with which collaboration is necessary.

  d. The general over-all problems of operation of the organization as a whole.

Relevant to
Status
System
(also *y*)

  e. Lines, scope, and source of directive and representative authority.

  f. Quality of performance of associates, superiors, and subordinates.

  g. Reaction and response of associates, superiors, and subordinates to person and performance.

  h. Grievances and information about method of presentation and handling.

  i. Suggestions and information about method of presentation and handling.

Relevant to
Reward and
Penalty system
(also *h, i,*
and *y*)

  j. Standards by which persons and their performance are measured by associates, superiors, and subordinates.

  k. Nature of rewards available for approved individual or team performance and of penalties for disapproved performance. Chief types of these are wage rates, relation of earnings to amount of work and output, promotion policies and schedules, tenure, personal approval and disapproval, special rewards and penalties.

  l. Nature of rewards and penalties available as result of membership in particular groups or the organization as a whole. (Chief among these are benefits, pensions, special privileges, emoluments, and reputation, or the absence of these.

  m. Nature of techniques, costs, and rules for achieving these rewards and avoiding penalties.

Relevant to Organizational Charter	*n.* Objectives, purposes, and functions of the organization and its subdivisions.
	o. Major policies of the organization with respect to public, employees, and company (if union) or union (if company).
	p. Place and significance of organization to larger groupings, e.g., of company to Bell System, of union to labor movement, of both to national economy.
	q. Character and significance of the organization's achievements and outside reputation.
	r. Traditions of the organization.
	s. Symbols of organization as a whole.
Relevant to Technology	*t.* Nature of materials and tools.
	u. Nature of relevant technological processes and theory.
Relevant to Thoughtways	*v.* Body of fact and principle required.
	w. Thoughtways which give system to knowledge and govern its utilization.
Relevant to Educational System (also *v* and *w*)	*x.* The educational system through which knowledge is acquired.
	y. Characteristics of the people with whom participants are associated in the organization.

OBJECTIVE OF THE COMMUNICATION

The basic objective of the communication is, or should be, to facilitate teamwork in line with the fulfillment of the purposes and functions of the organization as a whole, or that subdivision of the organization whose operations are concerned. This is done by action in line with certain subsidiary objectives, e.g., to provide information necessary for effective behavior, to direct or modify that behavior, or to furnish motivation for it. The first is the relevant objective from the point of view of the organization as a whole, although now one, now another of the subsidiary purposes is paramount in connection with particular subjects of communication.

ROUTE OF COMMUNICATION FROM ORIGIN TO INITIATOR TO RECIPIENT

A definition of the terms initiator, recipient, and origin will clarify the concept of route. The *initiator* is the person who has the authority to initiate or the privilege of initiating the communication. The *recipient* is the one from whom ultimate comprehension or behavior is expected. The *origin* is the source of the stimulus leading the initiator to initiate the communication. He may, for instance, be acting after counsel with or in line with decisions of higher authority, as when a department manager issues a communication from his office after a decision of the General Officers' Conference or the president of the union does so after a decision of the Executive Board. In such a case the Conference or Board is the origin, the department manager or the president the initiators. The recipient in this case recognizes that the communication comes to him from the department manager or president, though it may be stimulated by the actions or decisions of other people and may be transmitted to the recipient by intermediaries. The initiator then is that person from whom the recipient recognizes that the message comes in the form he receives it. If the department manager or president had merely acted as a transmitter of information which the Conference or Board wanted the recipient to receive *from the Conference or Board*, then the latter are the initiators.

Consider an example. A decision, let us say, is made by the proper authorities that it is necessary to reduce labor costs, and this decision, with instructions to act accordingly, is communicated to the Department Manager. If now an order to reduce labor costs were to go from the department manager to division managers, who then ordered district managers to reduce costs by combining jobs, who then ordered foremen to combine jobs of a particular nature, who then ordered employees to combine jobs in certain ways, the communication to the *recipient* employees, would come from the *initiator* foremen and that to the *recipient* foremen would come from the *initiator* district manager, etc.

Likewise if employees suggested to the foreman that jobs would be more satisfactory if combined, the foreman suggested to the district manager that jobs could be combined in certain ways, and the district manager suggested to the division manager that jobs of a certain appropriate type should be combined, the employee is the initiator and the foreman the recipient at the first stage, the foreman the initiator and the district manager the recipient at the second stage, etc.

These illustrations are oversimplified for the sole purpose of defining the *initiator* and *recipient*. They are not descriptions of the way decisions are made in this company.

In other words, whenever a more general order is made specific to bring it within the scope of authority and responsibility of a subordinate, or of a following person in the work-flow, or a particular suggestion is made in more generalized form to conform with the action appropriate to a superior or to a preceding person in the work-flow, a new communication with a new combination of initiator and recipient is set up. The test of an initiator is whether he has the authority or privilege essential for initiating the communication in the form and degree of specificity in which it comes to the recipient.

The *origin* in the first example above is the proper authorities; in the second example it is the employee or employees.

The *route* of the communication is the line of persons within the organization through whom it passes either in process of elaboration[1] from its origin or in process of transmission from initiator to recipient.

If it were transmitted by printed word and distributed by mail, this fact would be noted under *media*, but the printers and post-office employees would not fall within the definition of "persons within the organization" through whose hands it passed.

Should, however, one of the clerical staff disclose the contents of the communciation to a friend or friends, the description of the route would have to include this unauthorized grapevine as well as the line of responsible persons within the organization. Any leak via the employees of an outside organization, such as those of the printing firm, is regarded as sufficiently infrequent to make description unnecessary.

It will be realized that the route may involve no intermediate persons, but go directly from initiator to recipient.

TECHNIQUES OF COMMUNICATION

The techniques of communication may be classified as: Media, Language and Composition, and Manner of communicating.

[1] By process of elaboration we mean, for example, giving it increasingly more particularized form in downward communications and more generalized form in the case of upward communications.

a. *Media of Communication*

The media may include the spoken word directed either to individuals or groups, and be either face to face or proceed via mechanical instruments; or the written word in the form of memoranda, letters, bulletins, or printed materials.

b. *Language and Composition of the Communication*

This·feature refers to the type and kind of language and composition rather than to contents.

c. *Manner of Giving and Receiving the Communication*

This feature is of a different order than the others in that it is heavily dependent on the personality traits of the initiator, recipient, and intermediate transmitters. Yet the quality of the human action and reaction in the process is rightfully and necessarily included in any complete description of the system as experienced. Adjectives which might describe the manner of giving would include such words as patient, careful, respectful, quiet, dictatorial, etc., or their opposites. Adjectives which might describe the manner of receiving would include patient, attentive, respectful, interested, grateful, etc., or their opposites.

TIMING OF THE COMMUNICATION

This aspect of the Communication system refers to such matters as when the communication is made, how frequently, and how rapidly.

AUTHENTICATION AND CONTROL OF THE COMMUNICATION

Authentication of the communication is achieved in various ways through letterheads, signatures, seals, other communications (say information on who is responsible for what, or education on supervisory authority and privileges), and ritual attending the transmission or elaboration of the communication. This feature, in other words, includes those methods by which the recipient may be assured that he can depend on the authenticity of the communication.

The aspects labeled controls are essentially a summary of those aspects of the Functional Specifications, the Status system, and the system of Reward and Penalty which apply to those in the line of communications elaboration or transmission in performing communications functions. Controls are the features of these other systems designed to see that details, as expressed, accurately reflect the facts, and that no hitch occurs along the route in either the elaboration of the communication or in its transmission.

Relevance of Aspects of Communication System to Goal Achievement

Here are eleven aspects of the Communication system (in addition to subjects). The nature of these other aspects is not discussed in this interim report. It may serve to make clearer the conception of how organizational bonds affect goal achievement, however, to summarize briefly under several of the goals these other aspect of the Communication system (additional to subjects) which have an influence on their realization.

Respect is affected by Techniques, particularly by Language and Manner of communications.

Creature Comforts are affected by the Techniques and Timing (including Frequency and Speed) of communications.

Control is affected by the Route, Timing, Frequency and Speed, and Controls of communications.

Understanding is, of course, affected by all aspects.

Capacity Performance is affected by Timing, Frequency and Speed of the communications.

Integration is affected by the Objectives, Route, Frequency, Media, and Manner of communications.

Security is affected by the Objective, Route, Media, Timing, Frequency and Speed, Authentication, and Controls of communications.

Justice is affected by Objective, Language and Manner, Timing, Frequency and Speed of communications.

A thoroughgoing study of the whole range of subjects of communications and the other aspects of the Communication system, plus a testing of the degree to which each aspect aids or hinders participants in their attempts to reach their goals, would constitute a study in itself. No such comprehensive task is undertaken either in this interim report or in the monographs on this investigation which are to follow.

When in our final report we describe the Communication systems of this company and union in detail, it will become obvious that the system as a whole is heavily weighted with informal elements. This is not merely a reference to the so-called grapevine. Such an informal procedure is related closely to the feature we have labeled Route, but it scarcely describes the variety of arrangements among *origin, initiators, recipients,* and *transmitters* to which we have referred above.

When consideration is given to the several other aspects of the Communication system, it will be realized that this is inevitable. Formal attention is given by management and leadership in the company and union to those aspects labeled Authentication and Control, Media, and Timing, as well as to Route. But even in these aspects informal arrangements have been worked out. After observing the extent of these, we are inclined to agree with a number of our respondents who said in effect: "The organization would bog down in a single day if we had to count only on the recognized people and methods for getting or giving our information in the recognized way."

Reference to the list of twenty-five subjects of communication listed on the foregoing pages would underscore this conviction if any underscoring were necessary. The subjects are so numerous and so complex, the variety of personal, social, and operational needs so great, the capacities for delivery and receipt of communications so varied, that it is difficult to see how any management, however competent, could formally devise effective and efficient arrangements for doing this essential job completely. Even if able to do so, and to install such a system, its utilization by human beings would soon introduce modifications to meet uncontemplated situations. The variations in the training and therefore the habits of participants may be expected to contribute—along with the variations in their needs and capacities and objectives as individuals and members of the working team—to take the creation and control of the Communication system out of the hands of the recognized planners and administrators except at a few points where organizational effectiveness dictates a need for uniformity. Even in the latter case they cannot guarantee that plans and realizations will coincide. While this is true of all organizational devices or bonds, it is especially true of the Communication system.

Our respondents were reacting, as reported below, not to the planned system of Communication even in those areas where it *was* planned; they were reacting to planned procedures, which they had remade; but what is equally important, they were reacting to unplanned procedures which they themselves had made.

Degree of Satisfaction with Communication System

Perhaps the best way to get an over-all picture of the degree to which the problems of the people in the company and union are increased or reduced by the adequacy and clarity of communications is to consider Charts I and J.[2]

One difference between these charts and those in Chapter II (relating to satisfaction with Functional Specifications) should be noted. Whereas in Chapter II an absence of any dissatisfaction in the case of Functional Specifications led us to record the response as "satisfied" (thus giving a bias toward satisfaction), in this chapter whenever a respondent indicated that he received no information on the subject, his response was placed in the "dissatisfied" column. There was no system as far as he was concerned. This was an arbitrary choice, and has the effect of decreasing the accuracy of the proportions somewhat as indicating a true "subjective" reaction. (Some might receive no information, but not care; that is, in effect would be saying, "Nothing is enough for me.") Yet since the subjects were chosen as those particularly significant as an aid not only to organizational effectiveness but to goal realization, we felt that the scattered answers indicating no information should be classified as Unsatisfactory. We felt that little would be gained by those looking at the results for an indication of the relative efficiency of communications on the several subjects by adding a third "no response" category; and that a clearer picture of the degree of efficiency of the Communication system would result from a two-category comparison.

Since, throughout the discussion, the communication items will be referred to by the short titles used in the tables, it is desirable at this point to explain briefly the content of each item. In the case of every item it must be remembered that satisfaction or dissatisfaction is expressed with the *system* for getting this type of information. For instance, the proportion satisfied opposite the title Superiors' Reactions means satisfaction with the system for learning about superiors' reactions, and not with the reactions themselves. The system may not be clear or it may be inadequate when dissatisfaction is expressed. The letters in parenthesis indicate the group: Management, Employee, Union Officer, or Union Member, giving information on the item.

[2] The tables on which these charts are based (XII and XIII) are in the Appendix. They record (in tenths) the proportion of individuals in the groups indicated who said that the system for getting information with respect to the indicated subject was satisfactory. A guide to the interpretation of these tables has already been set forth in Chapter II.

Job Instructions

Getting information on what to do and how to do it with respect to one's job in the company or union. (Mgt., Emp., Off., Mem.)

Superiors' Problems

Getting information about the job problems faced by those holding superior status in the company or union. (Mgt., Emp., Off., Mem.)

Subordinates' Problems

Getting information about the job problems faced by those holding lower status in the company or union. (Mgt., Off.)

Employees' or Members' Problems

Self-explanatory. (Mgt., Off.)

Company Problems

Getting information about problems of operation and survival faced by the company as a whole. (Mgt., Emp., Off.)

Union Problems

Getting information about uproblems of operation and survival faced by the union as a whole. (Mgt.)

Company General Information

Getting information about uthe structure, policies, reputation, history, etc., of the company. (Mgt., Emp., Off.)

Union General Information

Getting information about the structure, policies, reputation, history, etc., of the union. (Mgt., Off., Mem.)

Personnel Policy Change

Getting information about some changes in company personnel policy which affect the work of participants. (Mgt., Emp.)

Changes in Rules

Getting information about changes in rules of procedure or operation in the union which affect officers' jobs. (Off.)

Approval Requirements

Getting information about whose approval is necessary (and what they expect) for getting ahead in the company or union. (Mgt., Emp., Off.)

Disapproval Standards

Getting information about personal or union conduct of which union officers would disapprove. (Off., Mem.)

Subordinates' Reactions

Getting information about subordinates' reactions to superiors and how they do their work for the company or union. (Mgt., Off.)

Superiors' Reactions

Getting information about superiors' reactions to subordinates and how they do their work. (Mgt.)

Members' Reactions
Getting information about members' reactions to union officers and how they do their job. (Off.)

Union Reactions to Company
Getting information about reaction of union officers to company practice and policy. (Mgt.)

Company Reactions to Union
Getting information about reaction of company officers to union practice and policy. (Off.)

Subordinates' Performance
Getting information on the quality of performance of subordinates for whose work the superior is responsible. (Mgt. Off.)

Grievance with Company
Procedure for registering a complaint about circumstances of work or treatment by company. (Mgt., Emp.)

Dissatisfaction with Union
Procedure for expressing dissatisfaction with union practice and policy. (Mgt., Off., Mem.)

Dissatisfaction with Company
Procedure by which union officers may express dissatisfaction about company's treatment of the union. (Off.)

Suggestions
Procedure for suggesting improvements in practice and policy to the company. (Mgt., Emp.)

It should be remembered further that when these questions are asked of management and employees, they have reference to the company Communication system; and when they are asked of union officers and members, they have reference to the union Communication system.

DANGER SPOTS

Several conclusions are suggested by a study of Charts I and J. First of all, where are the danger spots? Where is satisfaction with the Communication system relatively low? We again use the following arbitrary classifications: Satisfactory (.8 or more), Questionable (.5 to .8), and Unsatisfactory (less than .5).

Company

Consider first the management response in the light of this arbitrary basis for judgment. We have three departments responding to 17 questions, making a total of 51 responses. Of this number 39, or nearly four fifths, are in the Satisfactory group and the rest in the Questionable group.

Of the 12 responses in the Questionable group only 2 are attributable to Plant, while 4 are attributable to Commercial and 6 to Traffic managements. The relatively low proportion satisfied in Traffic is possibly due to the rotating trick system for assistant chief operators, an organization

TYPE OF COMMUNICATION	Traffic			Plant			Comm.	
	Mgt	E I	E II	Mgt	E I	E II	Mgt	Emp
Job Instructions								
Superiors' Problems								
Subordinates' Problems								
Employees' Problems								
Company Problems								
Union's Problems								
Company General Information								
Union General Information								
Personnel Policy Change								
Approval Requirements								
Subordinates' Reactions								
Superiors' Reactions								
Union's Reactions								
Subordinates' Performance								
Grievance with Company								
Dissatisfaction with Union								
Suggestions								
All Items								

LEGEND

Satisfactory

Questionable

Unsatisfactory

Irrelevant to this group

CHART I

Proportions Satisfied with Types of Company Communications

of their working time which makes regular and recurring contact with them more difficult than in the case of other first-line management groups.

All three departments indicate that getting information on Reactions of Superiors is less than satisfactory. The largest group of local management interviewed was, of course, first-line supervision. Their constant response to this question was "No news is good news." They assumed their superiors were satisfied if they were not reprimanded or corrected. But there were many complaints that they would prefer some more positive means of knowing where they stood. "Silence isn't always golden," said one, "especially when it comes from the brass." Both Commercial and Traffic (especially the former) managements find getting information on Union Problems and Union Reactions less than Satisfactory. In these two departments we found an interesting attitude which could almost be summarized: The union's problems and reactions are not really the concern of first-line supervision. At least two factors tend to encourage passing on to higher management any concern about union affairs or attitudes. There is a feeling that first-line supervision has little discretion in dealing with borderline interpretations of wages and working practices, and that higher management is concerned that "no precedent be set by the handling of local matters." Such convictions create a "don't stick your neck out" and "this is Bill's [i.e., higher managements'] headache" reaction. Since the chief way one learns about the union is through experience, the small amount of experience is mirrored as little opportunity to learn.

In addition to these items which are Questionable for more than one department, others are classified in this category by single departments. Traffic alone records as Questionable: getting information on Policy Changes, Subordinates' Reactions, and Superiors' Problems; Commercial alone: procedure relative to Grievance with Company; and Plant alone: procedure on Suggestions to Company.

If we turn now to the employee group, we find a considerably lower proportion satisfied on the whole. Since there are two groups of employees in Traffic and Plant and one in Commercial, and 8 questions, we have a total of 40 responses to consider. Sixteen of these, or only two fifths, fall in the Satisfactory group, and all but 3 of the remainder fall in the Questionable group. Of the 21 responses rated as Questionable, nearly half come from Traffic employees. Six are attributable to traffic operators, 4 to traffic supervisors,[3] 5 to outside and 4 to inside Plant, and 2 to Commercial. As in the case of first-line management in Traffic, we are inclined to assign the relatively less-satisfactory situation among Traffic employees, in part at least, to the rotating trick (changing hours) practice which increases the problems of contact for purposes of communications from

[3] Supervisor is an employee classification.

higher management. Only the response relative to getting General Information about the company is in the Satisfactory group for traffic operators, and that response and the one relative to procedure on Grievances are in the Satisfactory group for outside Plant. In the case of all employee groups except traffic supervisors, getting information about Superiors' Problems

TYPE OF COMMUNICATION	Traffic			Plant			Comm.	
	O	M I	M II	O	M I	M II	O	M
Job Instructions								
Superiors' Problems								
Subordinates' Problems								
Members' Problems								
Company Problems								
Company General Information								
Union General Information								
Changes in Rules								
Approval Requirements								
Disapproval Standards								
Subordinates' Reactions								
Members' Reactions								
Company Reactions								
Subordinates' Performance								
Dissatisfaction with Union								
Dissatisfaction with Company								
All Items								

LEGEND

Satisfactory

Questionable

Unsatisfactory

Irrelevant to this group

CHART J

Proportions Satisfied with Types of Union Communications

is ranked as Questionable; in all except Commercial, getting information about a Policy Change and about Approval Requirements are listed as Questionable. Getting Job Instructions is considered as less than Satisfactory by traffic operators and both Plant groups; getting information on Company Problems less than Satisfactory by both Traffic groups and by outside Plant. Traffic Operators find the Grievance procedure less than

Satisfactory, and all groups rate the Suggestion system as either Questionable (traffic supervisors and Commercial) or Unsatisfactory (traffic operators, outside, and inside Plant).

Union

We turn now to the discussion of the danger spots in the Communication system of the union. The situation is graphically set forth in Chart J.

Consider first the union officers' responses. We have three departments responding to 16 questions, making a total of 48 responses. Of this number 23, or nearly half, are in the Satisfactory group and the rest in the Questionable group. Of the 25 responses in the Questionable group, 6 are attributable to Commercial, 8 to Plant, and 11 to Traffic officers. Since union officers are also employees and subject to the same time schedules as employees, the rotating-hours system furnishes the same problem in communications to the union as it does to the company. The rotating hours furnish a special difficulty with respect to attendance at union meetings, a primary instrument of communication for the union.

All three departments indicate that getting information on Superiors' Problems and Company Reactions is less than Satisfactory. Traffic and Plant officers find getting information on Company Problems, Subordinates' Reactions, and Members' Reactions less than Satisfactory. Traffic and Commercial officers report getting Union General Information and Job Instructions in the Questionable group. Plant and Commercial officers likewise report getting information on Disapproval Standards held by union officers and Subordinates' Performance in the Questionable group. Plant officers are the only ones whose responses indicate that the process of expressing Dissatisfaction with the Union is less than Satisfactory, but a .7 proportion is close to Satisfactory. Traffic Officers are alone in recording as Questionable getting information on Subordinates' and Members' Problems, Changes in Rules, and Approval Requirements.

If we turn now to the member group, we find an entirely different picture. Since there are two groups of members in Traffic and Plant and one group in Commercial, and 5 questions, we have a total of 25 responses to consider. Only one of these is in the Satisfactory group. Inside Plant records as Satisfactory getting information on what they are to do and how they are to do it as union members. Both groups of Traffic members and Commercial members report as Unsatisfactory getting information about

Disapproval Standards used by union officers, and Plant members record this item as Questionable. In other words *all* groups of employees record as Questionable or Unsatisfactory getting information about Superiors' Problems, the Union in General, Bases of Disapproval by union officers, and the process for expressing Dissatisfaction with Union.

Variations Among Departmental Groups

The foregoing findings have suggested certain variations as between the departments in the proportions expressing satisfaction with the procedural adequacy and clarity of certain types of communications. Those variations may be brought to a focus by considering the ranking of the departments.

Company

Turn first to management. We may eliminate getting Job Instructions, Company General Information, and information about Approval Requirements as revealing insignificant variations among the departmental managements. Plant Management has the highest proportions among the three departments expressing satisfaction with respect to 6 of the remaining 14 types of communications, Commercial with respect to 2, and Traffic with respect to 1. Proportions satisfied are the same for Plant and Commercial on 4 items, and for Plant and Traffic on one item. Plant Management rates 15, Commercial Management 13, and Traffic Management 11 of the items as Satisfactory.

If the departmental standings on all items of communications are rated by averaging the numbers satisfied with respect to all items, we get the following results: Plant .8, Commercial .7, Traffic .7.

In the case of employees, of the 8 items Commercial employees rate 6, traffic supervisors 4, inside Plant 3, outside Plant 2, and traffic operators 1 as Satisfactory.

Commercial employees show an average proportion (in tenths) satisfied for the eight items of .8, Traffic Supervisors of .7, and the other three groups (Traffic Operators, Inside and Outside Plant) of .6.

Union

The relative ranking of the items by union officers indicates that communication procedures are Satisfactory with respect to 10 items in Commercial, 8 in Plant, and 5 in Traffic. The over-all average proportions (in tenths) satisfied with all 16 items are as follows: Commercial .8, Plant .7, and Traffic .6.

The members were questioned about 5 items. None except getting Job Instructions was rated as Satisfactory and that by only one group, inside Plant. The over-all average proportions (in tenths) satisfied with all five items are as follows: Inside Plant .6, Outside Plant .6, Traffic Supervisors .6, Commercial .5, and Traffic Operators .5.

VARIATIONS BETWEEN STATUS GROUPS
Company

Variations have also been observed between management and employees in the proportions satisfied. If reference is made to the averages just discussed, it will be seen that in the Commercial Department the employee average proportion satisfied is larger than the management average, but that the situation is reversed in Plant and Traffic where management average proportions satisfied are greatest. This fact is revealed in Table XIV.

TABLE XIV

AVERAGE PROPORTIONS SATISFIED FOR ALL RESPONSES RELATIVE TO COMMUNICATIONS
(In tenths)

Department	Management	Employee I	Employee II
Traffic	7	6	7
Plant	8	6	6
Commercial	7	8	

Union

It is obvious from the foregoing discussion of the degree of satisfaction with communications in the union organization that members on the whole are less satisfied with communications than are officers. The situation is clearly revealed in Table XV.

TABLE XV

AVERAGE PROPORTIONS SATISFIED FOR ALL RESPONSES RELATIVE TO
UNION COMMUNICATIONS
(In tenths)

Department	Officers	Members I	Members II
Traffic	6	5	6
Plant	7	6	6
Commercial	8	5	

FOCI OF SATISFACTION
Company

Another interesting comparison is between management and employees with respect to the order[4] in which they rate the satisfactory character of information on the several items about which both were questioned. A rough approximation to this order can be seen by a glance at Table XVI.

TABLE XVI

ITEMS OF COMMUNICATIONS IN ORDER OF PROPORTIONS EXPRESSING SATISFACTION
(COMPANY)

Order	All Management	All Employees
1	General Company Information	General Company Information
2	Company Problems	Grievances
3	Approval Requirements	Company Problems
4	Job Instructions	Job Instructions
5	Policy Changes	Approval Requirements
6	Grievances	Supervisors' Problems
7	Suggestions	Policy Changes
8	Supervisors' Problems	Suggestions

Several interesting suggestions arise from a consideration of this table. Both management and employees apparently express a higher degree of satisfaction with the means for getting general information about the company, its traditions, achievements, objectives, etc., than with any other item of communication. This is coupled with a high ranking in both groups (second for management, third for employees) of getting information on Company Problems. Another interesting finding is that although means for getting Job Instructions falls in the upper half in the order, it ranks fourth in each group. Approval Requirements and Policy Changes are apparently conveyed more adequately (relative to other subjects) to management than to employees. The proportion of employees satisfied with the Grievance Procedure causes this item to be ranked relatively higher on the satisfaction in the case of employees than in that of management. The relative position of the Suggestions system for improvement in operations or conditions of work (last for employees, next to last for local management) is worthy of note, as is also the position of getting information

[4] This order was derived by the simple and rough method of adding together the numbers of satisfied individuals in all three departments with respect to each item and then arranging the items in the order resulting from these totals.

about Supervisors' Problems (last in case of local management, third from last in case of employees).

In some cases these results fit the popular conception of the differences between management and employees in industry generally. In other cases they do not. The high degree of satisfaction of both management and employees with their means for getting information relative to the company's general character and its problems is at once a slight departure from this popular picture, so far as employees are concerned, and a tribute to the effectiveness of the Communication system in this company on these matters. The same could be said of the relative satisfaction with the process for getting Grievances taken care of on the part of employees; but the lower relative degree of satisfaction on the part of local management in this respect is somewhat unexpected.

Four possible explanatory factors in relation to this situation may be noted at this point. The grievance procedure for employees is regularized, is specifically defined, is reduced to written terms, to some extent is formalized, and is carried on with the assistance of union representatives who make this their business. Management, on the other hand, must use more informal methods, learn by experience, and operate "on its own." Moreover, the company officers are "employee" conscious and have probably given greater attention to planning for grievance procedures for employees than for their fellows in local management. The third factor we get from the interviews is that employees as a group more frequently present grievances than does local management; and the use of a procedure (coupled with the opportunity to share experiences) increases familiarity with it. A final factor is that in many cases local management is geographically separated from district management so that the opportunities required for the *informal discussion*, which seems the "appropriate and approved" way for management to get attention for its grievances, are less easily experienced.

That management should be more satisfied relatively with means for getting information on Approval Requirements and Policy Changes than employees is to be expected; that getting information relative to Supervisors' Problems should be least satisfactory of all for management is not. However, an objective factor should be here considered (which also applies to the ranking of Job Instructions). Since both of these items are matters of continual concern to management, because they are so intimately related to daily tasks, they require more information if that information is to be classed as "enough," and it needs to be clearer if it is to be classed as "clear enough." In other words the demand which must be satisfied is a large one. In one sense one can seldom get "enough" information on these points.

Union

The order of satisfaction[5] with the system providing information on the five items with respect to which both union officers and union members were questioned is revealed in Table XVII.

TABLE XVII

ITEMS OF COMMUNICATIONS IN ORDER OF PROPORTIONS EXPRESSING SATISFACTION
(UNION)

Order	All Officers	All Members
1	Dissatisfaction with Union	Job Instructions
2	Bases for Disapproval	Union General Information
3	Union General Information	Dissatisfaction with Union
4	Job Instructions	Superiors' Problems
5	Superiors' Problems	Bases for Disapproval

Several interesting suggestions arise from a consideration of this table, although the absolute differences in proportions, among officers and members respectively, satisfied with the several items make a comparison of the relative rankings of degree of satisfaction with the several items as between officers and members of little value.

An interesting juxtaposition which is both relative and absolute, however, is revealed in the position of the means for getting information about the bases on which higher union officers would be inclined to disapprove what is done by union officers and members respectively. Union members are least satisfied with the system on this point. Union officers, probably because of their more frequent personal contacts with higher union officers, are relatively well satisfied.

Although not more than an average of .6 of union members are satisfied with the process for learning what to do as union members, it is interesting to note that this item rates highest in their judgment as satis-

---

[5] This order was derived by the simple and rough method of adding together the numbers of satisfied individuals in all three departments with respect to each item and then arranging the items in the order resulting from these totals.

factory among the several communication items about which they were questioned, and that the system for getting general information about the union ranks next. The lowest relative satisfaction rating is accorded by members to those items which have to do with learning what their officers are up against and how their officers appraise their performance as union members.

Union officers are also relatively dissatisfied with the method for learning about the problems of their superior officers. The relatively low position among officers of the system relative to Job Instructions is also worthy of note, although the absolute difference in proportions satisfied with this item and the others which "outrank" it is not great. Nevertheless the fact that getting information relative to performance of duties as a union officer (Job Instructions and Superiors' Problems) is the least satisfactory of the items of communication cited is of significance.

Again we must point out, as we did in the case of management, that the importance attached to "knowing the job" is greater for officers than for members. In one sense they are aware that information on this point can hardly be enough no matter how effective the system for getting it. This may account for the relatively small numbers who are satisfied with the Communication system on this score.

RELEVANCE OF COMMUNICATIONS TO GOAL ACHIEVEMENT

Adequate information is essential if an individual is to act or respond in such a way as to achieve his goals. To relate each item of communication to a particular goal, however, would be not only difficult but confusing. Moreover each item may be, and is, related to the achievement of several goals. Any averaging therefore would tend to reproduce the general average for all types. It is worth pointing out, however, that the variations noted among exchanges and among different departmental and status groups in satisfaction with the communication would normally be reflected immediately in variation in ability to achieve certain goals, particularly those of understanding, control, capacity performance, integration, and security. Any appraisal of the effect of the Communication system on goal achievement must, however, take account not only of the adequacy and clarity of information and procedures on certain subjects but of other aspects of the Communication system as well, such as Route, Media, Language, Manner, Timing, and Authentication and Control. Since we are not considering these aspects in this report, it would not be useful to discuss the matter of relevance to goal achievement merely in terms of over-all satisfaction with communication procedures.

COMMUNICATIONS RELEVANT TO EFFECTIVENESS OF OTHER BONDS OF ORGANIZATION

We indicated in the introduction that the Communication system was a helper system to the other bonds of organization. We should now inquire to what degree it is furnishing information and procedures adequate to perform that service to the other bonds: Functional Specifications, Status system, Reward and Penalty system, and the Organizational Charter.

We may classify those communication items about which we asked questions in accordance with those bonds to which they are primarily helpers. The results are recorded in Tables XVIII and XIX. A difference of judgment is possible with respect to the allocation of certain of the Communication system items as helpers to the several bonds. The ones listed in these tables are, we believe, clearly relevant without any straining of interpretation.

TABLE XVIII

COMMUNICATION ITEMS CONTRIBUTING TO EFFECTIVENESS OF OTHER BONDS OF ORGANIZATION (COMPANY)

Bond	Contributing Items*	
	Employees	Management
Functional Specifications	1, 5, 9	1, 2, 3, 4, 5, 9
Status System	1, 15, 17	1, 11, 12, 14, 15, 17
Reward and Penalty	7, 10, 15, 17	7, 10, 11, 12, 15, 17
Organizational Charter	5, 7	5, 7

* Items from company questionnaire: 1. Job Instructions, 2. Superiors' Problems, 3. Subordinates' Problems, 4. Employees' Problems, 5. Company Problems, 6. Union Problems, 7. Company General Information, 8. Union General Information, 9. Personnel Policy Change, 10. Approval Requirements, 11. Subordinates' Reactions, 12. Superiors' Reactions, 13. Union's Reactions to Company, 14. Subordinates' Performance, 15. Grievance with Company, 16. Dissatisfaction with Union, 17. Suggestions to Company.

An averaging of the numbers satisfied with respect to those types of information represented by the question numbers in the columns opposite each bond reveals the situation disclosed in Tables XX and XXI.

TABLE XIX

COMMUNICATION ITEMS CONTRIBUTING TO EFFECTIVENESS OF OTHER BONDS OF
ORGANIZATION (UNION)

Bond	Contributing Items*	
	Members	Officers
Functional Specifications	1, 2	1, 2, 3, 4, 8
Status System	1, 15	1, 11, 12, 14, 15
Reward and Penalty	7, 10, 15	7, 9, 10, 11, 12, 15
Organizational Charter	2, 7	2, 7

* Items from union questionnaire: 1. Job Instructions, 2. Superiors' Problems, 3. Subordinates' Problems, 4. Members' Problems, 5. Company Problems, 6. Company General Information, 7. Union General Information, 8. Changes in Rules, 9. Approval Requirements, 10. Disapproval Standards, 11. Subordinates' Reactions, 12. Members' Reactions, 13. Company Reactions to Union, 14. Subordinates' Performance, 15. Dissatisfaction with Union, 16. Dissatisfaction with Company Dealings with Union.

Company

It would be anticipated from the previous discussion that each organizational bond is better served by the Communication system in the case of management than it is in the case of employees.

TABLE XX

PROPORTIONS SATISFIED WITH INFORMATION OR COMMUNICATIONS PROCEDURES SERVING
AS HELPERS TO OTHER BONDS OF ORGANIZATION (COMPANY)

(In tenths)

Bond	Proportions Satisfied					
	Employees			Management		
	Tr.	Pl.	Comm.	Tr.	Pl.	Comm.
Functional Specifications	6	6	8	8	8	8
Status System	6	6	7	7	7	7
Reward and Penalty	6	6	8	7	7	7
Organizational Charter	7	7	9	9	9	8

Among employees, only those in Commercial reveal a proportion satisfied which can be classified as Satisfactory. This they do with respect to getting information relevant to all bonds save the Status system. Employees in all other departments indicate proportions of satisfaction which must classify their degree of satisfaction with information or communications procedures as Questionable. Those with respect to the Organizational Charter come closest to achieving the status of Satisfactory.

In the case of management the satisfied proportions enable us to conclude that information and procedures relative to Functional Specifications and Organizational Charter are Satisfactory; and those relevant to the other two bonds, though falling in the Questionable group, are very close to the Satisfactory group.

Union

The information and communication procedures available to "help" the union's bonds of organization are less effective in the case of union members than in the case of union officers. In every case, save in that of Plant members relative to Functional Specifications and the Status system, the proportions fall in the .6 or the .5 groups for members. This is dangerously close to the Unsatisfactory category.

TABLE XXI

PROPORTIONS SATISFIED WITH INFORMATION OR COMMUNICATIONS PROCEDURES SERVING AS HELPERS TO OTHER BONDS OF ORGANIZATION (UNION)

(In tenths)

| | Proportions Satisfied | | | | | |
| | Members | | | Officers | | |
Bond	Tr.	Pl.	Comm.	Tr.	Pl.	Comm.
Functional Specifications	6	7	6	6	8	8
Status System	6	7	5	7	7	7
Reward and Penalty	5	6	5	6	7	7
Organizational Charter	5	6	6	6	7	7

The general picture for union officers is that in Commercial and Plant all bonds are served fairly well, the proportions of satisfied individuals falling in the .7 group except in the case of information on procedures relevant to Functional Specifications, where they fall in the .8 (Satisfactory) group. Traffic officers, however, report less satisfaction than officers in the other departmental locals with respect to items serving as helpers to all bonds.

VARIATIONS BY SIZE OF EXCHANGE GROUPS

In the case of Functional Specifications and the Status systems, we found that the size of the exchange influenced considerably the proportions of satisfaction revealed and that variations were marked in the case of certain types of responses. What was the effect of this factor in the case of the Communication system?

Company

The basic data for conclusions on this point with respect to management and employees are contained in Table XXII below. This table presents the average proportions (in tenths) satisfied with respect to all items of communications for each of the groups indicated.

TABLE XXII

AVERAGE SATISFACTION RATING WITH RESPECT TO ALL SUBJECTS OF
COMPANY COMMUNICATIONS

(In tenths)

| Dept. | Status | Size of Exchange Group | | | | Hdqt. | Div. | Dist |
		I	II	III	IV			
Traffic	Mgt.	8	7	8	8	8	9	6
	Empl. I	6	6	6	7	7		
	Empl. II	6	7	7	7			
Plant	Mgt.	8	8	8	8	9	8	8
	Empl. I	6	6	6	5	7		
	Empl. II	7	6	4	6			
Commercial	Mgt.	8	8	9	8	8	10	8
	Empl.	7	8	8	8	7		

The highest and lowest proportions satisfied for employee groups are indicated below:

| Employee Group | Proportions Satisfied | |
	Highest in Groups	Lowest in Groups
Traffic Operators	IV	I, II, III
Traffic Supervisors	II, III, IV	I
Inside Plant	I, II, III	IV
Outside Plant	I	III
Commercial	II, III, IV	I

The headquarters employees in Plant and Traffic have a proportion satisfied equal to any local group. This is not the case, however, with Commercial headquarters.

The highest and lowest proportions are indicated below for management in each department:

| Management Group | Proportions Satisfied | |
	Highest in Groups	Lowest in Groups
Traffic	I, III, IV	II
Plant	All the same	All the same
Commercial	III	I, II, IV

Division management reports a higher proportion satisfied than does any local group in Traffic and Commercial, and an equal proportion in Plant. District management has a lower proportion satisfied, however, than one or more local exchange groups in Traffic and Commercial. Headquarters management groups reveal proportions satisfied about equal to the average for local management groups.

Union

One can make only one generalization concerning variations according to size of exchange in satisfaction with the union Communication system. Members in Group I (the largest) exchanges reveal the lowest proportions satisfied in every department. The proportions (in tenths) are indicated in Table XXIII.

TABLE XXIII

AVERAGE SATISFACTION RATING WITH RESPECT TO ALL SUBJECT OF
UNION COMMUNICATIONS
(In tenths)

Dept.	Status	I	II	III	IV	Hdqt.
Traffic	Officers	6	6	6	7	7
	Mem. I	4	5	5	6	6
	Mem. II	4	7	6	6	
Plant	Officers	8	6	7	9	9
	Mem. I	6	7	6	6	5
	Mem. II	4	5	8	7	
Commercial	Officers	8	8	8	7	9
	Mem.	5	5	5	5	6

The highest and lowest proportions for members and officers are indicated below:

Member Group	Proportions Satisfied	
	Highest in Groups	Lowest in Groups
Traffic Operators	IV	I
Traffic Supervisors	II	I
Inside Plant	II	I, III, IV
Outside Plant	III	I
Commercial	All the same	All the same

Headquarters members show a larger proportion satisfied in Commercial than does any field local group.

Officer Group	Proportions Satisfied	
	Highest in Groups	Lowest in Groups
Traffic	IV	I, II, III
Plant	IV	II
Commercial	I, II, III	IV

Officers in the headquarters locals show a larger proportion satisfied than, or equal to, those in any field local group. The executive board[6] reports .7 satisfied, a proportion lower than headquarters local officers in Plant and Commercial.

SUMMARY

The system for transmitting information is properly regarded by organizers and leaders as basic to the functioning of any group. We have in this report discussed the reactions of workers in general terms to the system as it deals with several types of communications. This gives only a first approximation to an understanding of how well the system is working. Reference to the definition of the Communication system contained in the first part of this chapter will make it clear that any thorough-going conclusions on this matter would have to be derived from an analysis of many aspects of the system. Adequacy or inadequacy may arise from a situation as disclosed by the answers to a number of questions. Are all necessary or desirable items made *subjects* of communication? Are the *objectives* of communications clearly set forth and are they legitimate? Is the *route* clear and effective and is it a two-way street? Do the *media, language,* and *manner* used facilitate understanding? Is the *timing* good?

[6] Not shown in tables.

Is the system for *authentication* and *control* of communications working satisfactorily? Are all of these aspects such, in nature and in operation, that the several goals of the participants and of the whole organization are brought closer to realization?

Fully recognizing that our conclusions are only first approximations to the question, "How satisfactory is the Communication system in this company and union?" they nevertheless reveal certain areas of concern for those responsible for the welfare of these organizations.

Departmentally, with respect to employees (especially operators), management, union leaders, and members, Traffic shows the lowest proportions satisfied. We have suggested that a major factor contributing to this situation is the rotating of work hours.

Management shows a higher proportion satisfied in general than do employees; union officers a higher proportion than members.

For both management and employees the suggestion system and the means for obtaining information about superiors' problems would appear to require attention. Also relatively less satisfactory than other items in the case of management is the system for getting grievances taken care of and for being clear about superiors' reactions. Employees rate as relatively less satisfactory than other items, in addition to those named above, getting information about personnel policy changes and about the standards superiors use in approving or disapproving.

In view of the close to Unsatisfactory proportions of union members expressing satisfaction with all items of communication, a major task for the union in this area would seem to be indicated. Attention in the case of the system as it applies to officers might well be directed to the means for learning about superiors' problems, the duties and responsibilities of office, the reactions of subordinate officers, and about company problems and management's reactions to the union.

The largest exchanges on the whole show lower proportions satisfied than the smallest exchanges, but departmentally there is some variation from this general pattern.

Since we have labeled the Communication system a helper system to the other bonds of organization, it is of interest to see which of them, if any, are well served. Among both employees and management most satisfactory aid is given the Organizational Charter—that is, the concept of the company as a whole, its purpose, function, policies, affiliations, reputation, and the symbols, slogans, traditions, etc., which support it. Functional Specifications, the Status system, and the Reward and Penalty system are not so well served for employees in Traffic and Plant as is Organizational Charter.

As would be expected from foregoing comments, all bonds in the union are in need of greater support from the Communication system as far as members are concerned; but with the exception of Traffic they are fairly well supported in the case of union officers.

An effective and efficient means for acquiring and imparting information on the various subjects discussed in this chapter is not the only requirement for good and productive teamwork in an organization, but it is difficult to see how that teamwork can be maximized unless participants do "know the score."

V

REWARD AND PENALTY SYSTEM

W E HAVE seen in the foregoing chapters how a company or union society tries to suggest and support behavior which will achieve its objectives by means of systems of Functional Specifications, Status, and Communication. These bonds of organization help to weld a group of varied individuals into a functioning team which, through its teamwork, will do what the organization is set up to do. We have now to consider another such bond of equal importance with those already discussed, the Reward and Penalty system. Like the Communication system, it is a helper system for all the others—that is, it provides incentives and controls which attempt to assure the society that its participants will perform their work-flow tasks, carry on their directive and representative status functions, and communicate in a way which furthers the objectives of the company or union society.

Certain readers might prefer to use other terms such as "incentives" and "discipline." These may be more familiar to practical men. But they are too narrow for our use, though the items normally described by such terms are comprehended within the system as we define it.

From observation and interview we have gathered considerable material describing the system of rewarding and penalizing in this company and union as it is actually experienced by the participants. In attempting to organize the material we find that this experience places emphasis on the following aspects of the system:

1. Objectives
2. Kinds of behavior (and inferred human qualities) rewarded and penalized
3. Agents of reward and penalty
4. Bases of agents' power to reward and penalize
5. Techniques of reward and penalty
   a. Instruments and methods
   b. Manner
   c. Timing

A brief discussion of each of these will help to give content to our definition of this system.

OBJECTIVES OF REWARD AND PENALTY

The major objective of rewards and penalties is or should be to facilitate the teamwork toward the achievement of the organization's purpose. It is this major normal objective with which we shall be concerned in this report. It must be conceded that the system as existing might not, in all respects, be a help to the achievement of the organization's objectives. That would be true, for instance, in case the customary behavior expected of participants (and therefore rewarded) was poorly designed to achieve one or more of the organization's objectives. Or it might be true if customary and expected behavior ran counter to the society's objectives and was not penalized.

It must also be recognized that, since human beings are the primary agents of reward and penalty, the instruments and methods may be manipulated by them to serve purely personal ends which may or may not be consistent with those of the organization.

BEHAVIOR (AND INFERRED QUALITIES) REWARDED AND PENALIZED

The kinds of specific behavior which are rewarded and penalized will differ from one organization to another. Questions on this subject directed to participants in this company and union have, however, resulted in responses emphasizing by constant repetition certain major kinds of behavior which these people assume to be rewarded and the absence or opposite of which they assume to be penalized. These responses are reinforced by those received from other managers, union leaders, and employees in the course of other research projects we have carried on since 1932. The emphasis and the specific content may vary as between organizations. Yet the similarities in types of expected behavior are too clear to miss.[1]

[1] The list in Table XXIV is made up from answers to a number of questions, such as "What kind of behavior in others in the organization (employee, superior, subordinate, member, steward, officer, etc.) mark them as worthy of your support?" "If you could change places with ———, how would you act differently?" "What does a fellow in your position have to do to get ahead?" "What do you mean by getting ahead?" "What are the advantages of being an employee or member of this organization, and what does one have to do to realize those advantages?" "What standards of conduct do others in the organization have for you?" "What kinds of behavior are approved and what disapproved?" etc.

In Table XXIV these types are named in the right-hand column. In the left-hand column are listed the human qualities which, it is normally inferred, characterize a person who behaves in the way indicated. These items are tabulated not merely to provide a list but to provide a basis for certain observations and generalizations about the items which have a definite bearing on the effectiveness and efficiency of the system of Reward and Penalty.

Some repetition will be noted in both columns, this being a result of classifying a few items as relevant to several types of qualities and areas of activity.

Here are sixty-eight items of behavior which in some manner are normally rewarded in this company and union and in the other organizations we have studied. The items do not give all the answers we have recorded, but they are the ones which have appeared frequently and widely. We feel justified in saying with confidence that they are representative of the kinds of behavior which people assume are normally rewarded in the organizations we have studied, though the emphasis and content may vary from one organization to another. The specific definition of each item will also vary from one group to another.

A study of these general types of behavior does, however, suggest certain characteristics that we shall find to have an important bearing on the development of a Reward and Penalty system which is effective in accomplishing the objectives of the organization and efficient in providing participants with a realization of their goal experiences. Those whom we interviewed were aware of these characteristics. They are suggested by their comments. Most of them complicate the problem of administering rewards and penalties so that these will be considered just by those on the receiving end.

First of all notice that there is nothing absolute about such definitions of desirable behavior. They are relative to several factors. They are relative first of all to the objectives of the organization in question. Those objectives will determine both what types of behavior are emphasized and what specific acts define that behavior. There is a difference between the emphasis on and definition of these items of behavior in the union (a political organization) and in the company (a business organization). The definitions would be different in the union if it aimed ultimately to destroy private enterprise rather than as it does, to strengthen it. Con-

TABLE XXIV

BEHAVIOR AND INFERRED HUMAN QUALITIES NORMALLY REWARDED AND PENALIZED IN COMPANIES AND UNIONS

Inferred Qualities	Behavior

1. *Technical Skill*
  a. Job know-how
  b. Productive competence
  c. Versatility
  d. Accuracy
	1. *Productive Activities*
	  a. Contributes high quantity and quality of products and services
	  b. Does all that is required
	  c. Makes few mistakes

2. *Nontechnical Job Attributes*
  a. Steadiness and stability
  b. Adaptability
  c. Stamina and health
  d. Interest in job
	2. *Productive Activities* (*Continued*)
	  a. Continued service
	  b. Good work habits, timekeeping, and attendance to duties
	  c. Meets unexpected and new situations effectively
	  d. Produces effectively under pressure
	  e. Tries to improve job

3. *Mental Competence*
  a. Intelligence
  b. Mental alertness
  c. Mature judgment and common sense
  d. Imagination
  e. Reasonableness
  f. Ability to learn
	3. *Thinking*
	  a. Grasps instructions quickly, particularly those involving new methods and specifications
	  b. Invents new methods and tools
	  c. Contributes new ideas
	  d. Analyzes new problems immediately, carefully, and well
	  e. Is amenable to reason
	  f. Relates effects to their real causes and acts accordingly
	  g. Understands the problems of those he deals with
	  h. Takes points of view and reactions of others into account
	  i Resists being taken in by "wild-eyed" or "unsound" schemes and ideas

4. *Personal Attributes*
  a. Self-confidence
  b. Ambition
  c. Enthusiasm
  d. Emotional stability
  e. Energy
  f. Initiative
  g. Inclination to be satisfied
	4. *Stimulation and Control of Self*
	  a. Goes ahead on own initiative, but not too far
	  b. Tries to better self, but not so as to inconvenience or block others
	  c. Works hard and enthusiastically
	  d. Controls his emotions
	  e. "Looks before he leaps"
	  f. Avoids "griping"

TABLE XXIV (*Continued*)

BEHAVIOR AND INFERRED HUMAN QUALITIES NORMALLY REWARDED AND PENALIZED IN COMPANIES AND UNIONS

Inferred Qualities	Behavior

5. *Good Character*
  a. Honesty
  b. Responsibility
  c. Reliability
  d. Self-reliance
  e. Perseverance
  f. Conservatism
  g. Moral courage
  h. Discreetness
  i. Thrift and foresight
	5. *Ethical Conduct*
	  a. Gives full day's work for day's pay
	  b. Tells the truth
	  c. Takes responsibility well
	  d. Does what says will do
	  e. Sticks on job until it is finished
	  f. Depends on self rather than others
	  g. Follows the middle road
	  h. Sticks by convictions
	  i. Tends to his own business
	  j. Keeps mouth shut when should, avoids gossip
	  k. Takes the long view
	  l. Saves his money and sacrifices present for future gains

6. *Good Representative of the Organization*
  a. Aware of and committed to community standards
  b. An "ingrouper" culturally
  c. Well bred
  d. Leadership ability
	6. *Outside Activities*
	  a. Acts consistent with behavior expected by those outside the organization (and especially by customers)
	  b. Shows good manners
	  c. Dresses well
	  d. Takes active part in community affairs
	  e. Directs attention to those activities which are respected by most people and gets himself well known for this

7. *Capacity for Teamwork*
General
  a. Co-operativeness
  b. Social adeptness
  c. Unselfishness
  d. Democracy
  e. Group-centered
  f. Adaptability
  g. Reliability
  h. Aware of group's standards
  i. Tact, consideration, and courtesy
  j. Alikeness
	7. *Teamwork*
	General
	  a. Competent job performance
	  b. Works willingly with others on both pleasant and unpleasant tasks
	  c. Subordinates own interests to those of the group. Is loyal to the group
	  d. Contributes his share to group effort and results
	  e. Avoids major disagreements
	  f. Deals courteously, tactfully, and understandingly with others, particularly when under stress
	  g. Acts like a good fellow and a good sport
	  h. Shares the problems of the group and others with whom he deals
	  i. Acts consistently with behavior expected by others in the group

TABLE XXIV (*Continued*)

BEHAVIOR AND INFERRED HUMAN QUALITIES NORMALLY REWARDED AND PENALIZED IN COMPANIES AND UNIONS

Inferred Qualities	Behavior
Special for Teamwork with Associates k. Considerate l. Unassuming	*Special for Teamwork with Associates* j. Avoids domination of associates k. Takes leadership only when has capacity for leadership
Special for Teamwork with Superiors m. Deference	*Special for Teamwork with Superiors* l. Follows orders and instructions competently and willingly m. Avoids complaints and grievances, especially those involving the superior n. Senses superior's problems o. Is deferent to superiors, doesn't try to "run the show" p. Takes criticism well q. Is loyal to the organization r. Makes reasonable demands on superiors and organization
Special for Teamwork with Subordinates n. Leadership ability o. Fairness p. Knows his business q. "Human" r. Courage	*Special for Teamwork with Subordinates* s. Gives orders and instructions clearly t. Makes subordinates feel their interests are consistent with those of the organization and with his own u. Elicits rather than compels performance v. Shows interests in his subordinates' problems w. Sets his expectancies at the level of subordinates' capacities x. Accepts suggestions but doesn't lose his grip on the reins y. Maintains the dignity of his position but without ostentation z. Faces problems head on aa. Accepts responsibility for his own and his subordinates' performance (including mistakes) without attempt to alibi bb. Gives credit where credit is due and withholds it when not due cc. Backs up his subordinates

sider the difference in emphasis placed upon "outside activities" by a small establishment making house dresses and this public utility providing a public service. Consider the difference in the definition of "invention of new methods and tools" in a highly mechanized establishment using a continuous assembly line and in this establishment employing a large number of relatively independent craftsmen.

This last illustration suggests that emphasis and definition are also relative as between different groups of participants within the same organization. The specific content would be different for highly skilled craftsmen than for manual laborers, for employees than for management (and for different levels within management), for leaders than for members.

The emphasis and definition will vary also because some person or persons must clarify and state both. Fortunate is the organization in which all those within the organization with responsibility for doing so have consistent ideas and take consistent action on the matter. This was not always the case in this company and union. What, for instance, constitutes production of *high quantity and quality*? What is the base line? What is a *mistake*? What is the meaning of *hard* work, or someone's *share*, or for that matter *action expected by the group* or by a supervisor or leader? The meaning will vary according to the persons who influence the definition at particular times and in particular organizations. Particularly in the company there was evident a high degree of standardization in such definitions, and satisfaction was high in this respect in both organizations. But standards cannot eliminate personal differences entirely. Any organization in which this was accomplished would be pretty "inhuman," an organization of automatons.

All of this may seem like writing footnotes to the obvious, but such variations are critical problems in devising a system of Reward and Penalty which is effective and efficient. The variations are one reason why experience is not perfectly transferable. A person moving from one organization, department, exchange, or work group to another will have to learn the emphases and definitions characterizing the general behavior traits rewarded and penalized in the groups to which he comes. Until he does so, and to the extent of his ignorance, his position and activity in the (to him) new group is insecure and his sense of justice likely to be violated on occasion. He will soon learn, however, as he experiences the rewards and penalties applied to him.

The second characteristic of this list of rewarded behavior traits is that they refer to more than job performance in the narrow sense. If a person acts or fails to act in the ways indicated, that fact is regarded as evidence in answering at least three questions:

a. How does he do his work?
b. How does he get along with people?
c. How does his behavior indicate the kind of a person he is?

These questions are not mutually exclusive. Each is relevant to the others. How he gets along with people and the kind of a person he is are not matters alternative to how he does his work, for instance. Yet a major emphasis can be sensed in the relationship of certain traits to answering each of these questions. Counting those traits that have to do with getting along with people as evidence of job performance when they apply specifically to supervisors or officers, we get the following classification:

a. How does he do his work?   23 traits
b. How does he get along with people?   27 traits
c. How does his behavior indicate the kind
    of a person he is?   18 traits

Here is evidence that "capacity for human relations" is not a newly discovered requirement for effective performance within a company or union. It is a capacity which has been and must necessarily be the basis for the rewarding and penalizing of one by the many in such organizations.

A third characteristic of this list of traits and inferred qualities is that, in specific performance, some of them may to a greater or less degree be incompatible or, at least, may place conflicting demands on the time and energy of people. Such conflicts arose in the experience of our informants, for instance, between "contributing a high quantity and quality of products and services" and "acting like a good fellow and a good sport" or "acting consistently with behavior expected by others in the group." Conflicts arose between "inventing new methods and tools" or "going ahead on own initiative" and "following orders and instructions competently and well" or "being deferent to superiors." They arose between "being loyal to the organization" and "avoiding major disagreements." The examples could be multiplied.

There is no doubt a golden mean which one may find, but in view of the relative character of these traits when defined by particular people in particular situations, the location of this golden mean and the understanding of the kind of behavior it implies are not always easy for an individual.

Finally, notice that objective behavior even if clearly defined and understood by all parties is not the only thing which is being rewarded and penalized. It is inevitable when human beings are the object that they shall be rewarded not only for what they *do* but for what they *are*. A machine which does not perform as it is expected to perform is discarded because its "behavior" was unsatisfactory. A worker who does not and will not perform as he is expected to perform is fired not only because his behavior was unsatisfactory but because "we don't want *that kind of a person around here*." At least this is the inference drawn by the person who is fired, and it must be admitted that there are some grounds for his inference. It is difficult even for the person who gives the reward or inflicts the penalty to disentangle these two types of stimulus to such action. Always coupled together in his thoughts are the two elements, "this person deserves reward for what he has done" and "what he has done shows he has the right stuff and the right attitude." His emphasis may be on the first. The emphasis is certainly modified by his estimate of the second factor. It also frequently occurs that once unfavorable inferences as to a person's innate qualities have solidified in the mind of, say, a supervisor, a rebuttal of such inferences is difficult no matter what the person *does*.

From this latter situation arises one of the most difficult problems of administering rewards and penalties so that they will be considered just by the recipient, one which is prominent in our responses. It was clear that justice, in the mind of our typical respondent, is treatment in accordance with his conception of his own worth. When he is rewarded he interprets the event as a reward primarily for what he *is* as well as for what he *does*. A person is rewarded ostensibly for perfect attendance and timekeeping, or for quantity and quality of his production. In his mind he is rewarded also because the rewarder thinks he is faithful, dependable, and skilled, as indicated by such behavior. A person is penalized ostensibly for nonattendance to duties or for poor-quality work. In his mind he is penalized also because the penalizer thinks he is "not to be trusted," undependable, incompetent. Since he (the object) has a more intimate acquaintance with what he is, what qualities he really has, than the rewarder or penalizer can get by inference from his behavior, and since he has some over-all judgment of his own intrinsic worth in terms of these qualities, it is most difficult to reward him and penalize him in a way completely consistent with that personal estimate. The rewarding and penalizing for those behavior traits and inferred qualities which are relevant to getting along with people are peculiarly subject to this type of difficulty.

AGENTS OF REWARD AND PENALTY

The agents of reward and penalty are, of course, primarily people. The roster of agents is essentially the same for all participants in these organizations, though, as we shall see in a moment, their power to reward and penalize varies with a number of circumstances. There is a sense in which every participant in an organization is an agent of reward and penalty for every other participant.[2] But those on the roster will vary in importance for different groups and for different individuals. For instance, although higher management, foremen, union leaders, and employees might all be on the roster for each other, the order of importance might vary thus:

For Foremen	For Union Leaders	For Employees
Higher management	Employees (members)	Foremen
Employees	Higher Management	Other employees
Union leaders	Foremen	Union leaders
Other foremen	Other union leaders	Higher management

The order indicated is purely hypothetical and not a conclusion from observations in these particular groups. In our final report we shall indicate the actual observed order. The reasons for the order we shall discuss in a moment under the heading, Bases Agent's of Power to Reward and Penalize.

But others outside the circle of participants may be on the roster. The rewards and penalties given and imposed by these "outsiders" are not so

---

[2] By participants we mean those encompassed by the widest concept of the "society" we have used in our discussions, that is, the organized enterprise. Hence included in the roster are stockholders and union leaders.

directly influenced by the internal structure and activities of the organization as are those given and imposed by the "insiders." But their influence is felt on activities of participants in connection with organizational business nevertheless. The list is long of those outsiders who, to some degree, can reward and penalize people for *what they do in the organization* and for the results of their collective effort: community leaders, newspaper editors and writers, politicians, officeholders, public administrators, police, family members, priest or pastor, members of religious community, fellow members of clubs and associations, social contacts, neighbors, and supernatural powers. Of particular importance to the participants in this company is the Public Utility Commission. Although these outsiders will not be discussed as such, their relative influence is subject to the same determining factors as that of those within the organization.

Halfway between the insiders and the outsiders are the customers and stockholders, both actual and potential. Their ability to reward and penalize the organization, as a whole, is unquestioned. Their ability to do that to particular participants will vary with their closeness of contact with these participants.

BASES OF AGENT'S POWER TO REWARD AND PENALIZE

The relative extent to which these agents appeared as actual rewarders and penalizers to particular individuals and groups within an organization seemed to depend on several factors. These factors help to answer the questions, Why do these people have the power to reward and penalize? From whence comes their power? And they help us to understand whose rewards and penalties are relatively most effective in conditioning the behavior of particular groups.

In the following discussion the word *agent* will apply to the person who delivers the reward or penalty, and the word *object* to the person who receives it. The following questions suggest the major determinants of the agent's power which can be inferred from the comments of those interviewed:

1. Does the agent have a relationship with the object which is close and frequent enough to provide an opportunity for the exercise of his power?
2. How accurate is the conception of the agent as to what constitutes reward and penalty for the object?

3. How much importance is attached by the object to the judgment and action of the agent? Could he, for instance, afford to disregard it?
4. How closely does the reward or penalty coincide with what the object thinks he deserves?
5. How much power has the object to stimulate or to nullify or modify the judgment and action of the agent?
6. Is the judgment and action of the agent reenforced by the judgment and action of other agents?
7. Does the agent have available and does he control adequate instruments for making his judgment and action effective?

Variations in the answers to these questions as applied to the roster of potential agents will determine their relative power to reward or penalize individuals or a group of persons we have called objects. A brief discussion and illustration of the practical circumstances in each case will clarify this generalization.

Does the agent have a relationship with the object which is close and frequent enough to provide an opportunity for the exercise of power? This is the simplest and most obvious of determinants. The variation in this factor would probably arrange the power of certain people to reward or penalize an employee in a certain department in the following descending order: fellow workers in the work group, immediate supervision, union officers, management in the same department, management in other operating departments, management in general engineering and other staff departments, top management.

The ranking in power of the several agents indicated above will clearly differ from group to group as the pattern of interactions in that group varies. In general it might be expected that the same order would result, but the order of the first four might vary considerably. Ordinarily, for employees the frequency and closeness of contact would be greatest with fellow workers. But this would not be true in the case of employees who work pretty much on their own, as, for instance, coin-telephone collectors, station installers, or salesmen. The position of union officers will depend, so far as this test is concerned, on the number of functions which bring them into immediate contact with the employee.

If it is asserted that contacts with certain agents though less frequent are more important, the answer is that this situation is revealed by a later test.

At this point we may restate a circumstance which we have noted before, that, for certain groups of employees, contacts with customers is more frequent than those with any participants in the organization. Consider, for instance, telephone installers, operators, commercial representatives. The power of customers to reward and penalize in such cases is high relative to that of participants in the organization. This is similar to the situation of waitresses in a restaurant and salesmen of all kinds.

How accurate a conception does the agent have of what constitutes reward and penalty for the object? In this third determinant we have a factor which goes far to determine the effectiveness or ineffectiveness of a Reward and Penalty system. The influence of any reward or penalty used by an agent to stimulate or control behavior on the part of an object will depend on an agreement between the two as to what actually is considered rewarding or penalizing to the object. For instance, a promotion to a foremanship or to a higher level of management or to a union office may not be considered rewarding to an employee. We found a number of cases where this was true. A larger pay check as the result of production beyond that considered "proper" by one's workmates may fall in the same category. The possibility of a pension for which deductions from the pay envelope are made may not be a realistic reward for a mobile individual, particularly if he has no vested right in the accumulation. Union leaders have been known according to comments made, to miscalculate what particular contract items or service or relationship of leaders to members would be rewarding to the rank and file. Likewise a penalty which makes a martyr of an individual in the eyes of his fellows may actually be a reward, not a penalty, to a politically minded individual.

It is not likely that in any organization, agents will continue for long to administer "rewards" which are not considered rewards by a substantial number of objects. The lack of results from such a process would, after a time, provide a warning signal that something was wrong. A more real probability is that things which objects would, and do, consider rewarding will be neglected by agents. For instance, the rewarding experience of respect and control which can come from a high degree of employee or member participation in sharing in the determination of their conditions of work or activity is very unevenly implemented among different exchanges and locals.

The object's definition of reward and penalty is closely related to that of the individuals and groups he identifies himself with. This leads to the discussion of our fourth determinant.

How much importance is attached by the object to the judgment and action of the agent? Anyone who has attempted to reward or penalize another person will recognize the fact that the effectiveness of his judgment and action varies to the extent that he, the agent, is important in the eyes of the object. The same reward or penalty which was effective with one who cared a great deal about what the agent thought and did would be much less effective when applied to one with whom the agent "didn't count much."

The variations in such reactions to agents by the objects revealed by our material is great. They arise from differential answers to such questions as these: Is the object aware of the actual importance of the agent to him? Does he respect the agent? Has he some basic faith or philosophy which highlights the importance and significance of the agent? Can he afford to consider the agent more or less important?

It is scarcely conceivable that any junior in an organization would not consider the judgment and action of his superiors to be of importance. We have found none such. Yet his reaction does vary with the completeness of his knowledge of how rewards and penalties are actually determined and administered in the organization, with the length of his contemplated service, and, if that contemplated service is short, with the importance of his superior in affecting his future chances with another organization. And, even though from these points of view he recognized the high importance of the superior, some considered relatively more important to their particular interest the judgment and action of fellow workers, union leaders, a priest, or the fellow members of a religious community, family, etc. A reward from one he respects is much more valued, and penalty from one he respects is felt more keenly, than is either from one for whom he has little respect. The power of the former is much greater than that of the latter. Whenever the object of either penalty or reward reacts with "Oh, well, consider the source," the agent has less power than one about whom the object says, "Whenever he gives you the works, it means something." The economic philosophy of one man may make management or a union leader significant for him, and that of another may reduce them to low significance. Variant social philosophies and religious faiths have the same sort of differential effect. The importance of a priest is much less for an atheist than for a devout Catholic. The importance of the agent may rest in the fact that there is no way to escape the effects of his judgment and action. Consider the relative power of the employer over a man of specialized skill useful only to that employer, and over a man who is master of several skills; or the relative power of the union leader in a closed-shop and in an open-shop situation.

The variations in such circumstances will produce variations in the importance attached by objects to certain agents and hence variations in the power the latter have to reward and penalize.

Closely related to the last is the next determinant of the power of the agent: *How closely does the reward or penalty coincide with what the object thinks he deserves?* The lack of coincidence may have little influence on the agent's power in the present instance, but it will modify the respect in which the object holds the agent so that the latter's power is reduced on future occasions. It was noted in this connection that judgment or action of an agent, *whether favorable or unfavorable to the object,* which is inconsistent with what the object thinks he deserves undermines the respect in which the agent's judgment is held and hence eventually undermines his power.

The next determinant of the power of the agent noted also rests upon the reaction of the object. It might be labeled *the existence of counterpower.* In question form it is this: *How much power has the object to stimulate or to nullify or modify the judgment and action of the agent?* This counterpower may arise from a number of conditions. Some of these fall under the heading of special privileges, or favoritism. That is, an employee may have access to someone above his supervisor who, in turn, can modify either the judgment or the action of that supervisor with respect to the employee.

The object may have access to sources of judgment and appraisal alternative to those affecting the judgment of an agent, as when a foreman's judgment on suitability for work must be paired with the judgment of a personnel officer, thus providing the object with power, through contact with the latter, to modify the foreman's decision. The suggestion which would not be rewarded by a foreman may nevertheless be rewarded by higher management because it must be transmitted to them by the foreman, or because it circumvents him in its processing.

The object may counter the agent's power by seeking allies, as when he joins political hands to weaken the power of a union leader, or joins with his fellows in a "quickie" or a regular strike against a decision he considers penalizing by management, or when one member of management seeks the alliance with others of management in order to counter a non-co-operative (i.e., penalizing) action on the part of one employee or a group of them. Such alliance-making may extend beyond the participants in an organization, to politicians or religious leaders outside, for instance.

Another source of counterpower is the development of control and regulation of the instruments of reward and penalty utilized by the agent. The typical example of this, which also involves making alliances, is collective bargaining and the grievance procedure. Through such activities, employees gain some control not only in determining what the rewards and penalties and their instruments shall be but over standards for their application, and their actual administration.

The degree of power of the agent is always, other things being equal, inversely proportional to the degree of counterpower exercised by the object through such measures as these.

The next determinant of the agent's power is suggested by the question, *To what extent can the agent obtain the co-operation of other agents in acting consistent with his own action?* Will other workers join the agent in rewarding or penalizing one of their members, a union leader, a member of management, in the same way? Does management hang together in its treatment of employees or union representatives? Do all union officers back up their president in his attempts to exert pressure on management? Can management get the backing of the board of directors for a liberalized personnel policy? These are relevant to major problems. The problems, however, may be as simple as the ability of one employee to get the others to contribute to a Christmas present for someone he would like to reward.

Although rewards and penalties are frequently administered by individual agents, the agent's power in these organizations is mightily affected by the degree of co-operation or backing he gets in such judgment and action from other participants who are also considered as agents.

Finally we come to the most important determinant of all: *Does the agent have available and does he have control of the instruments and methods for making his judgment effective?* Since an understanding of the importance of this determinant presupposes an understanding of what these instruments and techniques are, and since these constitute the next aspect of the Reward and Penalty system to which we shall turn our attention, we shall postpone for the moment any elaboration on this determinant. The obvious generalization can be made, however, that the larger the number of such instruments and methods available to and controlled by an agent, other things being equal, the greater his power to reward and penalize an object.

INSTRUMENTS AND METHODS OF REWARD AND PENALTY

Table XXV presents an analytical summary of those instruments and methods which have appeared prominently in our studies of this company and union and of other companies and unions to date. They have been arranged as to types, with examples given for each type. The examples would, of course, be amplified or modified for any particular organization.

Several comments need to be made about the characteristics of these items. Notice first of all that some of them are forthcoming primarily as a result of individual qualities or behavior, others are forthcoming primarily as a result of a person being the member of a group. In the latter case they are not basically associated with any particular cause within the control of the individual. Such, for instance, are items like vacations, holidays, pensions, insurance, and recreational facilities. Yet arrangements in some organizations do provide for differential treatment to individuals with respect to such items, as when benefits are geared to length of service. Some items are both individual and group centered in their eligibility requirements, wages for instance. The general level of wages is rewarding or penalizing to all individuals in comparison with groups of individuals in other plants; but particular rates or differential earnings under an incentive plan are related to individual performance.

Notice in the second place that the most frequent form of penalty is merely a withholding of the positive reward, although in certain cases like fines, reprimands, ostracism, restrictions on choice of work, suspension, and discharge, they may be "positively" negative. It is fallacious, however, to ignore the mere withholding of positive rewards as a very real form of penalty.

Notice the agents who normally found these forms of reward and penalty available to them in this company. The following agents are involved in the several types of rewards and penalties as experienced by *employees*:

1. *Personal Approval*
   Management—particularly immediate supervisors
   Fellow workers, particularly in own work group
   Union officers
   Employees (for management and union officers)
2. *Money and/or Materials*
   Management and union officers (in determining general levels)
   Management (primarily in determining individual application—though union officers may participate through grievance procedure)
3. *Privileges and Prerequisites*
   Management predominantly
   Union officers in determining general levels in some cases
   Fellow employees (only if prerequisite awarded as result of group selection of candidates)
4. *Physical Comfort Facilities*
   Management
   Union officers
5. *Freedom*
   Management primarily
   Union officers through implementing appeal
6. *Enlargement of Functions*
   Management primarily
   Union officers
7. *Tenure*
   Management primarily, though union officers may participate in defining terms and by processing grievances
8. *Personal Advancement*
   Management
   Fellow workers with respect to opportunity for personal development
   Union officers
9. *Co-operation*
   Management
   Union officers
   Employees
10. *Adequacy of Judgment and Application*
    Management
    Fellow workers
    Union officers

TABLE XXV

INSTRUMENTS AND METHODS OF REWARD AND PENALTY

Rewards	Penalties
1. *Personal Approval* a. Commendatory attitudes b. Expressed commendation c. Acceptance by group d. Favors and preferential treatment	1. *Personal Disapproval* a. Ignoring or disapproving attitude and manner b. Expressed disapproval or reprimands c. Ostracism d. Withholding of favors and preferential treatment
2. *Money and/or Materials* a. Wage payment and wage improvement b. Bonuses (including profit sharing) c. Prizes with monetary value	2. *Money and/or Materials* a. Wage withholding and decreases b. Withholding of bonuses and prizes c. Fines
3. *Privileges and Perquisites* a. Time off (vacations, holidays, sick leave, earned days off, leaves of absence, etc.) b. Benefits (pensions, insurance, medical, compensation, stock purchase, etc.) c. Perquisites (membership in long-service or special achievement clubs, buttons, medals, certificates, executive dining and parking facilities, right to material symbols of standing, etc.)	3. *Withholding of Privileges and Perquisites* a. Withholding of time off and imposition of extra-work time b. Withholding of benefits c. Withholding of perquisites
4. *Physical Comfort Facilities* a. Satisfactory speed, time, and organization of work b. Satisfactory health and safety provisions c. Satisfactory recreational facilities d. Satisfactory washroom and eating facilities e. Physical work surroundings f. Tools and equipment g. Location and layout	4. *Unsatisfactory Physical Comfort Facilities* a. Unsatisfactory or increasingly unfavorable facilities: a,b,c,d,e,f,g
5. *Freedom* a. Choice of work and schedules b. Minimum supervision c. Adequate appeal	5. *Restriction* a. Restriction on choice of work b. Maximum supervision c. Denial of appeal

TABLE XXV (*Continued*)

INSTRUMENTS AND METHODS OF REWARD AND PENALTY

Rewards	Penalties

6. *Enlargement of Functions*
  a. Opportunity for suggestions
  b. Invitation to consultation
  c. Special assignments
  d. Access to training
	6. *Reduction of Functions*
	  a. Disregard of suggestions
	  b. Ignoring
	  c. Withholding of special assignments
	  d. Denial of opportunity for training

7. *Tenure*
  a. Commitment to continued employment
	7. *Denial of Tenure*
	  a. Suspension or discharge

8. *Personal Advancement*
  a. Promotion in status
  b. Opportunity for personal development
	8. *Withholding of Personal Advancement*
	  a. Withholding of promotion or demotion in status
	  b. Withholding of or lack of opportunity for personal development

9. *Co-operation*
  a. Active assistance
	9. *Lack of Co-operation*
	  a. Withholding of assistance
	  b. Sabotage

10. *Adequacy of Judgment and Application*
  a. Clear standards and requirements
  b. Accurate appraisal
  c. Nondiscriminatory application
  d. No exploitation
	10. *Inadequacy of Judgment and Application*
	  a. Unclear or absence of standards and requirements
	  b. Inaccurate appraisal
	  c. Discriminatory application
	  d. Exploitation

11. *General Satisfactory Relationship*
  a. Respected company or union
  b. Satisfactory higher-ups
  c. Satisfactory immediate supervisors
  d. Satisfactory associates
	11. *General Unsatisfactory Relationship*
	  a. Organization with poor reputation
	  b. Unsatisfactory higher-ups
	  c. Unsatisfactory immediate supervisors
	  d. Unsatisfactory associates

12. *Stimulating Work*	12. *Unstimulating Work*

11. *General Satisfactory Relationship*
   All

12. *Stimulating Work*
   Management

We may now return for a moment to a brief amplification of the last point made under Bases of Agent's Power to Reward and Penalize. That point was that one such basis was the availability of, and control over, the instruments and techniques of reward and penalty. There is obviously good reason why management has power as an agent in the minds of employees from the point of view of this determinant. Every one of these types of reward and penalty is available to them. Even when control of their general definition and application is shared with union officers, management usually has the final say in specific application to individuals. Fellow workers have available fewer types, but these are extremely important—namely, personal approval (particularly acceptance by group), personal advancement (in giving opportunities for personal development), co-operation, adequacy of judgment, and general satisfactory relationship.

Yet notice the number of instruments and methods which are available to, and at least partly in control of, the union leaders! It is little wonder that many managements which deal with unions view with alarm the problem of meeting their obligations as managers of an organization. For the instruments and methods of reward and penalty, formerly almost exclusively at their command, must now be shared with union leaders. Unless union leaders are unconcerned about the effective operation of the company, or about the importance of preserving management's part in the Reward and Penalty system as an important element in this bond of organization, they can ill afford to make demands for participation which isolate management too far from access to and control over the instruments and methods of reward and penalty.

In general, if employees and union officers wish to reward or penalize management, they have at their disposal personal approval, co-operation, and adequacy of judgment. These are, of course, powerful instruments in themselves; but when used to reward or penalize management, they are even more powerful in marking management as a success or failure in the eyes of its superiors, who, in turn, can apply a longer list of rewards and penalties.

Notice finally that each of these types of rewards and penalties is especially relevant to certain goal experiences of persons to whom they are applied. The major relationships are indicated below. The italicized goals in each case are the dominant ones to which the particular instrument and method is relevant. The others are of secondary importance.

1. Personal Approval
   Respect, integrity, security, justice

2. Money and/or Materials
   Creature comforts, security, respect
3. Privileges and Perquisites
   Respect, creature comforts, security
4. Physical Comfort Facilities
   Creature comforts, security
5. Freedom
   Control, capacity performance, justice
6. Enlargement of Functions
   Capacity performance, respect, control, integrity
7. Tenure
   Security
8. Personal Advancement
   Progress, respect
9. Co-operation
   Integrity, capacity performance
10. Adequacy of Judgment and Application
    Justice, control, understanding
11. General Satisfactory Relationship
    Respect, integration
12. Stimulating Work
    Capacity performance, integrity

One further comment should be made about this list of instruments and methods of reward and penalty. The tenth item on the list, Adequacy of Judgment and Application, is of a slightly different nature from the other eleven items. It is included in the list for the following reason: Before any reward or penalty can be administered equitably, there must be established standards of performance against which the particular performance of an individual can be measured; and the consistency of the particular performance with the expected performance or standard must be ascertained. The specific elements involved in the carrying out of these preliminary judgments are vital parts of the instruments and methods of reward and penalty. If they are inadequate to their task, the awarding of rewards or the imposition of penalties will fail to promote behavior which is conducive to the achievement of the organization's objectives; for in the minds of participants, rewards and penalties will have been applied where they ought not to have been applied, and will have been denied or avoided where they ought not to have been denied or avoided. Under such conditions, the system fails to suggest and support the types of behavior which further the organization's objectives, and it fails to contribute to the experience of justice for the participants in the organization.

Four problems in this connection were faced, in some cases, by those in these organizations who would like to make this instrument and method of reward and penalty effective and efficient:

a. The lack of objective measurements for performance.

b. The lack of objective measurements of the human qualities which variations in performance are presumed to indicate.

c. The lack of clear understanding of the relationship between performance and the possession of certain qualities.

d. The lack of objective determinants of whether the performance was actually accomplished and the inferred qualities were revealed.

As set forth above, these problems seem abstract, but in concrete terms they are realistically, and sometimes critically, presented to those responsible for the welfare of company and union. Let us attempt to interpret the abstractions in concrete terms.

We have said that the first problem is the lack of objective measurements for performance. In Table XXV are 68 behavior traits, the presence of which is normally rewarded and the absence of which is normally penalized in any company or union. How many of these are subject to objective measurements? By objective measurement we mean standards that are relatively independent of the points of view and prejudices of the person responsible for making the judgment. Among those which are most nearly subject to such objective measurement are certainly the following:

1. Quantity and quality of production and services
2. Number of mistakes made
3. Length of service.
4. Timekeeping and attendance to duties
5. Invention of new methods and tools
6. Contribution of new ideas
7. Avoidance of griping
8. Avoidance of major disagreements
9. Avoidance of complaints and grievances, especially those involving superior

Let us assume that the company and union have made use of the best measurements available on the above-listed points and of the most carefully set standards resulting from the accumulated experience of those charged with the welfare of organizations. This assumption we are ready to make after our intimate contact with the participants in this company and union. They have made use of accumulated experience of other companies and unions, though we must point out that the volume of recorded management experience to which the management of this company had access is considerably greater than the volume of union experience to which the union had access.

Even assuming maximum use of available standards on these nine points, however, we may recall that there are 68 behavior traits with respect to which individual participants in these two organizations are rewarded and penalized. What objective measurements exist for performance in relation to the other 59 traits? The answer is, *none*. The standards in the case of these remaining traits are relative to the person who makes the judgment, his nature, the time and circumstance which affect his judgment. Both organizations are therefore confronted with the fact that the measurement of the great bulk of behavior traits for which participants are rewarded and penalized is subject only to personal judgment and not to objective standards. Considering the variations in the human beings making these judgments, the attempts of the union to establish such standards as seniority as automatic indicators of eligibility for certain types of rewards is understandable. It is merely an attempt to substitute dependability of measurement for that uncertainty and confusion which attend dependence on the unpredictable judgment of individuals.

If the lack of objective measurement for required performance is apparent, the lack of such measurement for the human qualities supposedly indicated by performance is even more apparent. We have listed 48 such qualities in Table XXV. Of that number, objective tests have been prepared by psychologists, doctors, and "human engineers" for the following:

1. Job know-how
2. Productive competence
3. Versatility
4. Accuracy
5. Steadiness and stability
6. Stamina and health
7. Intelligence
8. Mental alertness
9. Ability to learn

10. Emotional stability
11. Alikeness
12. Leadership ability

Again, assuming that the company and the union had made use of the best available knowledge about such tests, there would still remain 36 qualities which are normally rewarded for which no objective tests exist. In the case of this predominant proportion, the organizations must depend on the judgment of the variously trained and conditioned persons they have placed in positions whose responsibilities include making such judgment. Again we are forced back upon the conclusion that the judgment of people, not objective evidence concerning the presence or absence of personal qualities, is the foundation upon which the administration of rewards and penalties is chiefly based. When it is remembered that those rewarded and penalized consider that their treatment is evidence of what their critics estimate them to be as persons, this fact becomes highly important. To put the matter bluntly, the creation of a sense of justice among the participants of an organization is dependent on people making judgments of other people without the assistance of objective criteria upon which such judgments can be made or by reference to which they can be defended.

The third problem arises from the fact that even where tests of intrinsic qualities of persons were available, management or leaders in these two organizations were not convinced that there is always a necessary connection between the test demonstration of the existence of the quality and the capacity of the individual to perform in a way presumably indicated as possible by the results of the test. Performance is the thing which is important to agents who are rewarding and penalizing. They are not reluctant to infer a quality of a person from his performance, but they are reluctant to infer the probability of performance from the demonstration of a quality in a test situation. Such reluctance tends to reduce further the reliance on objective evidence and increase the reliance on personal judgment in determining whether an individual "has the stuff" for which he should be rewarded.

Finally we must indicate that those responsible for rewarding and penalizing must depend largely on the judgment of people as to whether a candidate for reward or penalty *has actually performed* in a way consistent or inconsistent with the standards set. Certain of the 68 behavior traits can be observed and recorded without undue individual bias on the part of the observer. These are identical with most of those we have listed on page 128 above. But with respect to the other 59 items of behavior on the basis of which individuals are rewarded or penalized, no evidence is possible which is not colored by the personal presuppositions and prejudices of some individual who certifies that the expected behavior has or has not been observed in a candidate.

These comments on Adequacy of Judgment and Application are not intended as implied criticisms of the company and union which we are studying. They are summaries of the reports given to us by participants in these two organizations as to the problems they face in carrying on their tasks. Although it is not our policy at this point in our study to suggest conclusions, a suggestion from the above evidence is so clearly indicated that we cannot resist at this point making it explicit.

The majority of judgments on the basis of which rewards and penalties are made in an organization are so necessarily dependent on the inclinations and intelligence of individuals that they cannot be regularized, systematized, and made consistent for the organization as a whole. In the light of this fact, the only assurance that an organization can have that its participants will consider their rewards and penalties just is to have an adequate and efficient grievance procedure. In such a procedure lies the opportunity to correct personal judgments which must inevitably be narrowly conditioned and hence come short of those necessary for the achievement of effective and efficient operations of the organization as a whole.

The last two aspects of the Reward and Penalty system may be briefly mentioned. The *manner* in which rewards and penalties are administered obviously contributed to their effectiveness. Manner heightened the value of the reward by making the object aware that he was respected and important, or lowered the value of the reward by making the individual feel that it was grudgingly given. Likewise, penalties were made less or more severe as the manner of the agent softened the blow by assuring the object that he had not lost standing with the agent, or increased the blow by, say, "adding insult to injury."

The importance of *timing* arises from the fact that the effectiveness of reward or penalty in encouraging or discouraging certain forms of behavior is proportional to the immediacy and continuity of its application after the act. One employee, paraphrasing a famous economist, emphasized the importance of timing in these words: "In the long run it all works out and you get what you deserve. But in the long run, we're all dead. And if they want to get results by giving you a boost or a kick in the pants it better be done while you're living." The relation of timing of the reward or penalty to the encouragement or discouragement of the behavior to which it is applied is one of the most fundamental principles of learning theory.

We need not here recapitulate the several features of the Reward and Penalty system, a description of which we have found necessary in order to do justice to the comments of our respondents concerning their conception of the system as experienced in this company and union.

As in the case of the other bonds of organization, however, it is well to remind ourselves of the great significance of those areas of rewarding and penalizing which are beyond the limits amenable to formal planning and predetermined implementation. Even the *instruments and methods* used which can be consciously devised do not provide full coverage for all ways in which rewarding and penalizing is desired or desirable, or is carried on regardless of desirability. The full roster of *kinds of behavior and inferred qualities* for which participants are rewarded, and for the lack of which they are penalized, may all be relevant to the accomplishment of an organization's objectives. But not only their very nature but a determination of their presence or absence is subject to definition and determination in which objective (and therefore partially control-giving) evidence plays only a minor role. The possible variations in the facts which determine an *agent's power to reward and penalize* are great; the facts themselves are created by the behavior of individuals who vary in their capacities to understand and act, and are modified by situations in which participants find themselves. The resulting roster of *agents* for the several groups of participants includes those over whose actions and attitudes the planners and administrators have little control.

All of this is said not to provide a counsel of despair for those responsible for the welfare and effectiveness of organizations but to suggest the multitude of elements which are involved in understanding, to say nothing of providing for, the motivation and discipline of participants in an organization. Seen in the context of such an informal Reward and Penalty system, even those specific parts such as wages, pensions, bonuses, discipline for infraction of safety rules, fines, discharge or debarment from membership, and election or promotion to office are obviously not autonomous items of reward and penalty but integral parts of a whole system. They cannot be studied and their nature and administration improved as things in themselves and without reference to the whole system of Reward and Penalty experienced by those to whom they apply. If the task of knowing the details of this system in a particular organization seems difficult, if not impossible, this judgment does not obviate the necessity for recognizing the fact, attempting to identify the aspects of the system which affect the process of modifying its parts, and setting about to learn as much as is humanly possible about their particular character in the organizations in which one is involved.

Whether or not a manager or union leader does this, he may be assured, not merely by our attempts to picture the organization as we see it revealed in the reported experience of participants, but by his own observation, common sense, and intelligence, that the success or failure of his efforts relative to particular formal rewards and penalties will be greatly affected by the impact of the informal but real Reward and Penalty system into which these formal elements are introduced.

Degree of Satisfaction with Reward and Penalty System

The rewards and penalties used to suggest and support behavior which promotes the best interests of the company and union are numerous. In this preliminary report we shall not consider these in detail. But in order to get a first approximation to a judgment on the efficiency of this bond of organization, we shall consider the proportions satisfied with certain important aspects of it.

The questions asked of the participants, the responses to which are here recorded, are listed below. They are concerned first with a general reaction to the system. This reaction is revealed in answers to two questions. The interview contained several questions which gave those interviewed the opportunity to expound in detail on the rewarding elements in their association with the company and union and to make an over-all positive judgment on satisfactory factors in their experience with the organizations. These were followed by the first questions made the subject of this part of the report: "On the whole is there any place you would rather work? Why or why not?" put to management and employees, and "Would you be sorry to relinquish your union office? Why or why not?" put to union officers. The next question sought to learn if there were any major disadvantages to being an employee or member of the union as compared with those who worked for other companies or were members of other unions.

Following the report on questions on this general reaction is a report on several which tested satisfaction or dissatisfaction with the standards one must meet and the qualities he must have in order to be rewarded and escape penalties. The next question considered has to do with the adequacy of knowledge of the system of Rewards and Penalty. Finally a report is given on the proportions satisfied with several types of instruments and methods of reward and penalty which stand out as particularly important. In other words, we are seeking our first approximation to a rating of the efficiency of the system by asking, "Is it on the whole rewarding, are the generally shared advantages satisfactory, are the qualifications required considered to be justified, is the system clear, are important kinds of rewards working satisfactorily for participants?"

The specific questions, the responses to which are used for this purpose, are set forth below. The headings are the shorthand descriptions used to identify the questions in the tables and the discussion. The letters in parentheses indicate those groups of whom the question was asked— i.e., Mgt = Management, E = Employee, with respect to the company system; O = Union officers, M = Members, with respect to the union system.

QUESTIONS ON COMPANY SYSTEM

General Reaction

Job Rewarding[3] (E, Mgt)

On the whole is there any place you would rather work?

Why or why not?

General Rewards (E, Mgt)

Are there any disadvantages as an employee of this company or things which other companies do for their employees which you think should be done here? What?

Qualifications for Reward and Penalty

Superiors' Standards (E, Mgt)

Are there any standards of personal or work conduct expected of you by management which you think are unjustified? What?

Subordinates' Standards (Mgt)

Are there any standards of personal or official conduct those under you expect of you which you think are unjustified? Which?

---

[3] The first eleven questions (through Cooperation) were preceded by questions calling for a positive statement of the matter involved.

Associates' Standards (E)

Are there standards of personal or work conduct expected of you by your fellow employees which you think are unjustified? Which?

Union Officers' Standards (M)

Are there standards of personal or official conduct expected of you by union officers which you think are unjustified? Which?

Promotion Requirements (E, Mgt)

Would you make any changes in requirements for promotion in pay or status? In what way?

Understanding

Knowledge of System (E, Mgt)

Is your knowledge of requirements of approval and for getting ahead, and of whose approval is necessary, etc., adequate?

Instruments and Methods

Money (E, Mgt)

Do you think your pay is fair? Why or why not?

Progress in Status (E, Mgt)

Are you satisfied that your present position in the company in comparison with that of other people is fair? Why or why not?

Co-operation (E, Mgt)

Do you get good teamwork from the people with whom you work in doing your job?

Higher Management Backing (Mgt)

Do you feel you have adequate backing from higher management?

Employee Backing (Mgt)

Do you feel you have adequate backing from your employees?

QUESTIONS ON UNION SYSTEM

General Reaction

Job Rewarding[4] (O)

Would you be sorry to relinquish your union office? Why or why not?

General Rewards (O, M)

Are there any disadvantages to belonging to this union, or things the union should do that it is not doing? What?

Qualifications for Reward and Penalty

Officers' Standards (O, M)

Are there any standards of personal, work, or union conduct expected of you by union officers which you think are unjustified? Which?

[4] The first ten questions (through Cooperation) were preceded by questions calling for a positive statement of the matter involved.

Subordinates' Standards (O)

Are there any standards of personal or official conduct that junior officers or the rank and file expect of you which you think are unjustified? Which?

Management's Standards (O)

Are there any standards of personal or official conduct expected of you by management which you think are unjustified?

Promotion Requirements (O)

Would you make any changes in requirements for getting ahead in union status? In what way?

Understanding

Knowledge of System (O)

Is your knowledge of requirements of approval and for getting ahead, and of whose approval is necessary, etc., adequate?

Instruments and Methods

Money (O)

Do you think union officers should be paid less or paid more for doing their job?

Progress in Status (O)

Are you satisfied that your present position in the union is fair?

Co-operation (O)

Do you get good teamwork from the union people with whom you work?

Officers' Backing (O)

Do you feel you have adequate backing from higher officers?

Members' Backing (O)

Do you feel you have adequate backing from members of the union?

At the risk of repetition, we again remind the reader that these are not the only questions we asked those interviewed about the Reward and Penalty system. These are the ones which were definite enough to lend themselves to answers which could be easily counted. But when we have wrestled with the more difficult problem of coding and analyzing the open-ended questions, we may have to revise our present conclusions. Moreover had we known at the beginning the rich detail of the varied aspects of the rewards and penalties in these organizations, our questions would have been considerably modified. Since one of the purposes of our study was to learn what the significant questions are and how to ask them, our next study will profit immeasurably from this experience. Yet, even in this form, we believe that the answers to the questions as asked give us important indicators of the degree of efficiency of the systems of Reward and Penalty in these organizations.

In the case of those questions in which the respondent gave no indication of dissatisfaction, though no positive satisfaction was indicated, the answer was classified as Satisfactory, thus giving an upward bias in the findings to satisfaction.

GROUP	ITEM	Traffic			Plant			Comm.	
		Mgt	E I	E II	Mgt	E I	E II	Mgt	E
General Reaction	Job Rewarding								
	General Rewards								
	Summary								
Qualifications for Reward and Penalty	Superiors' Standards								
	Subordinates' Standards								
	Associates' Standards								
	Union Officers' Standards								
	Promotion Requirements								
	Summary								
Understanding	Knowledge of System								
Instruments and Methods	Money								
	Progress in Status								
	Cooperation								
	Backing of Management								
	Backing of Employee								
	Summary								
Average	All Items								

LEGEND

Satisfactory	▨
Questionable	◩
Unsatisfactory	■
Irrelevant to this group	☐

CHART K

Proportions Satisfied with Company Reward and Penalty System

Perhaps the best way to get an over-all picture of the degree to which the several aspects of the system are satisfactory to participants is to consider Charts K and L.[5]

[5] The tables upon which these charts are based (XXVI and XXVII) will be found in Appendix A. They record (in tenths) the proportions of individuals in the groups indicated who said that the particular feature was satisfactory.

DANGER SPOTS

Several conclusions are suggested by a study of Charts K and L. First of all, where are the danger spots? Where is satisfaction with the Reward and Penalty system relatively low? We again use the arbitrary classification: Satisfactory (.8 or more), Questionable (.5 to .8), and Unsatisfactory (less than .5).

Company

Management's response in the light of this arbitrary basis for judgment shows relatively few danger spots. We have three departments responding to 12 questions, or a total of 36 responses. Of this number, 29, or nearly five sixths, are Satisfactory and none are Unsatisfactory.

Plant and Commercial in all but two, and Traffic in all but three items, reveal Satisfactory proportions. Only Promotion Requirements is Questionable for all three departments. The General Rewards (such as pensions and other benefits) are Questionable for Traffic and Plant; Co-operation is Questionable for Traffic and Commercial. The only rewards which are considered seriously not adequate, however, are the generally shared rewards and the promotional requirements in Traffic and Plant. We shall comment on these presently.

If we turn now to the employee group, we find a somewhat lower proportion of individuals satisfied with the several aspects of the Reward and Penalty system as they experience it. But the situation is still one which in most aspects reveals a high degree of satisfaction. In the case of only two of the aspects does more than one department report a proportion satisfied of less than .7.

We have recorded the responses of five groups of employees (two each in Traffic and Plant, one in Commercial) with respect to 9 questions, or a total of 45 responses. Of this number, 24 or well over one half, are in the Satisfactory group and none of the rest in the Unsatisfactory group.

All three departments, and especially Traffic and Plant, show Questionable proportions satisfied with the same aspects management rated low in satisfaction: Promotion Requirements and General Rewards. Traffic and Plant (especially the latter) find Knowledge of System less than Satisfactory. Traffic and Commercial (especially the former) report proportions satisfied with Co-operation which place them in the Questionable group. Individual employee groups reveal Questionable proportions on the following items: Superiors' Standards (both Traffic groups), Money (inside Plant), Progress in Status (traffic supervisors). But in all of these latter groups the proportion satisfied is .7.

Union

We turn now to a consideration of the danger spots in the Reward and Penalty system of the union organization. The situation is graphically represented in Chart L.

Union officers in three departments responded to 12 questions, making a total of 36 responses. Of this number, 23, or nearly two thirds, are in the Satisfactory group. Although Traffic proportions satisfied in no case fall into the Unsatisfactory group, they are responsible for 6 or nearly one half of those responses which are less than Satisfactory. Commercial is responsible for 4 of them and Plant for 3.

In the case of two items, officers in all three departments reported Questionable or Unsatisfactory proportions satisfied. The first of these is the General Reaction item. The question here was whether they would like to relinquish their jobs as union officers. Remembering that we are dealing here with local union officers, the fact that such a job is not sufficiently rewarding to keep half of the Traffic officers, and more than half of those in the other two departments, from saying that they would not be sorry to relinquish their union job is a serious finding. The tone of the answers indicates that their service is rendered out of a sense of obligation and responsibility rather than in the expectancy of reward other than a clear conscience for duty done.

The other item, in the case of which proportions of responses are less than Satisfactory for all three departments, is the matter of monetary reward for union service. Half or more in Traffic and Plant, and nearly half in Commercial, expressed dissatisfaction with the arrangements for compensating union officers.

The requirements for getting ahead in the union were Unsatisfactory to half or more officers in Traffic and Commercial. This is a bit surprising in view of the high proportions satisfied that their present position in the union was fair. This apparent inconsistency we shall discuss below.

Two fifths of officers in Traffic and Commercial rated the co-operation they received from those they worked with not very rewarding, and half of Traffic officers had the same reaction to the backing they received from members.

It will be recalled that the rating of Satisfactory was given to those proportions satisfied of .8 or more. The half of the proportions which

GROUP	ITEM	Traffic			Plant			Comm.	
		O	M I	M II	O	M I	M II	O	M
General Reaction	Job Rewarding								
	General Rewards								
	Summary								
Qualifications for Reward and Penalty	Officers' Standards								
	Subordinates' Standards								
	Managements' Standards								
	Promotion Requirements								
	Summary								
Understanding	Knowledge of System								
Instruments and Methods	Money								
	Progress in Status								
	Cooperation								
	Backing of Officers								
	Backing of Members								
	Summary								
Average	All Items								

LEGEND

Satisfactory	
Questionable	
Unsatisfactory	
Irrelevant to this group	

CHART L

Proportions Satisfied with Union Reward and Penalty System

could not be so classified did not even approach this rating. Five of the Traffic responses came close (.5) to being rated Unsatisfactory, 2 of the Plant, and 2 of the Commercial responses were definitely in the Unsatisfactory group.

Union members were asked only 3 general questions about the system of Reward and Penalty within the union organization. The qualitative detail in their responses will provide ample material for indicating what the rewards and penalties of association within the union are. In this report we indicate only the general tenor of those responses. Since there are 3 questions and five member groups, we have a total of 15 responses. Of these only 2 indicate proportions satisfied which cannot be classified in the Satisfactory group. Three tenths of Commercial members feel that other unions reward their members in ways which this union might well emulate or that there are positive disadvantages to belonging to the union; and .3 of Traffic operators are not satisfied with their progress in status in the union. But on the whole the responses give indication that union members in all departments consider union membership rewarding rather than otherwise.

Variations Among Departments

Variations among the departments in proportions satisfied with the several particular aspects of the Reward and Penalty system in the two organizations have been apparent in the foregoing discussion.

The two tables below (XXVIII and XXIX) indicate the relative departmental standings when the total numbers satisfied in the case of all items are averaged.

TABLE XXVIII

Average Proportions Satisfied with Aspects of
Company Reward and Penalty System
(In tenths)

Department	Management	Employee I	Employee II
Traffic	8	7	7
Plant	8	7	8
Commercial	8	8	

The average proportions (in tenths) satisfied with the company system of Reward and Penalty do not vary departmentally as much as in the case of the other bonds of organization.

TABLE XXIX

Average Proportions Satisfied with Aspects of
Union Reward and Penalty System
(In tenths)

Department	Officer	Member I	Member II
Traffic	7	8	8
Plant	8	8	8
Commercial	8	8	

With one exception the departmental variations in average proportions satisfied with all twelve items of the union Reward and Penalty system are also slight. The exception concerns the Traffic officers. It may be worth recalling, therefore, in what aspects Traffic Officer dissatisfaction concentrated. Half were dissatisfied with the backing they received from members, with the monetary rewards for official performance, with the requirements for getting ahead in the union, and with their knowledge of the Reward and Penalty system itself. Two fifths were dissatisfied with the co-operation received from those with whom they worked on union business.

VARIATIONS BETWEEN STATUS GROUPS
Company

Variations have also been noticed between management and employees. Reference to Table XXVIII will indicate that the average proportions satisfied with respect to all twelve items are identical for the two groups in Commercial, but that Plant and Traffic managements reveal higher proportions satisfied.

Reference to Table XXVI in the Appendix will show that the general reaction to the system was practically identical for all management and employee groups. Indeed, in the case of only one item (Knowledge of System) with respect to only one department (Plant) do management and employees vary from each other by more than one tenth.

Union

Table XXIX indicates no variation between proportions of officers and members satisfied on the average in Commercial. In the other two departments, member satisfaction is higher than officer satisfaction. This variation, however, grows largely out of the fact that union officers' responses to nine questions not asked of members are considered in the averages. If only those responses to questions asked of both groups are considered, the officer and member proportions satisfied are quite similar.

FOCI OF SATISFACTION

If the first General Reaction question is not considered, there are seven items about which both management and employees were questioned in connection with the company organization, and about which union officers were questioned in connection with the union organization. If we rank the numbers satisfied with these several items in management, employee, and union-officer groups, we get the result indicated in Table XXX.

TABLE XXX

ASPECTS OF REWARD AND PENALTY SYSTEM IN ORDER OF NUMBERS
EXPRESSING SATISFACTION

Order	All Management	All Employees	All Union Officers*
1	Superiors' Standards	Money	General Rewards
2	Progress in Status	Superiors' Standards	Progress in Status
3	Knowledge of System	Progress in Status	Superiors' Standards
4	Money	Co-operation	Co-operation
5	Co-operation	Knowledge of System	Knowledge of System
6	Promotion Requirements	General Rewards	Promotion Requirements
7	General Rewards	Promotion Requirements	Money

* With respect to union organization.

This, of course, is a ranking within each group, and it must be remembered, in the case of management and employees, that the satisfaction *with* all of these aspects was high. With this in mind, however, it is interesting to notice the relatively high ranking of numbers satisfied, in all three groups, with the standards used by superiors for rewarding and penalizing—in other words, with the requirements placed on one in order to win approval and avoid disapproval by superiors. Also note the relatively high satisfaction with progress in status as a rewarding element for all three groups. It is interesting that among employees, who receive less money than management, satisfaction with monetary rewards heads the list, whereas, among management, it is halfway down the list. Remember we are here considering *local* management.

The most consistent relatively low-ranking item is the Requirements for Promotion. As we have indicated above, this is surprising in view of the relatively high position occupied by the reward, Progress in Status. Why should a group be satisfied more with the end results of the status-achievement process than with one of the factors (Promotion Requirements) which influences that result?

Without exhaustive analysis of the qualitative and descriptive materials gathered in connection with these and other questions, we cannot do more than record a general impression. When men thought of Promotional Requirements, they thought of formal company policy, seniority, promotion from within, discrimination against married women (notice that the low ranking of this item is due to the low proportions satisfied in Traffic and Commercial, employing large numbers of women), the relatively open-ended opportunities for certain crafts, etc. At least two suggestions might be offered as to why they, nevertheless, reported relatively little dis-satisfaction with their present status in the company. The first arises from comments similar to this: "No, these requirements work against me, but they are the same for all, and probably necessary from the company's angle, so why kick about it? My position is fair in comparison with that of others, all right." In other words, requirements which are personally disadvantageous are accepted as organizationally justified, and the conse-quences in personal achievement resulting from their application are not therefore considered unfair. Should this statement prove valid, a full and convincing frank statement of organizational necessities with respect to re-quirements for reward may contribute to acceptance of results, though the participants do not like the requirements.

Another suggestion is that Progress in Status is measured both in formal and informal terms. Typical of the formal status achievement is promotion to a higher position. Typical of informal status achievement is increasingly good standing with superiors and associates. The relatively high degree of satisfaction indicated with Superiors' Standards for approval is indicative that the requirements for this informal status are highly satisfactory. Even though this informal status does not lead to promotion in formal status, because, let us say, the person is barred by formal policies, or indeed by lack of openings, it is nevertheless valued in itself. Here is a case where the informal system may provide rewards which result "on balance" in an over-all satisfaction with the status acquired. In view of the decreasing number of chances for promotion rewards as one ascends the status hier-archy, this possibility of informal reward deserves careful attention.

Some of these remarks apply to union officers, also. Again remember-ing, however, that the present report is concerned with local officers, one peculiarity of the requirements for promotion should be mentioned. One of the requirements is that the person be "amenable to persuasion that he should take the office." Again, the low ranking of satisfaction with promotion requirements results from the exceptionally low ranking of this item in Traffic and Commercial. The feeling that "Plant runs the union anyhow," is widespread. One gets the feeling from reading the interviews that, in Traffic and Commercial, local union leadership is frequently considered a headache but to be accepted "since everyone should take his turn." In the words of a Traffic representative: "The requirements? Who knows what they are, except that you be willing to do your stint and take the gaff for a year or two?" If such were to prove the case, then a substantial proportion of local union officers might be expected to have a low opinion of the reward to be anticipated from meeting such requirements.

The lowly position of satisfaction with monetary rewards for union activity is worthy of note. Although the present report deals with responses only of local officers (who receive no pay for union activity), we may record an impression, received from reading the interviews with higher union officers, that demands on their pocketbooks by virtue of their union activities make the monetary item a penalty instead of a reward.

VARIATIONS BY SIZE OF EXCHANGE

The satisfied proportions of both company and union departmental groups are so consistently high in all size-of-exchange groups that there is no need to explain variations. The generally high level of satisfaction in all size-of-exchange groups when the average of all responses is considered is indicated in Table XXXI and XXXII.

TABLE XXXI
PROPORTIONS SATISFIED WITH ASPECTS OF
COMPANY REWARD AND PENALTY SYSTEM
(In tenths)

Dept.	Status	Size of Exchange Group				Hdqt.	Div.	Dist.
		I	II	III	IV			
Traffic	Mgt.	8	8	8	8	8	9	6
	E. I	7	7	7	7	8		
	E. II	7	7	8	7			
Plant	Mgt.	8	9	8	7	9	8	8
	E. I	7	7	7	7	8		
	E. II	8	8	7	8			
Commercial	Mgt.	9	8	8	9	8	8	8
	E	8	8	9	9	8		

The departures from this general rule, when specific aspects of the Reward and Penalty system are considered, tend to concentrate on the same aspects of the system for management and employee groups. In the case of four aspects, a proportion of one half or less satisfied was reported

TABLE XXXII

PROPORTIONS SATISFIED WITH ASPECTS OF
UNION REWARD AND PENALTY SYSTEM
(In tenths)

Dept.	Status	Size-of-Exchange Group				Hdqt.
		I	II	III	IV	
Traffic	O	6	6	8	8	7
	M. I	8	9	8	8	8
	M. II	8·	8	8	9	
Plant	O	8	7	7	8	8
	M. I	9	9	9	8	9
	M. II	8	8	9	9	
Commercial	O	8	9	7	7	8
	M	8	8	8	7	7

by at least one size-of-exchange group in each department. These four aspects are listed below together with the groups in which such a low proportion of satisfied individuals was found.

Aspects	Size-of-Exchange Group				Hdqt.	Div.	Dist.
	I	II	III	IV			
General Rewards							
Traffic Management	x					x	x
Traffic Employees	x	x	x	x			
Plant Management	x		x	x			x
Plant Employees		x	x	x			
Commercial Management						x	x
Commercial Employees					x		
Promotion Requirements							
Traffic Management	x						x
Traffic Employees		x	x	x			
Plant Management	x			x		x	
Plant Employees	x	x	x	x			
Commercial Management		x					
Commercial Employees	x				x		
Co-operation							
Traffic Management	x			x			
Traffic Employees	x			x			
Commercial Management							x
Knowledge of System							
Plant Employees	x	x	x				

No union-member group reported a proportion satisfied of one half or less, but union officers did with respect to half the aspects about which they were questioned. The aspects involved, and those groups of local union officers reporting one half or less satisfied, are listed below.

Aspect	Size-of-Exchange Group				
	I	II	III	IV	Hdqt.
Job Rewarding					
Traffic Officers	x	x			x
Plant Officers	x	x	x		x
Commercial Officers	x		x	x	x
Officers' Standards					
Traffic Officers		x			
Promotion Requirements					
Traffic Officers	x	x			x
Commercial Officers	x		x	x	x
Money Reward					
Traffic Officers	x		x		
Plant Officers	x	x	x		x
Commercial Officers			x		
Co-operation					
Traffic Officers	x	x			
Plant Officers					x
Commercial Officers	x		x		x
Members' Backing					
Traffic Officers	x		x		
Plant Officers			x		
Knowledge of System					
Traffic Officers		x		x	
Plant Officers			x		

SUMMARY

In the minds of the participants of this company and union is a conception of the Reward and Penalty system as experienced by them. The detailed conception as revealed in their responses will be reserved for our final report after more thoroughgoing analysis of those responses. Our purpose at this time is to indicate the outline of the aspects of the system which their descriptive comments make clear. In general character these aspects should be characteristic of any organization. We have found that the Reward and Penalty system as experienced can be described by the answers to the following questions:

1. What objectives does the system serve?
2. What kinds of behavior (and inferred human qualities) are rewarded and penalized?
3. Who are the agents of reward and penalty?
4. What is the basis of the agents' power to reward and penalize, and in what order of strength as agents are they therefore arranged?
5. What are the techniques of reward and penalty available and how are they utilized?

The character of each of these aspects has been elaborated in the text. Here let us briefly refer to certain matters of major importance to those who seek to understand and improve this part of an organization's structure.

Objectives may be personal as well as organizational. A large number of rewards and penalties are available particularly to management and leaders for their use as executives of their organization, that is, to further the organizational purpose. Care must be exercised that the tendency, ever present, to usurp these instruments and apply them for personal objectives is reduced to a minimum.

The long list of behavior traits and inferred personal qualities for which participants believe they are rewarded suggests that a large share of them can never be standardized and systematized. Yet organizational consistency requires progress in this direction. The major problems are two. These requirements are, in actual definition and use, relative to a number of factors and particularly to the personal peculiarities of people who must apply the requirements in particular cases. This fact determines what is meant by a particular desirable or undesirable trait, and whether or not it was revealed by a particular person and his performance. Moreover, the requirements refer not only to job performance in the narrow sense but to performance in human relations, and the definition of the latter requirements are peculiarly influenced by the person with whom the relationship is established.

It was noticed, too, that justice is hard to achieve because of the inference drawn by an object of reward or penalty that he is being rewarded or penalized for what he *is* as well as for what he *does*. There is ample opportunity for disagreement between agent and object on the measurement of the degree to which the object has met the former requirement.

We pointed out one characteristic of the roster of agents of reward and penalty in this company, that is, the relatively important position occupied by customers and stockholders, actual and potential. It would be unwise to forget also that the roster of agents includes not only management but employees and union officers as well. The system of Reward and Penalty is not one administered solely by management.

The description of the power of agents to reward and penalize did not ignore the concept of power as "individual force of personality and character," but it did indicate that this was important only as related to the operation of several basic determinants of power. If, for instance, it was desirable to increase the power of any agent to reward or penalize, this could be done by one or more of the following methods:

1. Establishing a closer and more frequent relationship with the object.
2. Getting a more accurate and adequate picture of what the object considered to be rewarding and penalizing.
3. Making the agent more important to the object.
4. Making rewards and penalties more adapted to and consistent with performance.
5. Reducing the object's power to nullify application of reward or penalty to him.
6. Obtaining backing of others.
7. Increasing the instruments and methods at his disposal.

The discussion of the number and variety of the instruments of rewards and penalty actually employed in these organizations again highlighted the fact that many of them cannot be regularized and standardized either in their nature or their application. The necessary dependence upon the peculiarities of individuals who judge and administer prevents that process, even to the degree that it is desirable. In view of this fact, the grievance system becomes a highly important safety valve.

Another significant feature of the list of instruments and methods considered by participants to be a part of the system of Reward and Penalty is that those advantages or disadvantages they shared with other participants, just because they worked for this company or were members of this union, were as important as those rewards and penalties which they earned as individuals. Here is one reason why the words "incentives" and "discipline" are not comprehensive enough to encompass the content of the system. It is customary to think of this system as that by which individuals earn or fail to earn rewards by virtue of what they do or are as individuals. But if our respondents' conception is accepted as defining what system of Rewards and Penalties is experienced by them, then a highly important place must be given to such things as vacations, holidays, various benefits, speed and time of work, health and safety provisions, recreational facilities, and other items which they share with other participants and to which individual performance is only indirectly related as a qualifying condition. They are distinctly not extras or lace or frills in their minds. They are an integral part of the system of Reward and Penalty which conditions their life in the organization.

The foregoing comments, we believe, although growing out of our observations and interviews in this company and union, are applicable to the structure and dynamics of any organization. The brief recapitulation of the degree of satisfaction with this system given below is applicable, of course, only to these organizations.

The general picture for both management and employees is that of a high degree of satisfaction with the system of Reward and Penalty in the company. There are few danger spots when the responses of groups for the company as a whole are analyzed.

In the union the general picture for members also reveals a high level of satisfaction. The situation is mixed for officers, who, of course, have much more intimate familiarity with the institutional processes than do members. The most serious finding was the, at best, neutral reaction toward the rewards of holding local union office. The chief particular foci of dissatisfaction in the case of two or more departments were on the matter of monetary rewards, requirements for getting ahead in the union, and the co-operation of those with whom they worked. Satisfaction was relatively high with respect to the other eight aspects of the system about which they were questioned.

Variations in proportions satisfied as between departments and as between management and employees were not as great as they were in the case of the other bonds—Functional Specifications, the Status system, and the Communication system. In the union, Traffic officers showed a lower proportion satisfied than did those in other departments.

In the relative ranking of satisfaction with particular aspects within their own groups, all three (management, employees, and union officers) rated Superiors' Standards and Progress in Status consistently high, and Requirements for Promotion consistently low. This apparent conflict in findings was explained.

Little variation worthy of note was found in proportions satisfied when the responses were analyzed by reference to size-of-exchange groups.

The Reward and Penalty system in general is, to judge from the reactions of participants, the most satisfactory bond that we have examined to this point in the two organizations.

VI

ORGANIZATIONAL CHARTER

WHEN a person makes statements such as, "I am a citizen of the United States," "I am a Princeton man," "I belong to the United Steel Workers of America," "I work for Shell Oil," "I am a Johnson"; the words Princeton, United Steel Workers of America, Shell Oil, and Johnson suggest to his mind a concept of these institutions having characteristics which distinguish them from other institutions of the same general type. The picture he has in mind contains elements which are very personal to him. But it also contains elements which he shares with all or most of the other people who could make similar statements about themselves. Most important for our purpose, it is a concept of the particular nation, university, union, company, or family *as a whole,* as an entity, different from, say, England, Yale, Brotherhood of Electrical Workers, Ford Motor Company, or the Fitzgeralds.

Awareness of this fact will introduce us to what we mean by the *Organization Charter*. The elements which contribute to the concept of any organization as a whole, as an entity, we label the Organizational Charter. It should be obvious that it ranks with Functional Specifications and the Status, Communication, and Reward and Penalty systems as one of the important bonds which weld a group of individuals together into a functioning team.

It is as impossible for a company or a union to exist as such without some characteristic Organizational Charter as it is for it to exist without a Status or Communication system. Its importance to effective teamwork is obvious and recognized, though in many cases relatively little attention is given by managers or leaders to making it explicit and clear to participants. Regardless of their efforts, however, a conception of the Organizational Charter does exist in the minds of participants, and it influences their behavior in many ways. This will become clearer as we spell out its nature in greater detail.

Every organization has a name. That name stands for something to all who are aware of it or use it. One might almost say that the organization has a character, an individuality, which makes the name real. The scientist will not accept any such reification or personalizing of an organization. But participants in these organizations are subject to no such scientific scruples, and generations of men have felt and thought about the organizations they belonged to as something real in themselves. If we are to report accurately the factors that mold the behavior of these participants, we must report that they think of the Southern New England Telephone Company and The Connecticut Union of Telephone Workers as having character and individuality *as organizations.*

Some elements of that individuality and character are comprehended by those outside as well as inside the organization, others only by the participants. Of what types are they? Although the types named below are categories devised to provide a classification system for the elements as reported by the participants in these two organizations, in explaining them we shall make reference to organizations more familiar to the general reader. For the types must be applicable to the analysis of the structure and dynamics of all organizations.

First then let us consider the *elements* of the Organizational Charter used to identify organizations. Suppose one were trying to explain the difference between Yale, Macy's, the Aluminum Company of America, the United Gas and Electric Company, and the United Rubber Workers of America. The easiest and most obvious thing to say would be that each had a distinctive *purpose* and *function.* Then he would note that there were certain larger groups of similar organizations, a sort of a family, with which each was identified: nonprofit educational institutions, private enterprise, retail outlets, manufacturing industries, public utilities, the labor movement. This *affiliation* or *identification* could be used to characterize the organization.

Then if one were to go on to distinguish between Yale and the University of Chicago, or between Macy's and Saks Fifth Avenue, or between the United Rubber Workers and the Amalgamated Clothing Workers, he would make reference to differences in *reputation, major policies,* or possibly in the *significance* of the role played by the two.

There are perhaps others, but these are the types of elements which came to the mind of our respondents when they attempted to give us a conception of the over-all character of their company and union. We may summarize them as:

Function or Purpose
Significance
Identification or Affiliation
Major Policies
Reputation

Participants become a *team* in part through sharing an awareness of the specific content of these types of elements.

Notice that in each case the element is rooted in the behavior of participants as a group or as representing the group. The reality of these elements of the Organizational Charter is in the purposes *affirmed*, the functions *performed*, the significance of the role *played*, the affiliations *made*, the major policies *set*, and the reputation enjoyed because of present and past *behavior* of the sort named.

The first aspect of the Organizational Charter then requiring definition is its *elements*. The second aspect which came to our attention may be labeled *determinants of scope and limitations*. The determinants are in the form of thought and action of participants and outsiders as well.

It is obvious that the degree of comprehension and acceptance of the elements by participants determines the scope of and limitations on the purpose, function, significance, affiliations, major policies, and even the reputation of the organization. At the very least, such factors determine what the *experienced* content of the Organizational Charter is for participants. As we have indicated before, it is the bond as *experienced* which serves well or poorly to weld the individual participants into a team. A definition of purpose and function to which a predominant portion of participants does not give assent or which it does not comprehend does not constitute a part of the Organizational Charter acting as a realistic bond of organization, no matter how positively asserted by the leaders of the organization. The same can be said of the significance, affiliations, major policies, and reputation of the organization. This is a major reason why one cannot learn the realistic character of the Organizational Charter by questioning company or union leaders or by reading their published speeches or documents.

The scope and limitations are further determined by the rights granted and obligations imposed on the organization from the outside. Outsiders affect the purpose and function of an organization in many ways. They may or may not accept the purpose as legitimate. They may give the organization the right to perform its functions under certain restrictions. They may impose on it the duty to perform those functions. By their judgments they help to establish the significance and reputation of the organization. It goes without saying that the pressures exerted from the outside are thoroughly influential in the setting of major policies. The most obvious action of outsiders is that taken in their organized capacity as government.

The second aspect of the Organizational Charter necessary for its definition then is called determinants of scope and limitations. To define that aspect we must describe the degree of acceptance and comprehension of the Organizational Charter by participants; and the rights granted, obligations imposed, expectancies held, and judgments made by outsiders.

One more aspect is important. By what *means* are the comprehension and acceptance of participants assisted and assured; and by what *means* are the granted rights, imposed obligations, expectancies, and judgments implemented? The most important of these means mentioned by the participants in these two organizations may be classified as *symbols,* both material and human, *slogans, documents, tradition,* and *folklore.* Seldom mentioned were two others we have noticed in other organizations, *ritual* and *formal statements.*

The Organizational Charter Described

Because the Organizational Charter is not as well recognized by many as are the other bonds of organization we have discussed, it will serve our purpose to define it more specifically by reference to its nature in these two organizations so that it may be clear how it ranks with the other bonds as an integrator of the many individuals who are participants.

The content of the three aspects of the Organizational Charter of the company and union may now be suggested by indicating the elements and means most frequently mentioned by our respondents. In the final report on this study we shall analyze the responses so that relative emphasis on the several items is indicated as between certain groups of participants, according, for instance, to department, status position, and size of exchange. Here will be recorded only those items which dominated the overall picture as revealed in the responses of all participants in the company and all in the union organizations.

Material for this section came from an open-ended question asked about each organization. It was asked toward the close of the interview in these terms: "We have been talking about parts of this organization, different features of your experience with the organization. Now let's think about the organization as a whole. The name of this organization stands for something in your mind. It calls certain things or pictures to your mind. What are those things? For instance, when you think about the United States what does that suggest to you? Now think about the Southern New England Telephone Company [*or* the Connecticut Union of Telephone Workers]." We took what came. The answers below record what was uppermost in their minds. Any comparison between the relative emphasis given to the separate items grows out of this fact, not from counting items on a check list.

COMPANY

The image of the company as a whole was composed of elements which may be classified into the following types in the order of the frequency of their occurrence in the response made. Numbers in parentheses indicate the number of times an element so classified was mentioned.

Purpose and Function	(898)
Significance	(641)
Reputation	(466)
Major Policies	(399)
Affiliation and Identification	(105)

Tentatively, the outstanding emphasis on those elements which suggest the purpose and function of the company would seem to indicate a strong unifying factor conducive to good teamwork in carrying out the company's tasks.

The statements which follow paraphrase the comments made by management and employees. They do not represent our judgment, but that of the participants themselves. The number of comments made by management and by employees are listed after each item. Illustrative material is not used unless it appeared to a significant degree in *both* management and employee comments. In listing the contents of each type of element and in the discussion of the elements themselves, the items are arranged in the order of emphasis given to them by those interviewed.

We may then outline the Organizational Charter of the company, as disclosed in the answers to our questions, as follows:

Elements

I. *Purpose and Function*
   a. To provide a necessary public service to the citizens of the state and all who have dealings with them (M, 66; E, 212). More specifically:
   b. To weld together, by providing the facilities for adequate communication, the people, families, businesses, industries, and institutions of the state with those of the nation and the world. To provide the necessary link between need, decision, and action when two or more persons are not in face-to-face contact (M, 61; E, 326).
   c. To provide jobs for people, and an organization in which their individual skills and efforts can be caught up in a joint effort to accomplish this task (M, 27; E, 134).
   d. To provide for quick and uninterrupted transmission of messages in emergency situations and regardless of mechanical or nature-induced problems (M, 27; E, 109).
   e. To do all of this at the least possible cost, with the highest possible efficiency, and at lowest possible rates to the customer (M, 19; E, 15).
   f. To make a profit (M, 3; E, 3).

II. *Significance*
   a. Its service is vital to all aspects of life. How would any one get along without telephones? Whether it is two people, businesses, or nations, this company helps to bring them as close together as the nearest telephone. The whole economic and social and political life of the community, nation, and world would bog down if the telephone system were blanked out (M, 78; E, 384).
   b. It is an expanding and developing company. The whole telephone business started in New Haven, and now look at it! More and better equipment and service every year, new forms of communications (M, 14; E, 90). (Note that identification with the Bell System is frequently evident in this and the next item.)
   c. This is a large company because it is a part of a system which encircles the globe and reaches every corner of the world (M, 14; E, 61).

III. *Reputation*
   The company has excellent standing with other businesses, with government, and people in general because (M, 66; E, 214):

   a. It is old and reliable.
   b. It is well run and well regulated (internally) and businesslike.
   c. It is fair, considerate, and has high standards of courtesy.

d. It has good financial policies and offers a stable and secure investment.

e. It is progressive and at the same time conservative.

f. It is a "good" employer.

It has a long record of fair dealing with its employees; is paternalistic, but not so as to damage self-respect. It is considered "the best company around to work for." It is a place where teamwork counts and is rewarded (M, 30; E, 156).

(This is the dominant tone so far as reputation is concerned. Several warnings should be given. The reputation with outsiders is reported not by them but by participants. Their judgment may be the same, but our evidence does not bear on this conclusion. Again, in the midst of this generally favorable response are a few discordant voices who report that the public is fed-up with poor service and nonattention of operators, installers, and repairmen to duty; that they think "all employees must be dead up there"; that the company is "smug" and counts too much on the unwillingness of its employees to qiut; that "pull, not skill, counts not only in getting in but staying in." We would expect this from the examination of the proportions satisfied with the several aspects of the other bonds of organization we have discussed. But the dominant tone is struck by the first characterization.)

IV. *Major Policies*

    a. To give dependable and consistently high quality twenty-four-hour service, no matter what the circumstances (M, 23; E, 110).

    b. To have the kind of personnel practices which build high morale and satisfaction among employees and promote efficient service for customers (M, 20; E, 110). (Most frequently mentioned in order of their frequency were security of employment, no firing for minor offenses, the chance and guidance to make a career, fair wage setting and administration, benefit and welfare plans, adequate transfer opportunities, don't let complaints become grievances.)

    c. Courtesy toward customers in voice, manner, patience, and safe driving in company vehicles (M, 18; E, 73).

    d. To provide good working practices (M, 8; E, 37). (Examples of these were almost inevitably related to the persons' own job.)

V. *Affiliation and Identification*

The Southern New England Telephone Company, of course, does not stand alone. In the minds of those who work for the company, it is identified most frequently with the Bell System (M, 14; E, 40).

Next it is a part of the network of public utilities which provide basic public services (M, 10; E, 20).

(Beyond these two, few suggestions were volunteered. Only 6 from management and 6 employees identified the company with private enterprise; 1 employee identified it with "the American System." In each group, 4 people expressed strong feelings of independence from any group.)

Means

No single portion of our material is richer in content than that which records the cues which suggest and the means which support the Organizational Charter just described. Those who work for the company have in their minds a wealth of things that call to mind the company, its functions, significance, policies, affiliations, and reputation. A mere listing of these would make a chapter in itself. They provide participants with a language that is spoken, seen, and heard which they recognize as distinctly their own. Since our purpose in this report is to make clear merely the existence and importance of such items as a part of the "structure of living" in the company, we shall simply illustrate by reference to those items which are repeated most frequently.

The cues and means can be classified into the following groups. Numbers in parentheses indicate the number of times responses made fit into these classifications:

Functional Symbols	(700)
People	(481)
Policy Slogans	(416)
Identifying Symbols	(411)
Structural Symbols	(305)
Folklore	(21)
Ritual	(8)

We may briefly illustrate each of these:

Functional Symbols (M, 93; E, 607)
By functional symbols are meant those which suggest the purpose and function of the company. Unless otherwise noted, they are mentioned by participants in all departments of the company. In the order of their frequency of occurrence they are as follows: telephones (223), poles and lines (149), switchboards, (123, chiefly Traffic), company vehicles (86), equipment not otherwise classified (72), directories (24).

People (M, 111; E, 370)

People may symbolize the company either as individuals or groups. In the order of frequency of occurrence they are as follows: other employees (208), operators (129 from all departments), subscribers (63), specific people, (59, chiefly two or three high officers in the company, but including, in addition to these, Alexander Graham Bell, Walter Gifford, former president Knight, and the president of the union), management (53), stockholders (5 from management, 4 from employees).

Policy Slogans (M, 99, E, 317)

The most repeated policy slogans were Spirit of service (132), Voice with a smile (122 chiefly traffic); No job is so important that you can't do it safely (122, about 100 from Plant). Others frequently used generally were More service for less cost, Courtesy is not rationed, There's always time for courtesy, Be accurate, then build up your speed, There's always time to do it right, The calls must go through, etc.[1]

Identifying Symbols (M, 52; E, 359)

The nature of these symbols will be clear from the following list arranged in the order of their occurrence: the Bell seal (129), name and initials of the company (90), advertising (78), flag (22), radio program (15), common language (14). The bond represented by this last item is underemphasized. Interviewers' struggles with learning the meaning of terms such as Dead Ace, Mabel, plugging, A.G., W.H., B.T.O., O.D's, B.Y's. "How are you making it?" M.D.F. and I.D.F., the load, the build up, the frame, the rack, the board, etc., indicated a common language, usually pertaining to the craft, which certainly would mark an outsider if he got into the group. Other symbols reminding workers of the company are the service button, the telephone bill, certificates of award, the color green, and (perish the thought), for one man, Reddy Kilowatt.

Structural Symbols (M, 56; E, 249)

The buildings and work surroundings are cues which suggest the company to other participants: The local exchange, "you can always tell them," "there's something about the architecture," "you hardly need a sign" (134). The more immediate work place or environment (129), the Headquarters building or White House (32).

Folklore (M, 5; E, 16)

Stories were told which re-enforced chiefly the significance and reputation and policies of the company. Those mentioned referred to the beginning of the telephone business, the early experiments of Alexander Graham Bell, the

[1] If these are not identical with the slogans taught, the interviewers are not to be blamed. This is the way they were reported.

New England hurricane, the Naugatuck and Illinois fires, the Mississippi flood. New stories, some of which may "catch on" and become folklore, are constantly being fed into this stream.

Certain omissions will occur to those familiar with the operations of the company. Why did ritual used by the company rank so low as reminding people of the company (4 each from management and employees), in view of the importance attached by management to the presentation of the Vail award and service pins, bouquets for long-service people, dedication of new buildings, retirement ceremonies? There is no mention of the Glee Club or the athletic teams, no mention of the *News Briefs* or the house organ, the *Telephone Bulletin*.

Scope and Limitations

We have no sure way of knowing the scope and limitations imposed on the Organizational Charter by the degree of comprehension and acceptance existing among employees, though, as we have indicated, the responses indicating the company's purpose and function and significance were numerous and were consistent as between management and employee groups. We should point out that the purpose of the company to make a profit was overwhelmingly shadowed by the other concepts of purpose among employees and local management.

The rights and obligations as defined for the company by outsiders acting through government were clearly evident. Almost more important, however, were the obligations imposed by the immediate contact of a great proportion of employees with the customers which included almost everyone in the state. The expectancies held by them were powerful determinants of the function and policies. The closeness of contact with them provided opportunity for a constant reminder not merely to management but to employees as well. The contact was not merely in work relations but in neighborhood and community relations as well. "Almost anyone else can sometimes meet someone who isn't a customer. I never can," expresses the power of this determinant of important aspects of the Organizational Charter.

One other outside influence must be mentioned, if it can be considered "outside" merely in an organizational sense. That is the union officers. There is little doubt that the expectancies and power of the union officers, backed by a consensus of their members, are significant factors in determining the policies of the company at least with respect to its employees.

UNION

The image of the union as a whole was composed of elements which may be classified into the following types in the order of the frequency of their occurrence in the responses made. Numbers in parentheses indicate the number of times an element so classified was mentioned.

Purpose and Function	(706)
Reputation	(218)
Affiliation and Identification	(189)
Major Policies	(158)
Significance	(142)

Tentatively, we are inclined to regard this relatively high emphasis on those elements which suggest the purpose and function of the union as a sign of strength.

In the discussion of the particular elements which follows, we wish again to underscore the fact that these comments paraphrase the remarks of union members and officers. They are not our words; they do not represent our judgment. They represent the Organizational Charter *as it appears to the participants themselves.*

The reader should also be reminded that the content for each type of element has been arranged in the order of the emphasis given to it by the respondents.

No illustration has been used unless a significant number of both officers and members made reference to it. The numbers in parenthesis beside the item indicate the number of times it was mentioned.

We may then outline the Organizational Charter of the union, as disclosed in the answers to our questions, as follows:

Elements

I. *Purpose and Function*
    a. "To get just and equitable wages for members and keep them increasing (O, 13; M, 125).
    b. To support and protect members "as a bulldog," standing by in case of need, making them feel secure (O, 16; M, 117).

c. To give members a chance of representation to management better than management itself could provide, and to help management obtain the workers' point of view and knowledge of their problems (O, 34; M, 98).

d. To give members the experience of unity and co-operation, a feeling they belong and are not alone (O, 14; M, 104).

e. To provide members with nonmonetary benefits in better working conditions, better attitude and respect from supervision (O, 16; M, 83).

f. To provide members with an instrument for settling their problems (in this order of importance: smoothing out of petty differences with management and other employees, major general problems discussed in collective bargaining, and grievances) (O, 16; M, 80).

II. *Reputation*

The reputation of the union is one of which a member can feel proud. Our officers are on the whole motivated by service to members and are co-operative toward management. Toward both they are fair, faithful, levelheaded, honest, tolerant, and considerate. The union has done good things for the workers and for management (O, 24; M, 165).

A scattering of critical comments were vehemently expressed by a minority in terms of "too conservative," "weak," "company dominated," "a bunch of cliques," "strong at the top and weak at the bottom," "not aggressive."

III. *Affiliation and Identification*

The union is, first of all, spiritually and functionally a segment of the entire union movement, but it is independent organizationally of any branch of the movement. In fact it is much more identified with the company than with any such *branch* (O, 24; M, 165).

IV. *Major Policies*

The major union policy is to serve the workers by bringing the management and the workers closer together and by establishing mutually advantageous relations between them. This involves reliance on reason and negotiation rather than on strife and strikes. It involves urging workers to give a fair day's work. It involves major attention to settling difficulties and grievances "right" rather than under pressure from either side (O, 33; M, 114).

In relation to other *telephone* unions the policy is one of maintaining complete autonomy; with respect to other unions the policy is embodied in the slogans, Telephone work for telephone people and Compromise only when forced to (O, 2; M, 6).

[Little mention was made of policies in relation to the community (M, 3).]

V. *Significance*

The union is strong and significant only in relation to its work for the members and in this company. On the national scene and in the union movement, it is "a small drop of water in a big pail." For members it is significant because "it gives freedom of expression; for management because it keeps them on their toes." (O, 17; M, 125).

Although some union officers have a conception of the significant role this small union can play in demonstrating, on a small scale, the possibilities in union management co-operation, and that "local autonomy is the real basis of democracy," etc., these larger ambitions are not shared by any significant number of members.

Means

We have discussed the elements which together make up the image of the union in the minds of local members and officers. What are the cues by which this image is brought to mind, which suggest it?. What are the means which re-enforce and make vivid that image? It will prove interesting to list them in the order of frequency of their appearance in the responses before discussing each of them briefly. They are:

1. Union Officers	7. Meeting Hall
2. Union Members	8. Union Office
3. Union Meetings	9. Miscellaneous Symbols
4. *Union Voice*	10. Miscellaneous Slogans
5. Union Card	11. Other Specific People
6. Union Name and Initials	12. Folklore

The most interesting feature of this list is that the cues which most frequently brought the concept of the union as a whole to mind arise from the contact with members and officers of the union. In each case these cues were mentioned 50 per cent more times than any other single cue. Of those who named union officers, about one fourth named particular people, the president in particular. As our research continues and we describe the Organizational Charter of other organizations, this relative significance of human symbols will no doubt furnish one clue to the typing of the organizations.

Union meetings rank next as a means making vivid the idea of the union. The emphasis is not, however, on meetings in general, but on particularly outstanding meetings. "Now you take that meeting last year when the ———— issue was up. Boy, that really got me. I see the union and what it can mean when I think of that meeting," might be used to illustrate this item.

The *Union Voice* is the union periodical. The name is apparently a happy one, since it enables the paper not only to suggest the whole scope of union functions to members but re-enforces the basic significance of the union as a channel for free expression and a chance to "get the low-down."

The Union membership card, the initials C.U.T.W., the meeting hall, the union office, require little comment save to indicate that they are relatively less important as material symbols than are the human symbols mentioned above.

Numerous symbols were mentioned, but aside from "The emblems in ———— Hall," "the ballot," they appeared to be individual rather than group possessions. "I think of a chain," "I think of a picture I once saw of a man swimming against the tide," are typical of such scattered items.

Slogans, like these miscellaneous symbols, were not near the surface of consciousness. No one of them was mentioned enough times to indicate their major importance. United we stand, *The Voice* is free, Don't be a free rider, Telephone work for telephone people, are examples of slogans that may have reference to the union in particular situations. One that is likely to become more important as suggesting the basic character of the union is, A telephone union for telephone workers.

No real folklore was disclosed in our interviews, although the stories about the break from the former "Association" and about union activity in the recent nationwide strike are on the way to becoming folklore.

Scope and Limitations

The scope and limitations to the Organizational Charter are set primarily by the degree of comprehension and acceptance on the part of the participants. Only the purpose and function of the union appear to be close to the level of consciousness on the part of members. This is important. It is probably more important that agreement should be forth-coming with respect to this aspect than with respect to any other. The evidence we have indicates, however, that the chief limitations on the scope of the Organizational Charter of the union result from a lack of comprehension rather than from a lack of acceptance of elements of the Charter by the members.

Since the union is not well known as far as people in the community are concerned and since its constitution and by-laws are self-created, those outside the union exercise very little influence upon its Organizational Charter. To be sure the public, acting through government in the form of the Wagner Act, did stimulate the formation of the union as an associa-tion independent of company management, but not to the extent which would have resulted from a joining with some branch of the labor move-ment. This break inevitably affected its practice but not its major policies, as revealed in the comments above. Its function has been enlarged, its significance and reputation have been determined, by its own efforts. The Wagner Act did not impose any obligations upon it, nor give it any rights it did not assume or develop under pressure from its own member-ship. The Taft-Hartley Act, so far as we can learn, has imposed no obliga-tions on it that it had not already assumed, nor has it given it any rights, through duties imposed on management, of which it has cared to take ad-vantage. The chief outside influence which is likely to affect its policies and identification in the future is likely to be a competing union.

As in the case of the company, we must name the men on the other side of the bargaining table an important outside influence. This is to say no more or less than the expectancies and power of management must inevitably make its impact felt on all aspects of the Organizational Charter of the union with which it deals.

DEGREE OF SATISFACTION WITH ORGANIZATIONAL CHARTER

The degree of satisfaction with the Organizational Charter is harder to measure by direct questions to participants than the degree of satis-faction with other bonds. This is particularly true since the nature of this organizational device has not been so well explored in the literature as have the natures of Functional Specifications and the Communication, Status, and Reward and Penalty systems. In this case it was even more true, therefore, that we had to develop from our evidence a conception of the content of the bond before we would know how to frame our questions adequately.

It became evident, however, that the Organizational Charter as revealed in the comments of our respondents had an important bearing on the realization of the goal experience of *integration* or wholeness.

This goal has three aspects: wholeness within one's self (self-respect), wholeness with one's immediate group (solidarity), and wholeness with the world of affairs and people beyond the group (relationship). As we looked over the some 65 items in terms of which the respondents thought of the company and of the union as a whole, many of them seemed specifically related to one of these aspects of *integration*. Thinking of the company or union in these terms would contribute to their experience of integration. Examples are given below of responses which could be thus related to a particular aspect of the experience:

Self-Respect
"I think of a company which meets your own standards of good conduct. You never have to be ashamed or apologetic."

"I think of a union that makes it possible to realize what in yourself you know is right and just. So you're proud to be a part of it."

Solidarity
"I think of a group of busy people working together in a team."

"I think of the union as a group of members and officers who stand together. It keeps you from being alone."

Relationship
"I think of the company as an important activity that links all of us up with people all over the world."

"I think of the union as a part of a labor movement that has been going on many years in all parts of the world, and so it gives me a part in that movement, too."

Lacking direct questions the responses to which could be counted, as was done in the discussion of the other bonds, we decided to count for each group the number of individuals who had made responses of this sort. No individual was counted more than once in connection with each aspect, though several of his responses could have been so classified. The following charts are not representative of proportions satisfied as are the tables in the other chapters, therefore. The Tables on which they are based

(XXXIII and XXIV in the Appendix) represent the proportions (in tenths) who spontaneously indicated in their description of the company or union Organizational Charter an element which would clearly contribute to the aspect of the goal of integration under discussion.

GOAL ASPECTS		Traffic			Plant			Comm.	
		Mgt	E I	E II	Mgt	E I	E II	Mgt	E
Integration	Self Respect	/////	/////	/////	/////	/////	/////	/////	/////
	Solidarity	/////	/////	/////	/////	▓▓▓▓	▓▓▓▓	▓▓▓▓	/////
	Relationship	/////	/////	/////	/////	/////	/////	/////	/////
	All Aspects	/////	/////	/////	/////	/////	/////	/////	/////

LEGEND

Satisfactory ▨▨

Questionable ▰▰

Unsatisfactory ■

CHART M

Proportions Experiencing Integration through Company
Organizational Charter

DANGER SPOTS

Several conclusions are suggested by a study of Charts M and N. First of all where are the danger spots? In what groups does the Organizational Charter give a relatively low proportion the experience of integration? We again use the classifications of Satisfactory (.8 or more), Questionable (.5 to .8), and Unsatisfactory (less than .5).

Company

The contribution to the goal of integration on the part of the company's Organizational Charter is indicated in Chart M.

A glance at the chart will reveal that, on the whole, there are no real danger spots. In every department, in every status group, with only four exceptions, the proportions are in the Satisfactory category. These four exceptions we shall discuss below. One who has read the description of the Organizational Charter as revealed in the responses of the participants will be prepared for the results of analysis disclosed here. The heavy emphasis on the good reputation, the significance, and the world-wide role of the company indicates that the company has a real asset in its Organizational Charter for welding its participants together in a functioning team.

Departmentally there is little variation, save in the case of Commercial, with respect to the solidarity aspect. Both management and employees reveal a Questionable proportion in this case. Solidarity, it will be recalled, refers to the experience of wholeness with all participants in the organization. At first glance this result will appear surprising to those familiar with the important role played by Commercial officials and employees in the operations of the company. They are the people who have a particularly heavy responsibility for bringing the customers and the company's activities together. Although local managements in all three departments are considered coequal in the over-all operation of the exchange, in the minds of the public the "telephone company manager" in their town is the Business Office Manager, a Commercial position. How then explain the fact that the concept of the company as a whole expressed by this group contained relatively few elements suggestive of solidarity with *all* participants in the company? Could it be that they, like the public, thought of themselves and their department as *the* company to a greater degree than those in other departments? Could it be that this almost unconscious sense of importance reduced their tendency to respond in terms suggestive of the solidarity of all participants? We make no judgment on this matter.

Although, as we have indicated, little departmental variation can be noted, Traffic which, in connection with other bonds, has had proportions satisfied relatively smaller than other departments, has the highest proportions experiencing integration through the Organizational Charter. This is true not only with respect to the aspect of relationship but with respect to the aspect of solidarity as well. The result might be expected in the first case, since the girl at the switchboard is a focal agent in tying the world together through communications.

Managements and employee groups show small differences, if any, in connection with any aspect.

Union

The Organizational Charter of the Union does not provide that organization with as adequate a resource. The contribution of this bond to the goal experience of integration for local officers and members is indicated in Chart N.

Of the 9 proportions reported for union officers, 4 are in the Satisfactory category, one in the Unsatisfactory category, and the remainder are classified as Questionable. Of the 15 proportions reported for union members, only 3 may be labeled Satisfactory, 9 as Questionable, and 3 as Unsatisfactory. Moreover, 5 of the Questionable proportions are dangerously near the lower limits (.5) of that category as we have defined it.

GOAL ASPECTS		Traffic			Plant			Comm.	
		O	M I	M II	O	M I	M II	O	M
Integration	Self Respect								
	Solidarity								
	Relationship								
	All Aspects								

LEGEND

Satisfactory
Questionable
Unsatisfactory

CHART N

Proportions Experiencing Integration through Union
Organizational Charter

The aspect with respect to which the union's Organizational Charter apparently makes the greatest contribution is that of Self-Respect, all union officers and Traffic and Commercial employee groups indicating Satisfactory proportions with respect to it.

The aspect which is least satisfactory is that of Relationship. This, it will be recalled, has to do with the contribution of the Organizational Charter to making members feel as partners in the world of affairs outside the union. A reading of the description of the Charter as given by members and officers indicates why this aspect is so meagerly represented. The independence of the union of any affiliations with the larger labor movement, its emphasis on bargaining functions rather than on political or social ones, are characteristics which give it little opportunity to stand for relations with the outside world in the minds of its participants. Indeed, in view of the above facts, the proportions to whom it made such a contribution may be considered large. It is not the purpose or function of this union to make any such contribution.

What is potentially more serious, however, is the low proportions in all member groups and among Plant officers who think of the union in terms of solidarity with all participants. We say "potentially" more serious because we have no indication of what proportions responding in these terms are necessary or desirable if a union is to maintain a solid front and be strong. So far as we know, no other union has submitted to this kind of a diagnosis; and we have, therefore, no standard for comparison. Of one thing we can be certain, however. It would be hard to imagine that 100 per cent response in such terms would be too high. The more participants to whom the union means "all of us working together as a team" the better.

The relatively small proportion in Plant and particularly among Plant officers indicating an association of the union in their minds with outside relationships and solidarity with all members is a puzzling result at first glance, just as was the small proportion in Commercial in connection with the company Charter. It is puzzling because our impression is that the Plant group tends to be powerful and important in the running of the union. Could an explanation similar to that suggested in the case of the company Charter be advanced here? Could it be that the very importance of the Plant group and its large activity with internal union affairs cause it to think of the union less than do those in other departments in terms of the solidarity of members in all departments and of external relations?

VARIATIONS BY SIZE OF EXCHANGE

No pattern is discernible in the case of responses with respect to either the company or the union Organizational Charter when the summary proportions are analyzed by size-of-exchange groups.

All divisional management and all district management with the exception of Plant indicated positive contributions of the company's Organizational Charter to all aspects of their experience of integration.

Since no pattern emerges, the tables recording the proportions are reproduced below without comment.

TABLE XXXV

PROPORTIONS EXPERIENCING INTEGRATION THROUGH
COMPANY ORGANIZATIONAL CHARTER

(In tenths)

Department	Status	Size of Exchange				Hdqt.	Div.	Dist.
		I	II	III	IV			
Traffic	Mgt.	9	9	8	9	8	10	10
	Emp. I	9	9	8	9	9		
	Emp. II	9	9	8	8			
Plant	Mgt.	9	9	8	9	9	10	9
	Emp. I	9	8	8	8	9		
	Emp. II	9	8	8	8			
Commercial	Mgt.	8	8	9	7	9	10	10
	Emp.	8	7	8	8	9		

TABLE XXXVI

PROPORTIONS EXPERIENCING INTEGRATION THROUGH
UNION ORGANIZATIONAL CHARTER

(In tenths)

Department	Status	Size of Exchange				Hdqt.
		I	II	III	IV	
Traffic	Officer	8	7	8	7	8
	Mem. I	5	6	6	5	6
	Mem. II	7	7	6	6	
Plant	Officer	6	6	7	6	5
	Mem. I	6	5	5	3	6
	Mem. II	5	5	3	5	
Commercial	Officer	7	8	7	6	6
	Member	6	6	4	4	5

RELEVANCE TO OTHER BONDS

The test of efficiency of the Organizational Charter is the degree to which it contributes to goal realization of the participants. This matter we have discussed in the foregoing pages. The test of effectiveness is the degree to which the Charter contributes to the effective functioning of the other bonds of organization. We shall first indicate how it might accomplish this, and then estimate whether or not it is adequate in these respects on the basis of the evidence contained in the section describing the Organizational Charter above.

How may this bond contribute to Functional Specifications? The most important part of the Organizational Charter is the definition of the purpose and function of the organization. Since the system of Functional Specifications defines the way in which individual tasks are to be performed, through participation in the functions of activity-area and specific-task teams, in order to achieve the organization's purpose and carry out its function, this element in the Organizational Charter becomes an all-important and indispensable component of the system of Functional Specifications. Since in both the company's and the union's Organizational Charter the purpose and function of the organization was revealed as understood and accepted in the responses of an overwhelming majority of participants, and since there was a high degree of agreement and consistency in the responses of participants in all departmental and status groups, we are safe in assuming that the system of Functional Specifications is well supported by a clear conception of the purpose and function of the organization as a whole in the case both of the company and the union. The definition of individual and team tasks may be improved, but that of the whole is understood and accepted. The first requisite for clear Functional Specifications is present, an objective and a sense of direction for the organization as a whole.

What are the contributions of the Organizational Charter to the functioning of the Status system? Chiefly these: it affects the tendency of participants to accept or not to accept the direction or representation of directors and representatives; it reinforces the authority delegated to or designated in the latter; it provides a guidepost for them in the administration and execution of their status functions. Let us discuss each of these effects in more detail, and then indicate how they are influenced by the Organizational Charters of this company and union.

As we found in discussing the Status system, the authority actually possessed by directors and representatives is determined as much by those to whom the directions are given or the representations are presented as by those from whom the authority is "received" in the normal meaning of that term. By the degree of their acceptance they can enhance, modify, or nullify the received authority. If the Organizational Charter presents an image to the participants of a strong, stable, high-standard organization, the tendency of participants to accept that direction and representation appropriate to the position of the director or representative is enhanced.

This does not mean that the latter by their personality, character, or skill cannot negate this tendency, nor that they can count on the Organizational Charter to make good all their deficiencies. It simply means that to their personal qualifications for gaining acceptance has been added another factor which is combined with those qualifications. Persons whose qualifications for gaining acceptance in these two organizations are excellent can, on the whole, count on reinforcement of the tendency to accept their direction and representation, and those with lesser qualifications find their deficiencies less of a handicap, because they are serving an organization whose Organizational Charter is one of which most participants are proud. When this is the case, nonacceptance of the director or representative would, in a sense, be nonacceptance of the company or union. Given the organizational Charter as a whole, as described, we judge that participants in both organizations would be reluctant to be involved in such an effect. Any indications we have given, of course, of the relative weakness of certain aspects of the Charter of either organization point to areas where it can be strengthened and the general effectiveness thereby increased.

With respect to a second effect of the Organizational Charter on increasing the acceptance of directive authority, there is no question in either organization. The degree to which both management and leadership are symbolic of the organization as a whole to participants adds considerably to their probable effectiveness in winning acceptance. Whether management or leadership is thought of as a group, or as particular people, the fact that they are among the most prominent symbols suggesting the character of the organization as a whole to participants should enhance their strength as directors and representatives. This situation can be more clearly seen if it were to be contrasted with a management which, far from symbolizing the company for which it worked, was thought to be a "tool" of absentee owners, or "putty in the hands" of outside influences; or a union leadership considered to be the "mouthpiece" of a national union officer, or a "henchman" for a particular party.

We make no judgment on the desirability of this situation from any point of view other than the strengthening of the acceptance of the direction and representation by management and leadership. We are reporters, not critics, of what we find. But the degree to which management's acceptance is enhanced by the idea that it and not the officers of the A.T.&T. are symbolic of the Southern New England Telephone Company, and the degree to which the acceptance of the union leaders is enhanced by the idea that *they* and not the officers of an international union are symbolic of the Connecticut Union of Telephone Workers, cannot escape any one who reads the 1500 interviews we have recorded.

We have said that the Organizational Charter may reinforce or reduce the authority delegated to directors or designated in representatives. This it may do for several reasons. If the purpose and function and major policies of the organization are clearly set forth, understood by, and acceptable to the participants, those who receive the authority in specific terms can understand its relationship to implementing those aspects of the Organizational Charter. Under such circumstances this result would, of course, be accomplished only if the terms of the authority as received were consistent with the Charter. If the significance of the organization is great, that fact amplifies the directive and representative authority which is received by directors and representatives at every level of the organization.

These points may be summarized by saying that men feel they speak with greater authority when that authority is received from a significant than from an insignificant organization, and when it is consistent with well-understood and accepted purpose, function, and policy of the organization as a whole.

In both the company and union, from this point of view, authority is enhanced by the clarity and acceptability of the purpose and function of the organization and, as far as we can learn, by the consistency between these aspects and the kind and amount of authority received. In the company, authority is also enhanced by the clarity and acceptance of major policies. In the union, in which participants do not call to mind such clear-cut policies or such outstanding significance of their organization, the authority received lacks this reinforcement.

In both company and union the delegated authority, from the point of view of those who receive it, might be strengthened by closer affiliation with a larger organization: the A.T.&T. in one case, some branch of the labor movement in the other. However, as we have seen, this might work to weaken that authority rooted in acceptance by the participants.

Finally we have said that the Status system can be influenced by the Organizational Charter by the kind of guidance it gives to directors and representatives in the administration and execution of their status functions. Primarily this comes from the statement of purpose, function, and policies of the organization as a whole. As we have indicated above, the guidance received from all three is clear and consistent in the company, and from the first two in the union.

Another point is that both management and leaders give a high place to employees and members as symbols to them of the organization. This fact augurs well for the kind of administration which is employee and member centered, and hence more likely than otherwise to involve sensitivity to their needs, a point of strength.

How may the Organizational Charter contribute to the Communication system? Primarily the contribution is made because the symbols, slogans, folklore, and ritual provide them with commonly accepted language tools which facilitate communication. Moreover, people who share them acquire a group feeling, a consciousness that "these folks in the telephone company, or the union, who use this language and understand these things are our kind." Acceptance and attention to communications from "our kind" is probably greater than from others.

The rich storehouse of such language and group-making tools in the company enhances the effectiveness of its Communication system. Their lack in the union weakens its Communication system. The policy of promotion from within and the stability of personnel in Plant and certain headquarters departments facilitates the acquisition and retention of these tools. The turnover in Traffic, Accounting, and in certain sections of Commercial retards the acquisition of these tools. The rotation in office of union officials and the turnover in membership mirrored from employee turnover furnish difficult problems in the acquisition and use of a common symbolic language for the union.

How can the Organizational Charter contribute to the effectiveness of the Reward and Penalty system? The reputation and significance of the organization are important factors in determining how rewarding it is to be associated with it. Particularly in the case of the company, and to a lesser but still marked degree in the case of the union, the reputation is such that participants are proud to belong, and feel that their respect from other participants and those outside the organization is enhanced by belonging.

As was suggested by some of the employees, there were disadvantages to being an employee of the company (in our terms, some things were penalizing), but "on balance" they wouldn't change. A heavy weight in the balances opposite the disadvantages was the reward of being a part of an organization with the reputation and significance attached to this company. The union could not count so heavily upon these aspects of its Organizational Charter to counteract any penalizing experiences, any disadvantages, associated with membership in the union.

SUMMARY

The elements which contribute to the concept of any organization as a whole, as an entity, we have called its Organizational Charter. We might say it is what the organization's name stands for, the things which give it "character" and "individuality," which make the name mean something to those who use it.

The Organizational Charter may be described by reference to its *elements*, the *determinants of scope of* and *limitations* on its contents, and the *cues* used to suggest and the *means* used to reinforce it.

We have classified the *elements* as function or purpose, significance, identification or affiliation, major policies, and reputation.

The determinants of scope and limitations of the Charter are, first, the comprehension and acceptance by participants; and, second, the rights granted and obligations imposed, the expectancies held and judgment made by outsiders.

The most prominent of the means used to reinforce the Charter are symbols (material and human), slogans, documents, traditions, folklore, formal statements, and ritual. These also serve as cues to suggest it.

Each of these aspects was described as revealed in the comments of the participants in this company and union. That description should serve both to make clearer the nature of the Organizational Charter and to underscore its services both to goal realization of participants and to the effective functioning of these people as a team.

The relative contribution of the Charter of the two organizations to the experience of integration on the part of the individuals involved was indicated. This contribution was much greater in the case of the company than in the case of the union. The contribution of each of the Organizational Charters to the efficient functioning of the other bonds of organization—to Functional Specifications, to the Status, Communication, and Reward and Penalty systems—was found to be, on the whole, favorable.

The potential values of the Charter in increasing both the efficiency and effectiveness of the organization should indicate to managers and leaders in all organizations the importance of giving close attention to the comprehension and acceptance by all participants of the Organizational Charter of their own organizations. Some concept of the organization, as a whole, is bound to develop. That conception of what the organization as a whole is and stands for which is rooted in first-hand experience is difficult to alter by "education." But misinformation can be corrected, elements not understood and appreciated can be supplied, cues which suggest and support what is true about the organization as a whole, can be developed. The relation of the Charter to participant satisfaction and effective teamwork and organizational strength would appear to make attempts to clarify and strengthen it worth the effort.

VII

WHAT OF IT?

WILLIAM G. SUMNER put three questions to students who submitted the result of their investigations to him: "Is it true? How do you know it is true? What of it?" The first two questions are universally accepted as tests of value for the work of those who attempt to record and analyze the facts of human relations in industry. The third is also accepted, but frequently goes unanswered, lest the social scientist appear to be "blowing his own horn." Nevertheless, those who read and use the results of research are interested in and desire to be informed about the scientist's conception of the significance of his work. This concluding chapter, therefore, is focused on the readers' interest in the answer to the question, What of it?

This book is an interim report in at least two respects. It is a first report on a specific research project, and it contributes to the definition of certain terms essential to the development of a usable theory of human behavior. That development is a major long-range objective of the Yale Labor and Management Center. We share this objective with our colleagues, not only in other industrial-relations centers, but in social and psychological research centers interested in other areas of human activity. The relation of this book to the other reports on the investigation of the telephone company and union has already been indicated in Chapter I. Its relationship to the long-range objective of the Center is the subject of this final chapter.

PATH FOR PROGRESS

In order to see its place in the progress toward that objective, it will be desirable to indicate the path we have laid out. The successive steps planned are listed and briefly described below:

1. Determination of the nature of the problem.
2. Development of a framework for classifying the determinants of human behavior.

3. Definition in realistic terms of the character of these determinants by reference to observed facts in the places and circumstances in which men are working and living.

4. Formulation of hypotheses concerning the casual relations between observed behavior and these determinants as described.

5. Progressive testing and reformulation of these hypotheses in a series of investigations carried on in the "laboratories" of industrial, business, and union operations.

6. Rephrasing of these hypotheses with reference to behavior in other areas of human relations, such as the family, schools, government bureaus, political parties, the church, scientific and recreational associations, the community, the state, and international organizations. The ultimate purpose of such an extension of hypotheses is a contribution to a basic theory of why men behave as they do which might provide a unifying and integrating frame of reference for the building of a social science not subject to the present limitations of departmentalism.

These are the guideposts we have set up to mark the path and our steps toward the realization of this objective. Each study of human relations in industry at the Center is undertaken only if it contributes to progress along that path, only if it is a step toward our ultimate goal. This does not mean that the subjects of investigation are not of immediate and practical interest to men of action faced with the need for decision on today's problems and issues. A glance at the research projects completed and under way, recorded in *Publications*,[1] will show any such conclusion to be unwarranted. It means merely that the results of applying the tests of immediacy of interest and practicality are not permitted to set aside the results of applying the basic test of scientific value.

Progress along this path can be made in a number of ways. There is, for instance, an extensive and stimulating literature of science and practical affairs offering wisdom and valuable suggestions for the scientist at every step outlined. The steps preliminary to actual field work might be taken by using the definition of the problem, the classification framework, and the hypotheses developed by one or more of the producers of this literature. Or one might attempt a synthesis of the ideas of a number of them and use that as a guide. Much fruitful current work is being done in this way. It has many advantages, particularly in the conservation of the efforts of contemporary scientists for the important tasks of fact gath-

[1] *Publications.* (New Haven, Yale Labor and Management Center, 1948).

ering and analysis, and in the maintenance of continuity of present with past thought. If the path as laid out by either of these methods is satisfying to any scientist, he should follow that path. On the frontiers of research there is little place for dogmatic assertions respecting exploratory methods.

We have found this literature of value chiefly as a rich source for suggesting a wide range of alternative clues to the interpretation of our data. We acknowledge our obligation to the intellectual labors of our colleagues.[2] Anyone familiar with the work of those named in the footnote below, and with our publications, will recognize the general and specific contributions of the former to the staff of the Center in our attempts to make systematic sense out of our observations and findings bearing on the structure and dynamics of human relations. Their contribution, however, was not to provide us with *a* definition of our problem, *a* framework for investigation, *a* set of hypotheses, or *a* method for testing them. Those who are enthusiastic about the work of particular social or psychological scientists will feel that we might have made more progress had we proceeded in that fashion. Whatever the ultimate judgment of the wisdom of our course, we have not done that. We have staked out our field of facts to investigate, and have then been guided by what definition of the problem, framework, and hypotheses and methods appeared to fit the facts we observed.

This approach has its weaknesses and its dangers, as we are well aware. But it has the advantage of enabling us to follow where the problem leads us. And it places upon us the burden of maintaining in our conclusions a consistency, not with the generalizations or methods of a particular man or school, but with the data of our own field studies and those of others

---

[2] Specific acknowledgment for contributions made over many years is difficult. Yet we feel impelled to indicate the chief writers whose works have given us insight and guidance. With apologies to any of them who feel they are improperly classified, we indicate their names. *Anthropologists and Sociologists:* Arensberg, Benedict, Chapple, Davie, Durkeim, Ellsworth, Ford, Gardner, Ginsberg, Keller, Lazarsfeld, Linton, Lynd, McConnell, Manheim, Malinowski, Mayo, Mead, Mills, Moore, Murdock, Pareto, Roethlisberger, Selekman, Sumner, Warner, Weber, Whitehead, Whiting, Whyte, Zimmerman. *Psychologists:* Allport, Dollard, Doob, Gardiner, Heron, Horland, Hull, Katz, Kornhauser, Lewin, Likert, McGregor, McMurray, May, Miller, Pigors, Shartle, Sheffield, Smith, Tead. *Economists:* Berle, Dunlop, Gordon, Hamilton, Hilton, Hoxie, Kerr, Llewellyn-Smith, Means, Myers, Palmer, Ross, Simon, Slichter, Veblen, Webb. *Industry and Unions:* Barnard, Bergen, Dickson, Follett, Given, Golden, Gomberg, Nyman, Planty, Ruttenberg, Scanlon, Spates, Starr, Watt, Williams. Members of our own staff are not listed here, though our mutual obligation to each other is great.

who have sought facts in first-hand contact with the human-relations situations which produced them.

First Steps

The present study, initiated in 1947, was undertaken after considerable thought had been given to Steps 1 and 2. The contributions of our colleagues had been considered as aids in providing a definition of the problem and in constructing a framework of determinants of human behavior which would be consistent with the data obtained from our field studies to that date. We started on this investigation, therefore, with the results of that thought as a basis.

The nature of the general problem for research (see Step 1) for those who would contribute to a unified social science we phrased simply as answering the question, Why do men behave as they do in particular situations? We have retained this objective, though the search for *why* has led us to a conception of causality which in fact narrows the question considerably. Actually our approach to the problem has led us in a search for stimulants to, and compulsions on, behavior under particular situations. It would not be inaccurate to say that the basic question we have practically in mind is not, Why *do* men behave as they do in particular situations? but rather, Why *must* men behave as they do, that is, by what factors are they impelled or compelled to behave in certain ways?

The attempts to answer this question and investigations related to this problem with which we were familiar, including those we had conducted since 1931, suggested the desirability of constructing a framework within which one could classify the main factors determining human behavior (Step 2). It was important to do this if for no other purpose than to guard against incomplete generalizations which ignored the impact of elements in human experience which had not been surveyed in a particular investigation. Heavily influenced by the insights contributed by social anthropology and by contact with the learning-theory approach to social psychology, we developed such a framework in 1944, which was labeled the *Structure of Living*.[3] It provided a satisfactory and promising classification system for the field-work data which had been gathered to that time. Hardly had this framework been outlined and used as a basis for further investiga-

---

[3] Reported in *Adaptive Human Behavior*. (New Haven, Yale Labor and Management Center, 1947).

tions, however, than the facts observed began to demand its correction and elaboration. Such modification was made and reported in revised editions of *Adaptive Human Behavior* in 1946 and 1948. Such changes did not alter the basic concept of a structure of living which suggested to, or imposed on, individuals socially sanctioned and reinforced forms of behavior determined on the one hand by the fact that such behavior must use and be consistent with the human, social, and natural resources available to a particular group or individual; and on the other hand by the fact that the behavior was designed to enable the group or individual to realize certain goals or standards of successful living. Further modification in detail of this structure-of-living framework is to be expected, and will be made as the observations recorded in further research require. This is Step 2 in our long-range plan.

PLACE OF THIS REPORT

The present study, therefore, assumes the progress made in taking Steps 1 and 2.

Step 3 follows the designing of an investigation, a major purpose of which is to fill the terms or categories involved in this framework (Step 2) with realistic content. The present investigation of this company and union was so designed. Revealed in our data, gathered through participation, observation, and interview, are experiences and reactions which define concretely the content of such general terms as goals, resources, reinforcements, and such more specific terms as Functional Specifications, Status system, Communication system, Reward and Penalty system, and Organizational Charter—all of which are categories involved in the structure-of-living framework.

Such definitions are not ends in themselves; they are a necessary prelude to fruitful systematic research. As elements in the structure of living which influence the behavior of men, their causal relation to that behavior can be the subject only of guesses until their nature is sufficiently determined to permit detailed description of their characteristics in particular situations.

It is a commonly accepted scientific and common-sense generalization, for instance, that a person's behavior is influenced by the behavior norms and patterns, the social system, of his own society. What is the nature of that society and social system? What of their features are significantly related to the shaping of behavior? We have found in analyzing the social environment furnished by these two organizations, as reported by participants, that the concept of *social resources* conditioning behavior which, in turn, was sanctioned and supported by *social reinforcements* was useful.

But these terms are too general for application to specific problems. What are the significant elements comprised in social resources? We found that, in general, our original classification of social resources as *materials, people,* and *ideas,* plus the organizational devices, or *bonds of organization,*[4] which bound them together, provided descriptive categories into which our data would fit without strain.

This in itself is a useful finding. It provides an estimate of the boundaries that encompass the territory of cultural elements which are relevant to the explanation of behavior. Perhaps it is better to say, at this point, that it provides a framework for the classification of those cultural elements *people were aware of* as influencing their behavior, since our data is supplied chiefly by their comments.

It may be asserted that the finding is not convincing, since we found simply what we were looking for in the first place. It is true that our interviewers asked a series of questions which were formulated in order to test the validity of the categories with which we started. Had these questions failed to stimulate a flow of information indicating the reality of a particular category as a pigeonhole for the data of experience, however, we were prepared to discard it; and we would have so reported.

Moreover, the interviews contained open-ended questions giving the respondent an opportunity to elaborate on the realities of his life in the organizations, and we were prepared to expand or modify our categories in the light of these responses. As it turned out, however, the general system of categories proved useful and comprehensive so far as our data are concerned. As has been indicated in the body of the report, however, the nature of the responses made necessary considerable revision in the conceptions of the detailed character and features of the several organizational devices, or bonds.

Even these categories, however, are too general to make possible definitive analysis of the causal relationship between observed behavior and the cultural elements found to exist. It is at this point that our findings have

---

[4] These bonds are: systems of Technology, Services, Functional Specifications, Status, Communications, Reward and Penalty, Organizational Charter, Thoughtways, and Education.

contributed most to providing us with tools for continuing research; tools we felt were missing or inadequate in our own work and in that of our colleagues. We suspect that many of our readers have sensed the futility of even the most suggestive of commentaries on the relationship of, say, the Communication system or Technology or the Status system or the Educational system to human behavior, because these systems were either described without any meaningful specification of their elements, or because they were illustrated by reference to isolated aspects unrelated to a systematic concept of the whole.

Certainly practical administrators are puzzled by such commentaries, and understandably so. For, if defined broadly, these categories are difficult to reduce to the elements in the social environment subject to their control, or affected by their necessarily specific decisions and acts; and, if illustrated by details unrelated to a concept of the whole system, they are not amenable to treatment in terms of any but the most elementary of "principles." But the practical men are not alone in their difficulty.

Frequently social scientists are chided by their more "scientific" colleagues for their failure to quantify their description of the environment so that useful mathematical tools may be devised for its analysis and control. Consider the relative ease with which the psychologist can describe quantitatively the size, shape, and arrangement of the maze into which he puts his rats; or the size, shape, height from floor, and resistance applied to the lever which controls the flow of food pellets at a measurable rate from an opening at a definable distance from the lever; in other words, the environment which conditions the rat's behavior.

We make no prediction as to whether social scientists will ever be able to achieve this objective of "scientific" methodology (and offer no comment as to its desirability), but we make this observation. It is meaningless to quantify general categories such as social resources, and even less general categories such as Communication system, unless their structure and detail is specifically and integrally known. It is useless to quantify specific and detailed aspects of such systems unless the relation of the detail to the whole is defined. On the whole we are impelled by the same drive to derive our conclusions through scientifically valid methods as the most ambitious and devoted of our colleagues. But as an essential step in progress toward that objective, we feel the necessity of moving by the slow process of accumulating evidence toward the realistic definition, in terms of human behavior and experience, of the quantities we desire to measure.

Such definition relative to the experience of people in contemporary "civilized" society is less well developed than that relative to those in "primitive" societies. Any student of modern American behavior owes a heavy debt to the generalizing thought of the ethnologists and anthropologists who have made such primitive societies the object of extensive and intensive investigation. But he can take their definitions of categories only as suggestive starting points for his own efforts.

Having assured ourselves by observing the consistency of our interview and observational data with the general types of bonds of organization postulated as a framework for the classification of that data, we had still the task of indicating a definition of the aspects of each bond which are relevant to its impact on the behavior of individuals who work with the social resources of which the bond is a part.

These aspects of several of the bonds are recapitulated below. They are described in greater detail in the foregoing text. They will be amplified by specific evidence in our final report on this investigation.

BONDS OF ORGANIZATION DEFINED

We turn then to a summary statement of the aspects of certain bonds of organization which may be considered important for the description of that bond as experienced by the participants in an organization or society; important because the detailed facts concerning the aspects, as experienced, will have an observable—and we hope after sufficient study, a predictable —effect on those subject to this experience.

Functional Specifications was defined as the system of job descriptions and of arrangements for association in work-flow operations which tie the function of the organization, as a whole, to the functions of individuals in the organization, through the functions of teams. In order to describe this bond as experienced in this company and union, it was necessary to describe: (a) the job description of individuals; (b) that of the organization as a whole; and (c) that of the several activity-area and specific-task teams by which the tasks of individuals and that of the organization, as a whole, are co-ordinated.

These teams are of work-flow and staff-line variety. The first may be described by means of a work-flow chart indicating the successive steps taken in the performance of the task assigned to or undertaken by that team in the production of goods or services coming out at the end of the work-flow stream. The second may be described by indicating the points at which, and the ways in which, staff functions contribute to the basic work-flow.

The *Status* system was defined as the system which placed participants in a vertical hierarchy of authority and deference with respect to direction and representation, and the arrangements by which the relationships involved were facilitated. In order to describe this bond as experienced in this company and union, it was necessary to describe both with respect to direction and representation:

a. The organization of positions
b. The scope of authority for each position
c. The source of authority (in delegation or designation *and* acceptance) for each position
d. Administrative methods employed for implementing and using authority
e. Techniques for assignment to and maintenance in positions of authority
f. Personal attributes of those in authority

The *Communication* system was defined as a helper system to the other bonds of organization providing the means by which essential information was transmitted from one participant to another in the organization. In order to describe the system as experienced in this company and union, it was found necessary to describe the following aspects:

a. Subjects (with particular attention to items necessary for the effective functioning of the other bonds)
b. Objective
c. Route
   1. Between origin and initiator
   2. Between initiator and recipient
d. Techniques
   1. Media
   2. Language and composition
   3. Manner of giving and receiving
e. Timing (including frequency and speed)
f. Authentication and control

The *Reward and Penalty* system was defined as that system by which desirable behavior is encouraged and undesirable behavior is discouraged.

In order to describe the system as experienced in this company and union, it was found necessary to describe the following aspects:

a. Objectives
b. Kinds of behavior (and inferred human qualities) rewarded and penalized
c. Agents of reward and penalty
d. Bases of agents' power to reward and penalize
e. Techniques of reward and penalty
    1. Instruments and methods
    2. Manner
    3. Timing

The nature of each of these aspects was described in some detail which need not be repeated here. That elaboration, however, represents a further necessary analysis for one concerned to understand the impact of this most important bond on human behavior.

The *Organizational Charter* we defined as the system of ideas and means which contribute to the concept of the organization or society as a whole, as an entity. One might say it is comprised of those ideas and means which give character and individuality to the organization when its name is employed.

In order to describe the reality of the Organizational Charter as experienced by the participants in this company and union, we found it necessary to describe the following aspects:

a. Elements
    1. Function or purpose of the organization
    2. Significance of the organization
    3. Identification or affiliation of the organization
    4. Major policies of the organization
    5. Reputation of the organization
b. Determinants of scope and limitations of the Organizational Charter
c. Cues which suggest and means which support the Organizational Charter

The question naturally occurs to the reader, How do you know these aspects of the several bonds are *the* aspects which are significant as determinants of human behavior? Basically the answer to that question lies in the fact that each question asked of our respondents was designed to elicit not merely his description of some aspect of his experience in the organization but his *reaction* in attitude and behavior toward it. Whether, therefore, his reaction was one of acceptance and conformity, or of resentment and rebellion, his answer pointed to a relationship between experienced fact and its effect on behavior. As listed above, the order indicates nothing about the relative importance of these aspects as determinants of behavior. In our final report based on complete analysis of the evidence, that order will be suggested.

We have characterized these aspects of the several bonds as necessary for the description of the bond *as experienced in this company and union.* We make no assertion that they are necessary for the description of the bond in *any* organization or society, though such an inference would seem plausible. We shall assume that this is true, however, in designing our study of the next organization which becomes our "laboratory." Others may find that such a possibility offers a suggestion for a framework for their own investigations of organizational facts whose relation to human behavior they are attempting to discern.

An even more practical possibility has been suggested by some executives in companies and unions who have seen preliminary reports concerning this framework. "Does not this list of bonds," they say, "provide a usable outline for exploring, in training courses, the realities of organizational life in this company and union? If these bonds are among the most important of the devices which weld a crowd of individuals into a working team, is not the first task of those responsible for developing teamwork to understand what they are as experienced by people in this company or union? Then cannot we, in training, move on from that point and ask how bonds with different features are more or less satisfactory to people and thus contribute more or less to stimulate them to active and co-operative effort advantageous to the organization? Eventually would we not begin to get a grasp on principles of teamwork that we could use because they indicated a relationship between how people behaved and the character of the bonds of organization which was to some extent amenable to modification by decision and action of leadership?"

We would welcome experimentation along such lines; for, if successful, it would go a long way toward laying the foundation for partnership between the men of action and the men of science which we believe is essential to the best performance of both.

When the whole roster of potential determinants of human behavior included in the structure-of-living framework is considered, it will be seen that this report covers only a portion, though, we believe, an important portion of them. The list considered in our final report will be longer, but still incomplete. The process of verification of concepts by reference to evidence is a slow one. But on our plans for continuing research in other companies and unions in a manner similar to that employed in this study rest our expectations of progressively more complete, accurate, and useful description. When we undertake our next investigation, the results of this one, recorded above, will give us a better idea of what to look for, a better understanding of what questions it is significant to ask, and a greater skill in shaping the questions so that they are more acurately focused on the experienced facts of organizational life. This, then, is the contribution of this report to Step 3 in the plan described at the beginning of this chapter.

NEXT STEPS

The contribution to Step 4 (formulation of hypotheses concerning the causal relations between behavior and determinants) will be indicated chiefly in our final report, since it requires a deeper and more comprehensive analysis of our data than that presented here.

Steps 5 and 6 obviously refer to future action. As soon as we have modified and corrected our framework, our terms, and hypotheses by subjecting them to the evidence gathered in this study and have corrected any shortcomings in our techniques of and equipment for research revealed by our experience, we shall turn to the next study of a different sort of organization, profit by its findings, move to the next "laboratory," and so on, in what we trust will be a continuing series of field studies carrying us in each case closer to our ultimate objective.

RELATIONSHIP TO WORK OF OTHERS

The foregoing has been an attempt to indicate the place of this particular report and the study on which it is based in a plan for realization of a scientific objective. It helps in part to answer the question, *What of it?* posed at the beginning of the chapter. Contact with the realities of organizational life in this company and union suggests in addition certain comments on generalizations made by our colleagues and practical men who also are trying to understand the structure and dynamics of human relations.

FORMAL AND INFORMAL SYSTEMS

The first of these generalizations is that the *formal* social system of any society offers an inadequate outline of the experienced reality of that system until it is supplemented by a description of the *informal* system. Our observations underscore that generalization in no uncertain terms; it has significance, not merely for guiding exploration and description of facts, but for suggesting the effects of those facts on behavior.

The meanings of formal and informal have become clearer to us in the light of our observations. The method frequently employed to illustrate the difference between the two is to present an organizational chart indicating the pattern of status relationships assumed to exist in an organization, and then to point out that in any organization there are informal groups which may help or hinder management in the performance of its functions or in the exercise of its authority as indicated by the chart. There is thus assumed to be an expected, or formal, pattern of relationships *and* an actual, or informal, pattern of relationships which take place "within" the first.

The illustration, of course, is just that, and does not represent fully the conception of the two systems as used by careful investigators or those who generalize from their findings. The conception as used by some, however, appears to draw its content almost entirely from the illustration. This occurs frequently enough to warrant emphasizing a point made clear by our evidence. The result of such use is both confusing and unrepresentative of the richness of the concepts for descriptive purposes. And if the descriptive value is not fully exploited, the analytical service of the concept cannot be fully realized. Perhaps this is one reason that, though practically every student of industrial organization and many managers pay their respects to the validity of the concept, so few have used it profitably in the analysis of any save a limited number of specific problems.

We have tried to point out, in each of the preceding chapters, that the substance of each bond is the behavior and relationships (whether formal or informal) of people. The first point to make here is that a formal and an informal aspect can be discerned with respect to every one of the bonds of organization described. These adjectives apply not only to the Status system but to the systems of Functional Specifications, Communication, Reward and Penalty, and to the Organizational Charter. In each of these cases there is a social system, together with factors which are essential to its operation, which is a part of an announced *plan* of organization. This announced plan is embodied in charts, memoranda, and in verbal and written explanations authenticated by seals, signatures, and other devices placing the stamp of official sanction upon them. We have found it useful to refer to this planned and announced system as the formal system of organization. Our usage here is, we believe, consistent with that of others of our colleagues who use the term, although it may cover a wider range of human relations than that to which some have applied it. The formal system represents the best efforts of those responsible for the activities of the organization as a whole—that is, normally, management or leadership—to reduce the complexity of human relationships in their organizations to a systematic description which *they* expect and assume will coincide with the normal pattern of relationships as men perform their work-flow tasks, exercise their directive and representative functions, communicate with one another, reward and penalize each other, and share a conception of the organization as a whole. This formal system is relatively static, not in the sense that it is unchanging, but that it changes only at intervals and is static in the interim between changes.

But when a description of the actual behavior and relations of people in an organization is undertaken and systematically portrayed, the patterns seldom coincide with those planned and announced by top management—that is, with the formal system. The peculiar individuals who make up the personnel of any organization or society (including management and leadership) have not only formally prescribed jobs to do under changing and unpredictable circumstances but varying capacities for doing them and varying goals they are attempting to satisfy in the process. That being the case, they introduce, through their day-by-day behavior, a multitude of variations into the planned and announced pattern formally descriptive, not only of their functional specifications and status, but of *all* of the bonds. The *variant patterns* of actual relationship and behavior we have found it useful to describe as the informal system.

Again, so stated, the concept is, we believe, consistent with that used by our colleagues. But it involves this amplification on the concept as used by some. It is not limited to informal groups among employees, serving individual and personal interests and desires of those employees. It involves a subtle and realistic modification of the planned and announced formal system in *all* of its aspects, and by every participant in the organization, including, incidentally, those who initiate and announce the plan. The latter may themselves introduce variations without going through the formality of announcing them.

This being the case, the description of the informal system is not complete with the description of informal groups having informal leaders and providing members with informal satisfactions distinguishable from the groupings, leadership, and satisfaction planned for in the formal system. Its description involves far more than this. It involves reporting the whole complex of informal and sometimes unlabeled adjustments made by actual behavior and thought in the structure of living within which people work and live.

These modifications in the Status system, for instance, provide not merely an informal organization of positions carrying informal directive and representative authority and functions; they establish an informal definition of the scope and source of authority, administrative methods, and techniques for assignment to, and maintenance in, positions of authority.

The modifications provide not only informal routes, and therefore informal human contacts, in the Communication system; they help to determine the subjects, the objectives, the media, the language, the timing, the authentication, and the control of communications.

The modifications not only set up informal work-flow teams within the system of Functional Specifications and define their tasks; they actually modify the formal job descriptions for the individual, for the organization as a whole, and for teams.

The modifications not only introduce instruments and methods of Reward and Penalty, unplanned by management, and hence designate "unauthorized" agents; they determine, informally, the objectives of that process, the definitions of the kinds of behavior and human qualities subject to it, the relative power of agents to reward and penalize, and the manner and timing of the exercise of their power.

The contribution of the modifications to the conception actually held of the organization as a whole, the Organizational Charter, is obvious.

Several conclusions are suggested by considering these findings. The informal aspect of life in an organization is not merely informal behavior and relations. This behavior and these relationships have contributed to the *structure* of the social system itself. Viewing all the participants in the group as contributors to their "society," the informal system they have created, is recognized and accepted, although possibly not by management or leadership, and it establishes expectancies as to behavior for all these participants. Along with the formal system, it places compulsions on the behavior of all alike—for instance, on the behavior of a formal "boss" like a foreman or the president of a company or union, and on that of an informal group leader.

This may seem like footnoting the obvious, but it is a footnote which students of human relations in industry might well make a part of the text. And it leads to a second conclusion, that, as factors influencing human behavior, the formal and informal systems *are not separable*. The fact that they can be distinguished for descriptive purposes does not warrant their distinction as separate determinants of behavior, save in cases in which they are in conflict. Our study of this company and union suggests that such conflict, which has interested a number of investigators, is likely to be less of a possibility than effective integration of the two systems, for the simple reason that when potential conflicts between them do appear, those who sense the discrepancy set to work informally to reconcile any differences. Without denying the danger of inconsistency and conflict between the formal and informal systems, we would suggest that the social system to which participants in an organization react, and which is an effective determinant of their behavior, is a synthesis of both formal and informal elements. People do not live in the midst of now one, now the other sets of elements. They experience the system as a whole, a whole which is continually, though slowly, being modified by the daily adjustments of participants.

This suggests a third conclusion. Management or leadership makes planned and announced, i.e., *formal,* as well as *informal*, contributions modifying this system. Such modifications are extraordinarily influential because they are initiated by the "boss." But employees and members also make contributions. In their volume and because they are responses to real needs of individuals, and because they are adjustments facilitating or handicapping the organization's work, these informal changes rate a significance equal to the others. Together *all* participants contribute to the structure of the social system which is actually experienced and in which *all* must live and work. The suggestion made by several investigators, and supported by many practical men, relative to the reason for resistance to changes introduced by management into the actual going system is certainly plausible. The suggestion is that this resistance is rooted in the awareness that what is being modified is, to a large extent, the work of their own hands and minds; that any change must be integrated, if they are to "live with it," into a social system built up in a significant way by their own adjustments in response to their own felt needs. The response to a threat to one's "craftsmanship" in the creation of a social system is quite understandably resisted in the same way as that to one's craftsmanship in the production of a material object or an idea. Such a reaction strengthens resistance based on other grounds, such as the effect of a change on security and comfort from, understanding and control of, or the integration and progress possible within the old ways and arrangements.

These conclusions point to a heavy and difficult task for management and leadership charged with responsibility for the rational development of organizational structure better to attain the aims of the organization. If their modifications find their effective real level only after reconstruction at the hands of every participant concerned, it would appear that they can *initiate* but not *make* changes. Once initiated, the change takes its course through the behavior of all affected, is modified by that behavior, and, as actually experienced, has become the creation of all of them.

It is scarcely conceivable that management and leadership do not recognize that such is the case. Indeed the experienced manager or leader may become skilled in anticipating the modifications to which others will subject his initiation, and develop his plans so that such modification will not require excessive change at the hands of his "partners." Moreover, he may take cognizance of an informal development which has grown up and announce it as a new recognized and sanctioned order of affairs, thus giving it formal status.

It can be further observed that among the management and leadership of these two organizations were those who recognized that the informal system was not merely a structural reality but a dynamic element in adjustment of the formal system to the reality of individual and organizational needs. Some, from particular experiences, labeled the informal patterns as nuisances interfering with the operation of the plans they had made. But this response was not general. In the judgment of many, the informal patterns did not spring from nowhere or from the devilish nature of un-co-operative individuals. If a pattern developed, they were willing to assume that it was generated by a felt need of partners interested in the effective performance of the organization. As such it could therefore be considered as a genuine suggestion which might well be embodied in the formal system of the organization.

Our contacts with other managements and union leaders reveal many who are aware of the utility of the informal products of such a partnership in suggesting lines for progressive developments in their formal systems of organization. It is not always true, however, in the organizations we are studying at the moment, or in others, that management and union leaders give full weight to the implications of the fact of such a partnership in considering the relations with and attitudes toward their employees or members appropriate to that partnership.

The factors of human nature and social structure which will determine the ultimate reconstruction of any modification that management or leaders initiate are not subject to careful and precise calculation. Nevertheless they are present as real factors remolding formal plans into informal reality, and will have this effect whether or not they are recognized and taken into account. To the degree that such factors are not understood, every managerial or leadership action introducing change into a social system— that is, into the organizational structure of his company or union—is a shot in the dark. If the light available for the relief of that darkness is at the moment inadequate, the fact furnishes only a problem in, and not a barrier to, increasingly effective management and leadership. Managers and leaders who have initiative and courage will no more abdicate in the face of a relatively unknown situation than will the medical profession quit in the face of polio, cancer, or the common cold. The indicated action on the borders of the unknown is systematic fact-finding and analysis. The darkness will not be dispelled by any proclamation, Let there be light. Nor, if light can be made available, is it good strategy to spend all one's time learning to "fly blind," however necessary that expedient may be at the moment.

INDIVIDUAL AND GROUP

Much time has been spent by psychologists and social scientists in debating whether the concepts of the *group, society,* and *social system* stand for anything real, something which acts *as such* to stimulate or condition the behavior of individuals. The reader will sense that we have used these concepts in a way that suggests an affirmative answer to that question. We have also spoken of subsystems within *a* social system, such as Functional Specifications, Status, Communication, Reward and Penalty systems, and Organizational Charter, as though they stood for things whose nature and structure could be studied and described and whose active influence, as real factors, on individual behavior, could be charted.

Much of this debate seems to have been needless, since it frequently was a battle of words to which the debaters gave different and frequently inconsistent meanings. But it has not been useless, for it has made sincere searchers for truth examine critically the real facts of life which they were attempting to represent by their words. It has given rise to an emphasis on the exploration of these facts by teams of psychologists and social scientists, or by individuals, within the area labeled *culture and personality*. The result of their labors and thought makes earlier debates on the subject appear a bit naïve.

Nor are the issues raised merely of academic interest. Those responsible for organizing and leading the activities of people in groups have generally assumed, as a basis for their actions, that a company, a union, a Communication system, a Status system, etc., were real entities upon which they could work and which they could manipulate. Many managers and leaders who sensed unfavorable human results of managerial and leadership action rooted in this assumption have sought to introduce a more "human" point of view. They have labeled the first assumption *impersonal*. They have spoken and written about "the human factors in management." They have warned managers and leaders not to forget that a company is composed of people, and that every one of these people is a different person. Such emphasis and warnings contributed greatly to underscoring the necessity for systematic study of human relations in industry, and to the development of a point of view making such systematic study possible. They stimulated the development of many "people-centered" techniques which have humanized life within organizations which had become, or were in danger of becoming, impersonal instruments with which people were simply manipulated.

This difference in point of view as to the basic character of a company or a union, and hence as to the most appropriate and effective focus of managerial and leadership effort, is the counterpart in the practical worka-day world of that confusion formerly existing in the ivory towers.

In observing the behavior and relations of people in an organization, one becomes aware of the danger in taking either the organizational (or structural) point of view or the individual-participant point of view as a complete guide either to analysis or to action. It sometimes would appear that practical industrial management and union leadership are subject to the same futile dichotomy between concepts of the organization and the individual which plagued the social scientists and psychologists. These managers and leaders are classified by others, and indeed by themselves, as interested primarily in the *organization* and its operations and success; or as concerned primarily with the *people* who work for the company, or are the members of the union, and their life and success.

We shall want to return to this matter in our final report, but even at this stage our research experience and conclusions may suggest a point of view which will prove useful to those who recognize and would like to avoid this "either-or" position.

The first suggestion is that since a society is an organized group of people, and a social system is created by the behavior of *all* members, the social system can only be discerned by observing the thought, action, and relations of people and the products of such behavior, and would cease to exist, save in historical description, if all members should cease to exist. In this sense it is fair to say that no society or organization is *real* inde-pendently of the people who make it up, and that no social system or organizational setup is *real* independently of the behavior and relationships or interactions of these people. This is a fruitful point of view, and it leads to the recognition of as great a practical need for understanding people and their relations with each other as does the most genuine humanitarian sentiment.

Perhaps the research man who comes into a company or union "cold" of necessity is struck more forcibly by this fact than the people who know their organization from daily contact. As the research man attempts to sketch an outline of the nature and structure of a society, he must observe people in action. In order to describe, for instance, the systems of Functional Specifications, Status, Communication, Reward and Penalty, and Organizational Charter, he must observe what people are doing. He sees them *functioning* and relating their activities to those of others. He sees them *exercising* direction and representation, *bestowing* and *accepting* or *rejecting* authority. He sees them *communicating* with each other. He sees them *setting* requirements for rewards and penalties, and *rewarding* and *penalizing* each other. He sees them *constructing* and *sharing* a concept of the organization as a whole. This is the raw stuff with which he must paint his picture of the structure of the organization. He recognizes the behavior of people as the *substance* of the systems. When he moves from structure to dynamics, seeking to learn not only *what* the organization is but *how* it works and *why,* the behavior and relations of people well-nigh constitute his only source of verifiable information.

In order to get a generalized conception of the organization, however, he seeks for *patterns* in such behavior, and he gives names to those patterns in order to be able to think and talk about them. At this point he arrives at a set of concepts, such as those we have labeled the bonds, or systems, of organization. These, he finds, are useless categories unless they are filled with behavioral content. The temptation arises, however, to think of them as real things in themselves, and, as we shall see in a moment, he faces not only a temptation but a necessity of assigning to them a reality more than the sum of the individual behavior incidents he has just observed.

This temptation also is present for the manager of a company or the leader of the union in even greater degree. The extent of his face-to-face contact with all the people, and his observation of them in action, is limited. If it is their behavior, as described above, which is the raw stuff of his organizational system, he sees little of it in its raw state. To him it is represented and visualized in organizational charts, written specifications, reports on performance, specific communication devices, etc. And the greater part of these reports is composed of summaries and makes use of averages or distributions in which the people involved and their individual behavior are lost.

Moreover, these practical men are responsible for acting on and modifying the patterns as such. This is in part what it means to be a manager or leader. They revise Functional Specifications, they reallocate authority, they introduce new media of communication, they change an incentive (reward) system, they try to "get across" the Organizational Charter. Dealing as they do with such labeled structural concepts, it is easy for them to think of these "things" as, in their own right, the objects of their attention, things which can be manipulated as a machine part can be manipulated.

But reference to our comments on the formal and informal systems will indicate the desirability of understanding these concepts of society, social system, and bonds of organization, not merely as terms, but as terms representing a content; and of recognizing this content to be the thought, action, and relationships of *all* the people involved, and the products of such behavior. By so doing, a manager or union leader will understand what was indicated above, that his behavior does not modify a system, but merely contributes a stimulus to such a modification. The ultimate modifications (of, say, a communication medium) is the work of many minds and hands, and is consummated by the behavior of every person concerned. It is this ultimate modification which is experienced as a condition or resource of life and work by participants, and constitutes the reality of the organizational system and its parts. Those who insist that "an organization is folks" have hold of an important truth, the significance of which is, and must be, recognized by every inductive social scientist, and which practical operators of organizations will find useful.

But it is not the whole truth. For these "folks," by their thought and action, create a social system and a society which has a reality greater than the sum of its parts at any particular time. Their behavior reveals patterns, and the fact that these patterns are known to characterize life in the group exerts a compulsion on the future behavior of their creators. Moreover, every participant, even though he is aware that his own behavior and that of his associates is the reality of the Reward and Penalty system, for instance, knows that his behavior, whether similar or dissimilar to that of his associates, has to be integrated with a pattern of customary practice which existed before he arrived on the scene; and that any pattern now experienced will be a real factor, to which a newcomer into the group will have to adjust and to which this man will have to add any modification inherent in his own behavior.

The company or union, therefore, is greater than the sum of its folks and their behavior because as a society, a social system, a structure of bonds of organization, it can be visualized, understood, and taken account of as something to which folks have to adjust by conformity or invention, and into which their inventions must be integrated; and because it is relatively permanent, that is, relative to the presence or behavior of any particular person who is associated with the company or union.

Every orientation or training program is a practical recognition of the fact that there is a real system, or systems, to which a new member of the society is to be introduced. This is the case regardless of the fact that human behavior and product constitute the *substance* of the system or systems. To be sure they will never experience a system save in interaction with people, and the newcomer might well be made aware of this fact. But he can be introduced to the general character of the several systems, *before* such experience, and will be able to recognize in his own behavior and that of others a consistency with or a departure from those systems.

Moreover, it was obvious to us, perhaps because of the large number of long-service people in these organizations, that, in a very real sense, the behavior tendencies of individuals, and perhaps their personality structure itself, had absorbed influences from the social systems of the company and union. It is a plausible inference that such individual tendencies and structure are different than they would have been had the social system involved been a coal company, a railroad, or a union of employees in such organizations. Whether we say this social system "became a part of individual behavior and personality systems," or "influenced the development of the individual," or "imposed compulsions on him," it is an active factor in its own right and can usefully be discussed and analyzed as such. The very contribution in behavior and product of the many individuals to the substance of the social system is affected, and even determined by, the fact that they have absorbed into themselves *this* social system and not some other.

One implication of this conclusion should strike those who are inclined to find the source of their human-relations problems in "difficult" people. If something goes wrong in an organization's operations, *cherchez l'homme* is their motto and guide to action. There is virtue in this tactic; for, as we have suggested, the man's behavior is, with that of others, the real stuff of the system that isn't working right. If his behavior is distorting or unbalancing the system, it is sensible to try to understand him and try to "straighten him out," after learning why his behavior is what it is.

But if our above observations are accurate, this search for *why* will probably lead not merely to the behavior impulse arising from peculiar characteristics rooted in the dark, unknown, innate qualities of an individual. What he is, as a source of what he does, will have been determined in some degree by the social system of this company or union which he has made a part of his own behavior tendencies and personality structure. Straightening him out, therefore, may involve work on not only that individual but on the social system to which he is conforming and which, in the act of conformity, he is making a part of *his* self.

The system of Functional Specifications in this company, for instance, permits, and even sanctions, the formation of teams for direct action between persons in one department with their "opposite number" in other departments, without specific clearance through the supervisors of these persons except in certain fairly well-defined situations, and always with the understanding that the supervisors are ultimately responsible. Of equal importance in establishing this system are the permission and sanction flowing from higher management, and the permission and sanction residing in the acceptance of those who form the team.

Now, let us say, an action in accordance with this system "balls things up," and this could have been avoided by clearance through the supervisors. It will accomplish only part of the straightening-out process to call the "guilty" individuals onto the carpet, or even to sit down with them and reasonably try to get them to modify their practice. Unless the system is altered (ultimately by the acceptance of the alteration by those involved), dealing with the man will have, at best, temporary results; and, at worst, may confuse him and make him so insecure that he does not know where he stands with respect to the system of Functional Specifications as he experiences it or with those people to whom he is related within that system.

Here, then, are a number of reasons a social system is more than the sum of its parts. There is another reason. The organization or society, considered as an organized group of individuals, has a set of *collective* functions to perform, within the areas set by the social system, and utilizing the bonds of organization. To be sure, these collective functions, as we have seen, are performed through the activities of teams, which in turn involve part performance by individual people. But it is meaningful to speak of a *collective* function, and the doer of that function (the organization) has a reality as a collectivity and not just as a number of individuals.

When individuals act as participants in the doing of this collective task, they act *for the company or union as a whole.*

Illustrations are numerous. A few will suffice. It is a function of the society through its social system to *reconcile* differences between the actions of particular people. It is a function of the organization to *co-ordinate* the behavior of its people. It is the function of the organization to *develop loyalty* in the participants to the organization. It is the function of the organization to *establish relationships* with other organizations. The behavior of the people who perform these tasks, the humanly devised techniques and tools they make use of in doing so, have patterns which can be used to describe the organization as a whole in action. The company or union is more than the sum of its parts in such areas, because it is functioning to relate the parts to each other, the parts to the whole, and the whole to other wholes.

In short, there appears to us no real substance to a society and social system aside from people, their thought, action, and relationships and the products of this behavior. But there are patterns to all of these, and the patterns, once established, can be visualized and understood; provide objective criteria by which conformity and departure can be measured; have a continuity of life which is greater than that of particular participants and their behavior; furnish resources which people can use; impose expectancies upon an individual's structure of behavior and personality; and are descriptive of collective behavior directed toward organizational objectives. And although such functions are performed through the behavior of individual people, these people, in such instances, act for and are the representatives of the organization in action.

That which performs a function has functional reality. But unless the human substance of the reality is correctly understood, the improvement or modification of the function is bound to be clumsily handled, and bound to elicit unexpected and probably disruptive reactions from the human beings who, in relationship to each other, compose the society and whose behavior and products of behavior are the real stuff of the social system.[5]

[5] The bearing of the findings of this investigation upon the clarification and use of the concepts of status and role, as these terms are used by anthropologists, may have occurred to some of our readers as it has occurred to us. These terms, so useful in analyzing the relations of an individual to his group and its social system, are clearly relevant to the interpretation of our findings. Our data contain much evidence on this point which we shall summarize in our final report.

The significance of this suggestion for practical management and leadership is clear. The attempt to understand, train for, and administer human relations must be based on a broader foundation than so-called principles of man-to-man relations. Knowing "how to win friends and influence people" is not enough. The complexities of the social system created by relations between people must also be understood. The interaction of the system with individual behavior tendencies and personality structures must be explored. Though the substance of the system is behavior and behavioral products, it has an influence in its own right.

Two types of managers and leaders who try to improve human relations are in equal danger of failure. The first is the man who "works on individuals" without the awareness that the individual is, in nature and action, inseparably bound up with the social system of the group. The second is the man who "works on the organizational structure or system" without the awareness that its substance is the behavior of all involved, and that by their behavior they are its creators.

MULTIPLE STRUCTURE OF LIVING

One cannot observe and record the experiences of people in an organization, for the purpose of describing the actual bonds of organization which weld them together, without noticing an outstanding fact. That fact is so consistent with common sense and everyday experience that the noticing hardly rates as a discovery. Yet it is worthy of emphasis because, though recognized, it is frequently not used as a tool for understanding or organizing human relations. Since the raw material of any bond is the thought, action, and relations of individual people in a company or union, it follows that, for each, the bonds as understood and experienced are to a greater or less degree different. Since the reaction of different people to the bond and their behavior in its presence is a response to the bond *as they understand and experience it,* their responses will vary accordingly. This fact of multiple contents of bonds has been discussed in a previous publication of the Yale Labor and Management Center[6] and will not be detailed here.

One point made in that publication receives, however, heavy under-

[6] See E. Wight Bakke, *Adaptive Human Behavior* (revised processed edition, 1950). In this publication, reference is made not only to the five bonds of organization discussed in this report but to all other elements in the structure of living as well.

scoring from our evidence. Though the actual bonds vary in content for each individual, the variation is greater as between certain groups of individuals than as between individuals within these groups. For instance, it varies more between management and employee groups than it varies among the members of these groups. The same categories of bonds[7] can be used to classify the data of experience reported by management and employees, or by union leaders and members, but the experience content reveals that they face a bond which in substance is not the same for all of them. This generalization can be pushed further to indicate that the content varies as between departmental representatives of all of the groups mentioned. What is equally important is that the content varies as between first-line, middle, and top management and leadership.

What we are suggesting here is that, for purposes of charting the relationship between a social system and observed behavior, it is not sufficient to define *a* company or union system of Functional Specifications, Status, Communication, Reward and Penalty, or Organizational Charter. For the company or union system is not the only one which is realized *in the experiences* of participants. There are sufficient similarities, however, in the content experienced by *all* management and *all* employees so that it is meaningful to attach the labels of management and employees to each bond, and also meaningful to attach labels descriptive of status and departmental groupings within these larger classifications.

So long as we do not forget this variation which arises from the actual experience of different individuals, it is legitimate and helpful to visualize this series of ever more comprehensive groups of people, each having essentially similar experiences and therefore sharing similar conceptions of the bonds of organization; and this series includes the company or union.

The fact that management and employees report a different description of, say, the Status or Communication system does not necessarily mean that there is a planned and announced bond for management and another for employees, though in actuality this is often the case.[8] But even if the planned and announced bond were identical for the two, it would be understood and experienced differently; and, therefore, as a factor influencing behavior, *be* different.

[7] I.e., Functional Specifications, Status system, Communication system, Reward and Penalty system, Organizational Charter.
[8] See next section.

This fact is implicit in some of the findings reported in this book and will be made explicit in our final report. It suggests that some of the most difficult problems in developing teamwork in an organization may arise from a lack of consistency in the experienced content for different groups of bonds assumed to be "the same for every one."

Many, perhaps most, of these inconsistencies cannot be removed by rational planning or action. Since they arise from and are defined by differences in experience, the experience itself would have to be changed. But it is just common sense for a manager or leader who "uses" these bonds as instruments of administration to recognize the fact, know as much as he possibly can about what the substance of his implements is for those with whom he works, and to make his judgments and decisions and to take his action in the light of this knowledge.

HIERARCHY OF SOCIAL SYSTEMS

Not only is it clear from our observations that the social system, or bonds, supposedly the same for all participants, is given varying content by experience, and that the system *experienced* by individuals is the real and actual one affecting their behavior, but that the system contains elements for some which others have no opportunity to experience at all. In other words, the actual behavior and relationships which constitute the substance of any experienced bond are characterized by their relevance to the scope of the society, or subdivision of it, whose function is promoted. Put into simpler terms there are, say, a Communication and a Reward and Penalty system serving as a framework for the functioning of each specific-task and activity-area team, which in structure and operation take their content from behavior and relationships essential to the functioning of *that* team. One who is not a member of a particular team, and has no part in its function, does not experience these bonds as a part of the social system within which he lives and works. Although he may, of course, know about these features, they are not a part of his pattern of living.

At a more generalized level of the society or organization, say the general management level, there are also such bonds which form a part of the social system which the department managers alone experience as they perform the task, assigned to their team, of co-ordinating the operations of the several departments. Those bonds, very real to them, are not a part of the social system experienced by the employees in their departments.

We may indicate parenthetically that this is one further reason for thinking of human relations in a company or union, not merely as "relations between people," but as "relations between people whose behavior tendencies and personality structures are responses to experiences with particular social systems the content of which is not the same." The problem is not simply that they live in different "worlds." The practical problem arises from the attempts of people in two groups (say management and employees, or leaders and members) to work out, for relations *between* them, a satisfactory division of labor, a status relationship, a means of communication, a method of rewarding and penalizing each other, and a common conception of the organized society for which they work. Their behavior in such attempts will be suggested by the systems relevant to these activities which they have experienced in their own worlds. The suggestions for the relationship between them arise for each from comparable relations among the members of their own groups. Different worlds produce different suggestions, and their reconciliation in an appropriate arrangement is frequently difficult.

These observations have an important bearing on the matter of company-union relations. They suggest that, for purposes of accomplishing the functions assigned to the company and the union in their *joint* task, those involved become *a* unique society, that is a group of people organized for a purpose. That both company and union participants are, for definite purposes, organized as *distinct* societies does not negate this fact. Representatives from each organization are thrown together in the carrying out of their joint function. Through their behavior and relationship they develop a social system pertinent to the effective discharge of that joint function and providing a framework for their joint activities and thought. The patterns of that behavior and relationship among those involved can be described, for them as an organized group, as the Functional Specification, Status, Communication, Reward and Penalty systems, and Organizational Charter of *that* group.

If anyone doubts the reality of this, he might contemplate the damage to the work-flow in collective bargaining if a lawyer or officer of the company or the union, or a government mediator, who was not acquainted with these bonds or systems as developed by the group, were to step in and stubbornly or in ignorance act contrary to the behavior sanctioned by their social system.

We will resist the temptation to give examples of this from our evidence, since the identity of individuals would be clearly revealed. But we can indicate that the consequence of such interferences, after a brief disturbance, was an effort on the part of *both* management and union representatives to set the "out-grouper" straight, those representatives with which he was identified, of course, doing so in private and not in the joint meeting. It was as though those involved from both management and the union realized that any immediate tactical advantage resulting from the violation of the social system pertinent to their joint function was outweighed by the preservation of the system within which heretofore they had accomplished mutually satisfactory results.

We have labeled this joint society, including people with an attachment both to a management and to a union group, the *organized enterprise.*[9] We shall, in our final report, indicate the bonds which are specifically characteristic of the social system of this society.

Although this is a concept that was not sufficiently clear in our minds at the start to suggest interview questions bearing sharply on the formation of this society, enough evidence has come to light to permit not only description but an amplification of the problem of its formation and operations. Through behavior and relations suggested to them by experience with a management system on the one hand, and a union system on the other, they face the most difficult task of creating a social system appropriate to the organized enterprise.

It should be said immediately that this concept of the organized enterprise implies no particular qualitative character which could be described by such words as efficient, smoothly running, friendly, businesslike, or peaceful. It could just as probably be described by adjectives carrying an opposite meaning. Since the bonds of organization are patterns of actual behavior, the adjectives applied must describe the quality of what is observed. The division of labor might be inefficient. The Communication system might be unstable and ineffective. War—that is, striking—might be an instrument of rewarding and penalizing, etc. It happens that the social system of the organized enterprise which we are observing

[9] The concept is suggested and explained by Neil W. Chamberlain, Assistant Director of the Labor and Management Center, in the *Journal of Political Economy,* June 1944, pp. 97 ff.

reveals few behavior patterns which could be so characterized. But the system would not disappear, but only change its character, if it did.

If societies, including the organized enterprise, or companies, or unions could be characterized as such only when legitimately described as efficient, businesslike, friendly, etc., the social scientist would simply have to invent another term to describe organized groups which fell short of such elegibility. We see no need for, and no scientific virtue in, such a tactic.

It should also be said that this concept of the organized enterprise no more involves a "washing out" of the distinct interests and organizational structures and systems of the two (company and union) societies than the concept of a team involves the washing out of the individuals who make it up. But it suggests an approach to the study of union-management relations supplementary to that customarily employed by many students, including the author. The customary approach is to study the internal systems of the union and company, and then discuss their joint activities as "foreign relations" between the two. This is a basic step in understanding why people from both groups behave as they do in relation to each other. But an equally important step is the one here suggested, that attention be given to the study of joint activities as the behavior of people within a single society which we have called the organized enterprise. For the social system created by the behavior and relations of people involved in joint functions exerts compulsions on their behavior and thought which parallel in importance those exerted by their participation in a company or a union society.

Neither approach is complete without the other. The contribution of company men and union men through their behavior to the social system of the organized enterprise will stem from the fact that their behavior tendencies and personality structures have become adjusted to the social systems of the union *or* the company. But once established, that mutually experienced social system assumes an active role affecting the behavior tendencies and personality structures of those participating.

One of the most difficult of all problems in effective operation of the organized enterprise is that the compulsions from its social system and those of the company and union systems are frequently incompatible; and since not all members of the company and union are active face-to-face participants in the joint functions, those excluded do not understand the compulsions arising from the participation of their representatives in the joint society. This problem is not different in nature, but only in degree, from that posed by the relations between leadership and the rank and file within the union, or between top management and first-line supervisors, or between all management and employees in the company.

If that fact is recognized, it seems reasonable to suppose that the attempt to discover principles of human relations *within* a company or union will yield results applicable to the relationship between them. But basic to the possibility of such applicability is the view of any self-perpetuating, functioning group organized for a purpose as a society having a social system similar in outline to other social systems, but differing in specific content.

In Conclusion

The flow of materials from the research activities of the universities, companies, and unions designed to get at the fundamentals of human relations is relatively meager. It is small relative to the production of studies on tactics and techniques for improving human relations. It is small relative to the reports on technical engineering problems and the basic sciences available for their solution. When a research project which tries to make systematic sense out of the underlying factors in human relations is reported, therefore, expectancies are raised that it will "give all the answers." It will be a long time before these anticipations are fully realized.

Practical men in companies and unions, puzzled and perplexed by the complexities of their human-relations problems in day-by-day operations, will understand that the unraveling of the underlying factors of human nature, of the structure and dynamics of organizational life, of the relations between individual behavior and the social systems of organizations, is a task no less difficult than managing or leading men. If the product of such unraveling is to be more than a set of "bright ideas" from the ivory tower, the process itself must involve the most careful and painstaking analysis of observed behavior and its determinants. As a preliminary step, the terms and concepts used must be rigorously tested and made consistent with the actual facts of life, an interpretation and understanding of which is sought.

The limited purpose of this first report is to take that preliminary step.

If we hope eventually to develop principles of effective teamwork, either for scientific or operational use, then it is important that we have an accurate conception of the nature of those organizational devices or bonds which weld a group of individuals into a functioning team. Those *bonds of organization* described in this report are not the only elements in the structure of living which influence the activity, thought, and relationships of people in an organization, but they are elements of primary importance, since they furnish a large part of the framework and a significant number of the patterns for the expected behavior of participants. That framework and those patterns make the participants in the organization aware of what kind of behavior is expected of them. They set up boundaries of appropriate behavior suggesting, supporting, and limiting action and thought. They are as effective in their sphere of influence as are the size and shape and arrangement of an office or workshop in determining the possible physical movements of individuals.

It has seemed to us important, therefore, to develop an outline of the elements in these bonds of organization which must be described for an organization if one is to report what those bonds are like *in the experience* of participants, and how they influence behavior.

The social scientist who seeks to establish significant causal relations between observed behavior of people and the social system within which they live and work can profit from a sharpening of the detail in his conception of the character of that system. Likewise the practical executive who seeks to modify the behavior of participants of initiating changes in certain aspects of the social system of his organization requires detailed knowledge of the aspects and character of that system into which he desires to introduce a modification.

We trust, therefore, that this report on the character of these five bonds of organization—Functional Specifications, the systems of Status, Communication, Rewards and Penalties, and the Organizational Charter—together with the suggestions for testing their efficiency and the comments on general implications of our findings, will contribute to the systematic thinking of both scientists and executives about the structure and dynamics of human relations.

APPENDICES

APPENDIX A

I. TABLES FOR DEPARTMENTS DISCUSSED IN TEXT

TABLE VI
PROPORTIONS SATISFIED WITH COMPANY STATUS SYSTEM
(In tenths)

Status	Item	Traffic			Plant			Comm.	
		Mgt.	E. I	E. II	Mgt.	E. I	E. II	Mgt.	E
Directive System	General Reaction	8	5	5	8	6	7	6	6
	Position Fair	9	8	7	9	8	8	8	8
Directive Authority	Double Reporting	9	3	5	9	7	7	8	9
	Backing of Higher Management	9			9			9	
Directive Acceptance	Of Superiors	7	5	7	7	5	7	4	5
	Backing of Employees	8			9			9	
Representative System	Grievances	8	7	8	9	8	8	7	8
	Suggestions	8	4	6	7	4	4	9	7
	Attention above Supervisor	7	7	8	9	5	7	8	5
Technique	Promotion Requirements and Methods	7	5	6	8	5	5	7	7

TABLE VII
PROPORTIONS SATISFIED WITH UNION STATUS SYSTEM
(In tenths)

Status	Item	Traffic			Plant			Comm.	
		O	M. I	M. II	O	M. I	M. II	O	M
Directive System	General Reaction	7	7	7	7	8	7	7	7
	Position Fair	8	8	8	9	9	8	9	8
Directive Authority	Double Reporting	9			9			8	
	Backing of Officers	8			8			9	
Directive Acceptance	Superiors	9	7	7	6	7	7	7	9
	Backing of Members	5			7			8	
Representative System	Dissatisfaction with Union	8	6	6	7	7	7	8	5
Techniques	Promotion Requirements	5			8			4	

TABLE XII
PROPORTIONS SATISFIED WITH TYPES OF COMPANY COMMUNICATIONS
(In tenths)

Type of Communication	Traffic			Plant			Comm.	
	Mgt.	E. I	E. II	Mgt.	E. I	E. II	Mgt.	Emp.
Job Instructions	8	7	8	8	6	7	8	8
Superiors' Problems	7	5	8	8	6	6	8	7
Subordinates' Problems	9			9			10	
Employees' Problems	8			9			8	
Company Problems	9	6	6	9	8	7	8	9
Union Problems	7			8			7	
Company General Information	9	8	8	9	8	8	9	9
Union General Information	8			9			8	
Personnel Policy Change	7	6	6	9	5	6	8	8
Approval Requirements	8	7	7	8	6	5	8	9
Subordinates' Reactions	7			8			8	
Superiors' Reactions	7			6			6	
Union Reactions to Company	7			8			5	
Subordinates' Performance	8			9			9	
Grievance with Company	8	7	8	9	8	8	7	8
Dissatisfaction with Union	8			9			9	
Suggestions to Company	8	4	6	7	4	4	9	7
All Items	7	6	7	8	6	6	7	8

TABLE XIII
PROPORTIONS SATISFIED WITH TYPES OF UNION COMMUNICATIONS
(In tenths)

Type of Communication	Traffic			Plant			Comm.	
	O	M. I	M. II	O	M. I	M. II	O	M
Job Instructions	6	6	7	8	8	7	7	6
Superiors' Problems	5	5	6	7	7	6	7	6
Subordinates' Problems	7			9			9	
Members' Problems	6			8			8	
Company Problems	6			6			9	
Company General Information	8			8			9	
Union General Information	7	5	7	8	7	6	7	6
Changes in Rules	7			9			9	
Approval Requirements	5			8			8	
Disapproval Standards	8	4	4	7	5	5	7	4
Subordinates' Reactions	6			7			8	
Members' Reactions	7			7			8	
Reactions to Union	5			7			7	
Subordinates' Performance	8			7			7	
Dissatisfaction with Union	8	6	6	7	7	7	8	5
Dissatisfaction with Company	8			9			9	
All Items	6	5	6	7	6	6	8	5

TABLE XXVI

PROPORTIONS SATISFIED WITH CERTAIN ASPECTS OF COMPANY
REWARD AND PENALTY SYSTEM

(In tenths)

Group	Item	Traffic			Plant			Comm.	
		Mgt.	E. I	E. II	Mgt.	E. I	E. II	Mgt.	E
General	Job Rewarding	9	9	9	9	9	9	10	9
Reaction	General Rewards	6	5	6	5	6	6	8	7
	Summary	8	7	7	7	7	8	9	8
Qualification	Superiors' Standards	8	7	7	9	9	8	9	9
for Reward	Subordinates' Standards	8			9			10	
and Penalty	Associates' Standards		8	8		9	9		9
	Union Officers' Standards	9			9			9	
	Promotion Requirements	6	5	6	6	5	5	7	7
	Summary	8	7	7	8	7	7	9	8
Understanding	Knowledge of System	8	7	7	8	6	5	8	9
Instruments	Money	9	8	9	8	7	8	8	8
and Methods	Progress in Status	9	8	7	9	8	8	8	8
	Co-operation	5	6	5	9	8	8	7	7
	Management Backing	9			9			9	
	Employee Backing	8			9			9	
	Summary	8	7	7	9	8	8	8	8
Average	All Items	8	7	7	8	7	8	8	8

TABLE XXVII

PROPORTIONS SATISFIED WITH CERTAIN ASPECTS OF UNION
REWARD AND PENALTY SYSTEM

(In tenths)

Group	Item	Traffic			Plant			Comm.	
		O	M. I	M. II	O	M. I	M. II	O	M
General	Job Rewarding	5			4			4	
Reaction	General Rewards	9	8	8	10	8	8	9	7
	Summary	7			7			7	
Qualifications	Officers' Standards	8	9	9	9	9	9	10	9
for Reward	Subordinates' Standards	8			9			10	
and Penalty	Management's Standards	9			9			10	
	Promotion Requirements	5			8			4	
	Summary	7			9			8	
Understanding	Knowledge of System	5			8			8	
Instruments	Money	5			3			6	
and Methods	Progress in Status	8	7	8	9	9	8	9	8
	Co-operation	6			8			6	
	Officers' Backing	8			8			9	
	Members' Backing	5			7			8	
	Summary	7			7			8	
Average	All Items	7	8	8	8	8	8	8	8

TABLE XXXIII

PROPORTIONS EXPERIENCING INTEGRATION THROUGH COMPANY
ORGANIZATIONAL CHARTER

(In tenths)

Aspect of Integration	Traffic			Plant			Comm.	
	Mgt.	E. I	E. II	Mgt.	E. I	E. II	Mgt.	E
Self-Respect	9	9	9	9	9	9	10	8
Solidarity	9	8	8	8	7	7	6	7
Relationship	9	9	9	9	8	8	8	8
All Aspects	9	9	9	9	8	8	8	8

TABLE XXXIV

PROPORTIONS EXPERIENCING INTEGRATION THROUGH UNION
ORGANIZATIONAL CHARTER

(In tenths)

Aspect of Integration	Traffic			Plant			Comm.	
	O	M. I	M. II	O	M. I	M. II	O	M
Self-Respect	10	8	9	10	7	6	9	8
Solidarity	7	5	5	5	6	6	8	6
Relationship	7	5	5	3	3	3	5	3
All Aspects	8	6	6	6	5	5	7	5

II. TABLES FOR DEPARTMENTS NOT DISCUSSED IN TEXT

TABLE II A

PROPORTIONS SATISFIED WITH CERTAIN RESULTS OF FUNCTIONAL SPECIFICATIONS

(In tenths)

Question and Goal	Exec.		Accting.		Eng.		Dir.[1]	Hs.[2]	Ds.[3]
	M	E	M	E	M	E	E	E	E
Job Instructions (Understanding)	9	7	8	8	10	9	10	8	10
Use of Abilities (Capacity Performance)	8	4	9	5	8	2	5	6	8
Scope of Freedom (Control)	9	9	9	8	8	8	10	8	7
Teamwork (Integration)	9	7	9	8	9	9	9	7	3
Respect for Job (Respect)	8	8	10	6	10	8	7	8	4
Fatigue (Creature Comforts)	9	9	8	8	2	8	10	8	3
Steadiness (Security)	9	8	8	8	10	8	8	8	6
Fairness (Justice)	10	8	9	7	7	8	8	7	8
Average—All Items	9	8	9	7	8	7	8	8	6

[1] Directory [2] House Service [3] Dining Service.

TABLE VI A

PROPORTIONS SATISFIED WITH COMPANY STATUS SYSTEM
(In tenths)

		Exec.		Accting.		Eng.		Dir.	Hs.	Ds.
	Status Item	M	E	M	E	M	E	E	E	E
Directive	General Reaction	9	7	9	6	7	6	7	8	10
System	Position Fair	10	8	10	8	10	7	9	8	10
Directive	Double Reporting	9	7	8	6	10	6	10	9	9
Authority	Backing of Higher Mgt.	9		9		9				
Directive	Of Superiors	4		6		7				
Acceptance	Backing of Employees	10		10		10				
Representative	Grievances	10	6	9	7	7	7	8	8	10
System	Suggestions	9	6	6	7	8	6	5	6	7
	Attention above Super.	8	7	10	8	9	9	5	6	10
Technique	Promotion Requirements and Methods	8	5	9	5	7	5	8	6	9
	Average—All Items	8	7	9	7	8	7	7	7	9

TABLE XII A

PROPORTIONS SATISFIED WITH TYPES OF COMPANY COMMUNICATIONS
(In tenths)

	Exec.		Accting.		Eng.		Dir.	Hs.	Ds.
Type of Communication	M	E	M	E	M	E	E	E	E
Job Instructions	9	7	8	8	10	9	10	8	10
Superiors' Problems	8	5	8	6	8	6	9	4	7
Subordinates' Problems	5		9		10				
Employees' Problems	8		8		9				
Company Problems	9	8	9	7	10	10	8	7	8
Union's Problems	7		8		5				
Company General Information	10	9	9	9	9	9	10	9	9
Union General Information	8		9		8				
Personnel Policy Change	10	8	9	8	10	6	10	6	9
Approval Requirements	10	8	9	8	8	7	9	8	10
Subordinates' Reaction	8		8		10				
Superiors' Reaction	7		6		8				
Union's Reactions to Company	6		9		7				
Subordinates' Performance	9		9		10				
Grievance with Company	10	6	9	7	7	7	8	8	10
Dissatisfaction with Union	9		9		8				
Suggestions to Company	9	6	6	7	8	6	5	6	7
Average—All Items	8	7	8	7	8	8	8	7	8

TABLE XXVI A

PROPORTIONS SATISFIED WITH CERTAIN ASPECTS OF REWARD AND PENALTY SYSTEM

(In tenths)

Group	Item	Exec. M	Exec. E	Accting. M	Accting. E	Eng. M	Eng. E	Dir. E	Hs. E	Ds. E
General Reaction	Job Rewarding	10	9	10	9	10	10	10	9	10
	General Rewards	6	8	8	9	5	8	7	8	9
	Average	8	8	9	9	7	9	8	8	9
Qualifications for Reward and Penalty	Superiors' Standards	9	10	9	8	10	9	9	9	10
	Subordinates' Standards	9		10		10				
	Associates' Standards		9		9		10	9	9	10
	Union Officers' Standards	9		10		10				
	Promotion Requirements	8	5	9	5	7	5	8	6	9
	Average	9	8	9	7	9	8	9	8	9
Understanding	Knowledge of System	10	8	9	8	8	7	9	8	10
Instruments and Methods	Money	8	9	9	8	8	8	10	8	6
	Progress in Status	10	8	10	8	10	7	9	8	10
	Co-operation	9	7	9	8	9	9	9	7	3
	Management Backing	9		9		9				
	Employee Backing	10		10		10				
	Average	9	8	9	8	9	8	9	8	6

TABLE XXXIII A

PROPORTIONS EXPERIENCING INTEGRATION THROUGH COMPANY ORGANIZATIONAL CHARTER

(In tenths)

Aspect of Integration	Exec. M	Exec. E	Accting. M	Accting. E	Eng. M	Eng. E	Dir. E	Hs. E	Ds. E
Self-Respect	9	9	9	8	10	8	10	8	9
Solidarity	8	6	9	7	9	8	9	7	5
Relationship	9	7	9	7	9	8	10	7	5
Average	9	7	9	7	9	8	9	7	6

APPENDIX B

TABLES UPON WHICH WORK-FLOW CHARTS ARE BASED

RESIDENCE INSTALLATION SPECIFIC TASK TEAM
(Large Exchanges)

Step	Person	Status	Others	Function	Papers	Inflow	Outflow
I	Service Representative (Comm.)	VII	Customer	Receives request for service from customer. Writes up *Form 1532*. Makes out *Credit Card* and *contract* for service, *Form 400*. Clips 3 forms together and sends to Service Order Group.	#1532 Credit Card #400		
2	Service Order Clerk (Comm.)	VIII		Receives 3 *forms* from Service Rep. Assigns order number and teletypes order on Service Order *Form 250*. Copies go via teletype to Plant Assignment Clerk. Retains *C copy*. Temporarily files this *copy*. *Credit card* and *Form 400* are returned to Service Rep. *Form 1532* is placed with completed day's work and filed. (End of *Form 1532*)	Same as above and Form #250		To Plant
3	Assignment Clerk (Pl.)	VII		Receives 6 copies of Service Order *Form 250* from Commercial Office (referred to hereafter as I.W., A.D., A.R., T., D., and D.D. copies). Checks station list, L.I. file, to see if any useable equipment at the location. Also checks street index file to determine location of cable terminal to be used. Hands 6 copies of *Form 250* to Facilities Assigner.	Forms #250; I.W., A.D., A.R., T., D., & D.D.	From Comm.	

				Forms	To Traffic Directory
4	Facilities Assigner (Pl.)	VII	Receives 6 copies of *Form 250* from Assignment Clerk. Assigns underground and aerial cable pairs and pair in terminal to be used to connect station with Central Office. Provides technical information (zoning, etc.). If outside construction needed (this not assumed in this chart) prepares *Order Form 265* to Construction Dept. or Plant Engineering. Assigns telephone number from list of numbers furnished by Traffic and prepares *Telephone Number Card (T.N.C.)* Prepares *Form 1571* for use by Framemen. This form perforated into two parts, one to cover work on Main Distributing Frame (M.D.F.), the other to cover work on the Intermediate Distributing Frame (I.D.F.). Sends *Form 1571* to Order Clerk in Repair Service Bureau (Step 5a). Hands *I.W. copy* with *T.N.C.* attached, the *A.D. & A.R. copies* to Dispatcher. Sends *T copy* to Traffic (Step 5b) and the *D & D.D. copies* to Directory Dept. (Step 5c.)	Forms #250 I.W., A.D., A.R., T., D., D.D. Form #1571 T.N.C. (Form #265)	
5	Dispatcher (Pl.)	VII	Receives *I.W. copy* with attached *T.N.C.*, *A.D.* and *A.R. copies.* Separates and reviews these. If review indicates special equipment needed, he orders it. Assigns each installer a daily quota of work using the *I.W. copies.* Files corresponding *A.D. copies* in tills for each installer to be used in dispatching each installer and recording his completions. *A.R. copies* are held in a numerical order file. Sends *I.W. copies* with attached *T.N.C.* for each installer to Foreman of Installers.	Forms #250: I.W., A.D., A.R., T.N.C.	
5a	Order Clerk (Pl.)	VII	Receives *Form 1571* from Facilities Assigner. Adds any additional information necessary and forwards it to Foreman of Central Office Repairmen.	Form #1571	

Step	Person	Status	Others	Function	Papers	Inflow	Outflow
6a	Foreman of Central Office Repairmen (Pl.)	VI		Receives *Form 1571* from Order Clerk and distributes to Framemen as orders to make necessary connections in the Central Office.	Form #1571		
7a	Framemen (Pl.)	VII		Receives *Form 1571* and completes necessary connections on M.D. Frame and I.D. Frame. Returns completed *Form 1571* to Foreman of C.O. Repairmen. (This Central Office work usually should have been completed before the Installer is ready to make corresponding installation.)	Form #1571		
8a	Foreman of C.O. Repairmen (Pl.)	VI		Receives completed *Forms 1571* from Framemen and sends them to Plant Clerk to file locally.	Form #1571		
9a	Plant Clerk (Pl.)	VII		Receives *Forms 1571* from Foreman of C.O. Repairmen and files locally. (End of *Form 1571*.)	Form #1571		
5b	C.O. Clerk (Tr.)	VII		Receives *T copy* of *Form 250* from Plant and temporarily files.			
5c	Mail Clerk (Dir.)	VII		Receives *D. & D.D. copies* of *Form 250* from Plant. Distributes to compilation clerk.	Forms #250: D. & D.D.	From Plant	
6c	Alphabetical Compilation Clerk (Dir.)	VII		Receives *D & D.D. copies* and temporarily files.	Forms #250: D. & D.D.		

6	Foreman of Installers (Pl.)	VI	Receives *I.W. copies* and attached *T.N.C.* Distributes to the Installers in the order arranged by the Dispatcher.	Form #250: I.W. T.N.C.	
7	Installers (Pl.)	VII	Receives *I.W. copies* & attached *T.N.C.* Installs and tests telephone. Places *T.N.C.* on telephone set. (End of *T.N.C.*) Provides customer with *directory* and instructs him on use of equipment. Records date, type of equipment used, and accounting information on *I.W. copy*. Calls Dispatcher, reports completion and gives him the same information to post on *A.D. copy*. Prepares his *Daily Time Sheet (Form 244c)* showing S.O. number, time required, date, and accounting information. Returns completed *I.W. copies* and *Form 244c* to Foreman of Installers at end of day. (Step 8b.)	Form #250: I.W. T.N.C. Form #244c	
8b	Foreman of Installers (Pl.)	VI	Receives completed *I.W. copies* and *Forms 244c* from Installers at end of each day. Checks them for accuracy. Sends *I.W. copy* to Installation Clerk and *Form 244c* to (Disbursement) Accounting. (See Step 12a.)	Form #250: I.W. Form #244c	To Accounting
8	Dispatcher (Pl.)	VII	Receives *call* on completion of each installation from Installer. Enters date, type of equipment used and accounting information on *A.D. copy* as reported by Installer. Pulls corresponding *A.R. copy* from numerical file and gives both copies to Installation Clerk.	Forms #250: A.D., A.R.	

Step	Person	Status	Others	Function	Papers	Inflow	Outflow
9	Installation Clerk (Pl.)	VII		Receives *A.D. & A.R. copies* from Dispatcher. Transcribes information from *A.D. copy* on *A.R. copy*. Prepares *S.O. Completion List.* (*Form 251*) in 6 copies (AD, AR, T, D, C, and I or Installation copies). Records order number and telephone number on *Forms 251* as each job is completed. As each page of *Form 251* is filled, reports by telephone or teletype the order number and telephone number to Traffic and Directory Departments. As each page is filled, it and corresponding copies of *Form 250* (A.D. & A.R.) are forwarded as follows: *A.D. copies* of *250* and *251* are sent to Service Order Clerk in Repair Service. (Step 10a.) *A.R. copies* of *250* and *251* are given to the Assignment Clerk. (Step 10.) *T. copy* of *251* is sent to Traffic. (Step 10c.) *D. copy* of *251* is sent to Directory (Step 10d.) *C. copy* of *251* is sent to Commercial (Step 10b.) *I. copy* of *251* is held on file. Also receives completed *I.W. copies* from Foreman of Installers. Pulls corresponding *I. copy* of *251* out of holding file. Files I.W. copy locally and *I. copy* in numerical order. (End of *I.W.* and *I. copies*.)	Form #250: A.D. & A.R. Form #251: A.D., A.R., T., D., C., I.		To Traffic, Directory Commercial
10	Assignment Clerk (Pl.)	VII		Receives *A.R. copies* of *Forms 250 & 251* from Installation Clerk. Posts completed order information on *Assignment Records*, and forwards *A.R. forms* to Auditor of Receipts in Accounting. (Step 11.)	Form #250: A.R. Form #251: A.R. *Assignment Record*		To Accounting

| | | | | | To Accounting |
					From Plant
10a	Service Order Clerk (Pl.)	VII	Receives *A.D. copies of 250 & 251* from Installation Clerk. Makes *Line Card* for each new customer, recording telephone number, equipment and circuit data from *A.D. copy of 250.* Files Line Cards locally. (End of Line Card.) Forwards *A.D. forms* to Auditor of Disbursements in Accounting.	Form #250: A.D. Form #251: A.D. Line Card	To Accounting
11a	Supervisor of Mat. & Station Rec. & Clerk in Auditor of Disbursements (Acct.)	V VI	Receives *A.D. copies of 250 and 251.* Records information on *Disbursements Accounting Forms* and *Retirement Statistics Forms.* Then sends 250 *A.D.* to Field Reports Reviewer.	Form #250: A.D. Form #251: A.D. D.A. Forms Retirement Statistics	From Plant
12a	Field Reports Reviewer (Acct.)	VI	Receives *244c.* Receives *A.D. copies of 250.* Compares with *Installers Time Report, 244c* (See Step 8b). Sends to Station Statistics Section.	Form #250: A.D. Form #251: A.D. Form #244c	
13a	Station Statistics Clerk (Acct.)	VI	Receives *A.D. copies. Marks completed.* Holds one month and sends to main filing section.	Same as above	
14a	Several		Receive *A.D.* copies of 250. Disbursement procedure.		
10b	Service Order Clerk (Comm.)	VII	Receives *C copy of 251* from Plant Installation Clerk. Draws *C copy of 250* (retained in Step 2). Marks it completed, enters telephone number from 251, and sends to Service Rep. in charge of this account.	Form #251:C Form #250:C	From Plant

Step	Person	Status	Others	Function	Papers	Inflow	Outflow
11b	Service Representative (Comm.)	VII		Receives completed C copy of 250, draws related Form 400 and Credit Card, enters telephone number, completion date, etc. and files last two in her other accounts. (End of Form 400 and Credit Card.) Initials C copy of 250 and returns to S.O. Clerk.	Form #250:C Credit Card Form #400		
12b	Service Order Clerk (Comm.)	VII		Receives C copy of 250 and files. (End of C copy 250.)	Form #250:C		
10c	C.O. Clerk (Tr.)	VIII		Receives T copy of 251 via teletype from Plant Installation Clerk. Draws T copy of 250 (See Step 5b) and posts information from teletype 251 on it. Records name, number, and address in Information Book. Also corrects Intercepting Book. In manual offices necessary information is entered in Panel and Jack, Multiple Check, and Line Records. Multiple Jacks printed, and lamp cap checked. Receives typed 251 and checks with T copy of 250. Initials T copy of 250. If in dial office sends T copy of 250 to Dial Assignment Office.	Teletype #251 Form #250:T Typed #251 Information Book Intercept Book Other Records	From Plant	
11c	Daily Assignment Clerk (Tr.)	VIII		Receives T copy of 250 and enters necessary information in her Connector and Line Finder Record. Returns T copy to C.O. Clerk.	Form #250:T Connector & Line Finder Record		
12c	C.O. Clerk (Tr.)	VIII	Printer	Receives T copy of 250 and files. (End of T copy.) Receives new Daily Addenda from Directory via printer. (Step 10d.) Removes old reprint and inserts new in Daily Addenda Book which is used by Information Operators.	Form #250:T Daily Addenda Daily Addenda Book	From Directory via Printer	

						From	To
1od	Compilation Clerk (Dir.)	VII	Printer	Receives D copy of 251, draws relevant D & D.D. copies of 250. (See Step 6c.) Enters completion date. In large exchanges, hands this to typist for transmission to Printer who returns *Daily Addenda*; one copy of which comes to Directory and several to Traffic (See Step 12c). Files *D copy* of 250, and sends *D.D. copy* to Directory Delivery. (End of *D & D.D. copies* of 250.) Orders checked against monthly reprint at end of month.	Form #251:D Form #250:D & D.D. Daily Addenda Monthly Reprint	From Plant	To Traffic
11	Order Section File Cl. in and of Rec. (Acct.)	VII		Receives A.R. copies of 250 and 251. Checks the two, sorts by types and sends 250 A.R. to advance Payment Clerk.	Form 250:A.R. Form 251:A.R.	From Plant	
12	Advance Payment Clerk (Acct.)	VII		Receives *A.R. copies* of 250. Writes in charges and necessary information. Sends back to Order Section File Clerk.	Form #250 A.R.		
13	Order Sec. File Cl. (Acct.)	VII		Receives *A.R. copies* of 250. Arranges alphabetically by exchanges. At billing time, passes them to Toll Special Clerk.	Same as above		
14	Toll Special Clerk & others (Acct.)	VII	Customer	Receives *A.R. copies* of 250. Billing process (5 steps) ending by sending *A.R. copies* to Order Section File Clerk and *bill* to customer.	Miscellaneous		To Customer
15	Order Sec. File Cl. (Acct.)	VII		Receives *A.R. copies* of 250 and files. (End of *A.R. copy*.)	Form #250: A.R.		
15e	Customer			Receives bill and pays $3.50 installation charge.	Bill	From Accounting	

PREPARATION FOR NEGOTIATIONS SPECIFIC TASK TEAM
(Union)

Step	Person	Status	Others	Function	Inflow	Outflow
1	Members in Local Meeting	V		Meet, raise and discuss suggestions for contract changes in "conditions."		
2	General Representative	III		Receives *Suggestions*, summarizes and semi-annually presents to Central Committee.		
3	Central Committee	II III		Receives *Suggestions*, sifts, drops some and presents remainder to Executive Board, through Executive Board member who is Chairman of Central Committee.		
4	Executive Board	II I		Receives *Suggestions*, sifts and evaluates in terms of total union interests. Drops some and presents remainder to Bargaining committee through President who is Chairman of both.		
5	President	I		Receives Suggestions, organizes *Report* on basis of these, those coming from steps 1a, 1b, 2b, 1c, his own study, and his notes on grievances and experience with contract negotiations.		
6	Bargaining Committee	I II	Anyone co-opted by Comm. particularly Gen. Reps.	Receives *Report* and that from Executive Board members on conditions (2c) and also that from Statistical Committee (1a) on wages and conditions. Sifts suggestions. Seeks further information if necessary on wages from Gen. Reps. Calls in anyone necessary on particular issues. Arranges priorities and suggests bargaining points and supporting arguments. Reports to Ex. Bd.		
7	Executive Board	I II		Receives *Report*, discusses, modifies or approves, and authorizes Bargaining Committee to proceed on plan.		
8	Bargaining Committee	I II		Receives *Authorization*, prepares final case and approaches negotiations.		

				From	To
1a	Statistical Committee	II III	Collects, analyzes and organizes *Data* on wages and conditions and developments for comparative purposes. Undertakes special *Studies* for President. Keeps file for Bargaining Committee. Submits *Report* on wages to Bargaining Committee.		To President and Bargaining Committee Steps 5 and 6
1b	Members	V	Suggest condition changes to President (Step 5) or to Officers (Step 2b).		To President
2b	Officers	II–IV	Receive or initiate *Suggestions*, and transmit to other officers or President (Step 5).	From Members	To President
1c	Grievance Handlers	II–IV	Report important and recurring grievances to President (Step 5) or to Executive Board Members.		To President and Executive Board Members
2c	Executive Bd. Members	II	Receive comments on important grievances and transmit to Bargaining Committee (Step 6).	From Members	To Bargaining Committee

GRIEVANCE SPECIFIC TASK TEAM

Step	Union Persons	Status	Company Persons	Status	Others	Functions	Papers
1	Member	V	Employee	VI		Experiences grievance and formulates for presentation to local and/or general representative *or* management.	
2a			Employee Supervisor	VI V	(Union Officer)	Explore grievance and provide remedy, if possible. Invite union in if adjustment is to be made (adjustment must be consistent with terms of contract). If no settlement, referred to higher supervisor.	
3a			(Employee) Supervisor Intermediate Supervisor	(VI) V IV	(Union Officer)	Explore grievance and provide remedy, if possible. Invite union in if adjustment is to be made (adjustment must be consistent with terms of contract). If no settlement, referred to higher supervisor.	
4a			(Employee) Supervisor Intermediate Supervisor Staff Supv.	(VI) V IV III	(Union Officer)	Explore grievance and provide remedy, if possible. Invite union in if adjustment is to be made (adjustment must be consistent with terms of contract). If no settlement, referred to higher supervisor.	
2	Member Local Rep. General Rep.	V IV III				Group explores grievance, gets facts, explains rights, and prepares case for presentation to first step of formal grievance procedure.	
3	Member Local Rep. General Rep.	V IV III	Employee Immediate Sup. Intermediate Supervisor	VI V IV		Union reps. present grievance. All explore facts and attempt to settle. If can't, sign joint statement for use at next step and submit to next meeting.	Joint Statement A

GRIEVANCE SPECIFIC TASK TEAM (Continued)

Step	Union Persons	Status	Company Persons	Status	Others	Functions	Papers
4	(Member) Local Rep. General Rep. Ex. Bd. Member	(V) IV III II	(Employee) Immediate Supv. Intermediate Supervisor Staff Supv.	(VI) V IV III or II		Receive *Report* from previous meeting, explore further, and attempt to settle. If can't, sign joint statement and submit to next meeting.	Joint Statement B
5	(Member) General Rep. Ex. Bd. Member	(V) III II	(Employee) Staff Supv. Dept. Gen. Mgr.	(VI) III or II II		Receive *Report* from previous meeting, explore further, and attempt to settle. If can't, sign joint statement and submit to next meeting.	Joint Statement C
6	(Member) Pres. and Union Grievance Comm.	(V) I II	(Employee) Pres. and Mgt. Grievance Committee	(VI) I II III		Receive *Report* from previous meeting, explore and attempt to settle. If can't, sign joint statement; and if the grievance concerns the true intent and meaning of a provision of the contract or a question as to the performance of any obligation thereunder, either party may submit to arbitration.	Joint Statement D
7	Concerned Parties		Concerned Parties		3 Arbitrators	Receive *Report* and evidence, and render decision which is transmitted to parties.	Evidence Decision
8	Employee		Management			Comply with decision.	

APPENDIX C

FRAMEWORK OF ANALYSIS

The framework of analysis employed in this study has been briefly described in *Adaptive Human Behavior,* a Labor and Management Center publication. The major assumptions which underlie this theoretical framework have been set forth in two additional Center publications entitled *Teamwork in Industry* and *From Tactics to Strategy in Industrial Relations.* A brief recapitulation of those assumptions will be of aid to the reader in understanding the significance of the topics of, and the terms used in, the chapters of this book. They are as follows:

1. A company or a union is a small society. That is to say, it is composed of individual people who are related to and work with each other, materials, and ideas within a framework of certain organizational devices or systems toward an organizational objective.
2. These systems through which people (and the materials and ideas with which they work) are bound together into a functioning whole may be classified as the following *bonds,* or devices, of organization. Here they are merely named. Five of them were defined in some detail at the beginning of the several chapters.*
   a. Organizational Charter
   b. Functional Specifications system
   c. Status system
   d. Communication system
   e. Reward and Penalty system
   f. Technology
   g. Services
   h. Thoughtways
   i. Educational system
3. The significance and effectiveness of each aspect, part, or technique in the organization (for example, house organ, union paper, incentive plan, wage rates, seniority agreement, pension plan, organizational charts, etc.) are determined not only in terms of what it is in itself but in terms of its relationship to one of these systems, or bonds, of organization.

* See p. xxviii for the present (1966) concept of the number and organization of bonds.

4. The test of *effectiveness* of these systems, or bonds, of organization is their degree of positive contribution to the operations and objectives of the organization as a whole, and to the strength of the other bonds.

5. The test of *efficiency* of these systems, or bonds, of organization is their degree of positive contribution to the goal realization of the participants in the organization.

6. The chief goals held by the participants in an organization are as follows:
    a. The desire for
        1. *Security* in
        2. *Progress* toward
        3. *Justice* with respect to
    b. The following achievements, considered to be standards of successful living in terms of the participants' own environment and experience:
        1. *Respect* of one's fellows
        2. *Creature comforts*
        3. *Control* of own affairs
        4. *Understanding*
        5. *Capacity performance*
        6. *Integration* or wholeness within oneself and in relation to the world of things and people about one.

7. Each bond of organization can be tested for *efficiency* therefore by ascertaining the degree to which it contributes to the realization of each of these goals on the part of individuals or groups of participants. The judgment can be made more pointed by considering, in testing the efficiency of each bond, the degree of realization of only those goals most relevant to it (e.g., in case of the Communication system, the goals of understanding, control, integration, and security).

8. In addition to the people, materials, and ideas, and to the bonds of organization which weld them together, and to the goals toward which they are striving, the *structure of living* of the participants in any society includes human and natural resources, and the reinforcements (folklore, symbols, slogans, etc.) for socially desirable behavior. This structure of living is then a framework for classifying the major determinants of behavior.

9. When this structure of living is in disequilibrium—that is, when it provides inadequate resources for goal achievements, when its parts lack consistency, contain rigidities, or are subject to threats—the members of the society experience tensions and anxieties which stimulate them to adaptive behavior.

APPENDIX D

METHODOLOGY

This report is based on (a) observations made by the director and associate director in a series of exploratory orientation conferences with management and union officers; (b) on a study of the work-flow processes made in one medium-sized local exchange and at headquarters; (c) on an analysis of the decision-making process relative to the transfer problem; (d) on the general observations made by interviewers during their period of training in the company (each was trained for some job) and after they had finished interviews at each exchange; and (e) on interview material gathered in the course of lengthy interviews (lasting from three to eight hours) with about 1500 respondents.

The basic sampling techniques contemplated that several conceptions of a universe were to be satisfied. The sample was chosen to be representative of employees and management, officers and members, in each of the operating and headquarters departments. Toward this end, employee and member names were chosen at random from the seniority lists of the company: every fifth name in the case of most departments, every tenth name in three cases (Traffic, Accounting, and Directory [Commercial]) in which there were large numbers performing identical operations. To this list was added a group chosen in cases where the random method did not hit upon a member of a basic craft. It was not intended by this process to make the craft sample statistically adequate, but to assure us that we had represented in our general sample every major occupational group present in the organizations.

First-line and substaff supervision were sampled on a one-in-five basis. All management on the divisional, staff, and levels above was, with few exceptions, interviewed, as were all executive-board members and general officers of the union.

In this report we have used all material from all sources in developing a definition of the bonds of organization. In analyzing the degree of satisfaction with the bond we have made reference to interview materials on only the three operating departments found at the field level: Traffic, Plant, and Commercial. The discussion refers to these departments. In our final report we shall, of course, consider the degree of satisfaction in all departments. However, in order that those in the company and union who are working in these other departments may see how their groups compared with those in the operating departments, we have included in the Appendix duplicates of the basic Proportions Satisfied tables for each of the bonds for the following groups: Executive, Accounting, General Engineering, Directory (Commercial), House Service, and Dining Service.

We are impelled to suggest to the reader several guides to the interpretation of our findings.

In the first place, although the reader may properly consider this a report on the reactions of participants merely to particular features of the company and union, the questions designed to reveal these reactions have a certain pattern related to an underlying theory of human behavior and the framework of factors determining that behavior. The questions were designed to tell us whether the bonds of organization were enabling patricipants to realize their goals, their standards of successful living. The goals were determined not from introspection or from a summary of psychological literature, but from the conclusions of a series of investigations by the director of the study since 1931, in which an attempt was made to isolate and define the objectives toward which management and union leaders, employees and union members, were directing their efforts.

The questions, therefore, were framed systematically to elicit responses which were not merely interesting to management and leaders as revelations of employee reactions toward this or that specific feature of the organization. They are grounded in the assumptions set forth above that significant reactions are a product of the degree to which particular and definable devices of organization in a functional group are enabling individuals to realize a particular and definable set of goals or standards of successful living. It is this set of assumptions which determined the questions asked. It is the fact that the questions were shaped within this framework which makes the responses to them significant, not only from the point of view of those who wish to know "what this group thinks about this or that," but from the point of view of those who wish to develop a realistic theory of why men behave as they do.

This is a report on responses to specific questions. The questions have to do with individuals' experiences with clearly identifiable and important aspects of the systems labeled organizational bonds. The responses—their variations as between management and employees and union officers, the variations as between different departments and exchanges of varying sizes—these are interesting in themselves. But we must warn that the proportions of satisfaction as revealed in summaries of the responses do not enable one to say at this point: "The whole system of (say) Functional Specifications, as we have defined it, is operating at some specified degree of efficiency." When the much more complicated and time-consuming analysis we are engaged in at present is finished, an analysis which involves focusing the respondents' answers to a number of questions on certain standards of efficiency, we shall come much closer to being able to make such a statement.

The purpose of this preliminary report is much more limited. Fifty of the questions asked of our informants were designed to elicit a spontaneous judgment as to whether a particular feature of the working environment was predominantly satisfactory or predominantly unsatisfactory, as well as to obtain detailed comments on the informant's experience with that feature. The spontaneous judgments can be analyzed quickly, and the proportions in the several groups to whom the feature was predominantly satisfying recorded in tables. This has been done, and this preliminary report sets forth a number of conclusions suggested by a study of those tables.

Several additional comments need to be made. As suggested above, this is a report on symptoms. It is a report on what proportions of individuals in the several groups indicated predominant satisfaction or dissatisfaction with particular features of their working environment. It is not a diagnosis of *why* they labeled those features in that way. It is in effect a survey of reactions of participants in the organization to experience within that organization, not an analysis of the details of that experience or the sources of their reactions. Such an analysis in depth is in process, but is not finished.

Even this preliminary analysis, however, is of interest to those who are trying to make systematic sense out of the phenomena of human behavior and relations. As we have indicated, the plan for interviewing was developed out of a definite conception that an organization is a small society, that is, a group of individuals welded into a working team by certain bonds of organization. Moreover, the questions designed to test satisfaction or dissatisfaction with these bonds were developed after a careful consideration of how each bond might affect the progress of the individual toward achievement of satisfying experience. The degree of satisfaction was assumed to be directly related to the extent of realization of his major goals. The answers to each question, therefore, are an aid to appraising *some* bond in terms of its contribution to helping the individuals to realize *some* goal. Accordingly, this report is rooted in a systematic conception of the nature of organizations and of the impact of experience with the features of that organization upon goal realization of the participants. Our underlying assumption is that goal realization promotes, and goal frustration retards, productive and efficient teamwork within an organization.

Another comment should be made about the statistical validity of the findings. In the first place the responses were classified into only two categories:

predominantly Satisfactory and predominantly Unsatisfactory. In rating the responses, the benefit of the doubt is given to satisfaction or dissatisfaction, as seemed most appropriate. The proportions, therefore, have an upward bias toward indicating satisfaction, or a downward bias toward dissatisfaction, in particular cases. These decisions were revealed in the text for each group of questions.

In the second place, the numbers involved, particularly in breakdowns, are not sufficient to justify comparisons in terms of percentage points. This report deals with the responses of those 1022 participants whose assignments are to a local exchange. About 478 assigned to Headquarters' sections and departments are not included except in particular tables, where they are clearly identified. Numbers are particularly inadequate when breakdowns by the four size-of-exchange groups are considered. In view of this fact, the tables in the report record the proportions satisfied on a particular point simply in tenths.

One further warning should be added. The findings in this report are peculiarly influenced by the conception of the organizational bonds necessarily held by the director of the study in order to shape specific questions. It was inevitable, in the formulating of the questions, that their content should be influenced by that conception. That conception has been amplified and modified by a consideration of the extensive materials gathered in the course of the training for and participation in jobs in the company on the part of our interviewers and in the interviews themselves. The description and definition of the bond in the first part of each chapter is not that with which we started. It is the original definition as modified by the results of our study. Since, however, the questions were influenced by our original conception, we now find ourselves without information on matters which our present conception suggests are important. This shortcoming will of course, be corrected before undertaking our next investigation. This fact does not reduce the value of our findings so long as the reader realizes the limits it imposes on the nature of generalizations which can legitimately be made.